PRO FOOTBALL

♦ ♦ ♦

COLLECTOR'S LIBRARY

PRO FOOTBALL

◆ ◆ ◆

Four decades of Sports Illustrated's finest
writing on America's most popular sport

Oxmoor
House®

copyright ©1993 by Time Inc.
All Rights Reserved

SPORTS ILLUSTRATED is a registered trademark of
Time Inc.

ISBN: 0-8487-1169-6
Library of Congress Catalog Card Number:
93-085398

Manufactured in the United States of America
First Printing 1993

Published by arrangement with:
Oxmoor House, Inc.
Book Division of
Southern Progress Corporation
PO Box 2463
Birmingham, Alabama 35201

SPORTS ILLUSTRATED PRO FOOTBALL
was prepared by:
Bishop Books, Inc.
611 Broadway
New York, New York 10012

Cover photograph: Walter Iooss Jr.

The following stories are used by permission of
the authors acknowledged:
The Scout Is a Lonely Hunter by George Plimpton
A New Life by Gary Smith
Deep Into His Job by Ed Hinton

Contents

♦ ♦ ♦

Introduction

◆

There is an old bromide in sportswriting that sits around in bottom drawers and back cabinets and never quite gets cleaned out: "The smaller the ball, the better the writer." It was a slap from the old days when the established sportswriters never budged from the baseball press box and the new kids were sent to try to make sense of pro football madness. Of course, it was never true then and it's not true now. If this Sports Illustrated Collector's Library edition on the best pro football writing in the magazine's 40-year history doesn't prove it, nothing does.

Who could read Dan Jenkins on 1966's bar-hopping, girl-shopping night-stopping Joe Namath and not wake up with a hangover? Who could read George Plimpton on the unending travels of an underpaid pro football scout and not ache for a motel pillow? Who could read Frank Deford on the untimely death of Kansas City Chiefs running back Joe Delaney and not need to swallow down a lump in the throat?

Great baseball writing is different from great football writing, but great football writing can often be more captivating. Pro football is not like baseball. There is not another game tomorrow and another 160 after that. It is right here, right now. It is grown men willingly hurling themselves into each other for the sake of an extra yard of sod. It is a three-hour train wreck. It is the gritty and the graceful and the gargantuan all thrown together in the bottom of a bowl under the huge ticking sound of a clock that will soon hit 00:00. It is not a pastime. It is a passion.

Over the years, SI has matched some of its best writers with pro football's greatest moments. For this special anthology, we have included Paul (Dr. Z) Zimmerman on Dwight Clark's cuticles-catch to give the San Francisco 49ers the 1984 NFC title. John Underwood on perhaps the greatest football game ever played, San Diego's 41–38 overtime win over Miami. Rick Reilly on John Elway's cardiac-causing drive in 1992. Tex Maule on the Giants-Colts classic OT thriller in 1958, and many others.

Actually, in 40 years of covering pro football, we had enough great material to fill a few CD-ROMs. Naturally, we had to leave out some very good pieces by some very good writers. We apologize to you and to them. Still, I believe the ones we settled on are unforgettable.

So it's official. The "smaller-ball" theory is dead. If there's one thing SI has proved over 40 years, it's that it's not the size of the ball but the size of the mind that makes for riveting writing.

Enjoy the proof.

MARK MULVOY
Managing Editor

GAMES

♦ ♦ ♦

The Best Football Game Ever Played

BY TEX MAULE

UNITAS. MARCHETTI. GIFFORD. AMECHE. BERRY. MANY OF THE
GAME'S ALLTIME GREATS PLAYED IN THIS NFL TITLE GAME, AN
OVERTIME THRILLER BETWEEN THE NEW YORK GIANTS AND
THE BALTIMORE COLTS. TEX MAULE HAD NO QUALMS ABOUT
CALLING IT THE GREATEST GAME OF FOOTBALL EVER PLAYED.

Never has there been a game like this one. When there are
so many high points, it is not easy to pick the highest. But
for the 60,000 and more fans who packed Yankee Stadium
last Sunday for the third week in a row, the moment they
will never forget—the moment with which they will eternally
bore their grandchildren—came when, with less than 10 seconds to play and the clock remorselessly moving, the Baltimore Colts kicked a field goal which put the professional
football championship in a 17–17 tie and necessitated a historic sudden-death overtime period. Although it was far from
apparent at the time, this was the end of the line for the fabulous New York Giants, eastern titleholders by virtue of
three stunning victories over a great Cleveland team (the last
a bruising extra game to settle the tie in which they finished
their regular season), and the heroes of one of the most

courageous comebacks in the memory of the oldest fans.

This was also a game in which a seemingly irretrievable loss was twice defied. It was a game which had everything. And when it was all over, the best football team in the world won the world's championship.

The Baltimore Colts needed all their varied and impressive talent to get the 17–17 tie at the end of the regular four quarters. Then, for eight and one quarter minutes of the sudden-death extra period, in which victory would go to the first team to score, all of the pressure and all of the frenzy of an entire season of play was concentrated on the misty football field at Yankee Stadium. The fans kept up a steady, high roar. Tension grew and grew until it was nearly unbearable. But on the field itself, where the two teams now staked the pro championship and a personal winners' share of $4,700 against a losers' share of $3,100 on each play, coldly precise football prevailed. With each team playing as well as it was possible for it to play, the better team finally won. The Baltimore Colts, ticking off the yards with sure strength under the magnificent direction of Quarterback Johnny Unitas, scored the touchdown which brought sudden death to New York and the first championship to hungry Baltimore.

This game, unbelievably, managed to top all the heroics of the spectacular Giant victories which had led up to it. The Colts won because they are a superbly well armed football team. They spent the first half picking at the small flaws in the Giant defense, doing it surely and competently under the guidance of Unitas. The Giant line, which had put destructive pressure on Cleveland quarterbacks for two successive weeks, found it much more difficult to reach Unitas. Andy Robustelli, the fine Giant end, was blocked beautifully by Jim Parker, a second-year tackle with the Colts. Unitas, a tall, thin man who looks a little stooped in his uniform, took his time throwing, and when he threw, the passes were flat and hard as a frozen rope, and on target. He varied the Baltimore attack from time to time by sending Alan Ameche thumping into the Giant line.

The Giant defense, unable to overpower the Colts as it had the Browns, shifted and changed and tried tricks, and Unitas, more often than not, switched his signal at the last possible second to take advantage of Giant weaknesses. Once, in the first quarter, when the New Yorkers tried to cover the very fast Lenny Moore with one man, Unitas waited coolly while Moore sprinted down the sideline, then whipped a long, flat pass which Moore caught on the Giant 40 and carried to the 25.

Then the Giant defense blocked a field goal attempt which followed, and Charley Conerly, the 37-year-old Giant quarterback who played one of the finest games of his long career, caught the Colt linebackers coming in on him too recklessly. He underhanded a quick pitchout to Frank Gifford, and Gifford went 38 yards to the Colts' 31; a couple of plays later the Giants led 3–0 on a 36-yard field goal by Pat Summerall.

In the second quarter, with the probing and testing over, the Colts asserted a clear superiority. They had gone into the game reasonably sure that their running would work inside the Giant tackles, and sure, too, that the quick, accurate passes of Unitas to receivers like Moore and Ray Berry could be completed. The first quarter reinforced that opinion and the second quarter implemented it. A Giant fumble recovered on the Giant 20 by Gene Lipscomb, the 288-pound Colt tackle, set up the first touchdown. Unitas punctured the Giant line with Ameche and Moore and sent Moore outside end once when the Giant center clogged up, and then Ameche scored from the two and it all looked very easy.

It looked easy on the next Colt foray, too. This one started on the Baltimore 14 and moved inevitably downfield. The Colt backs, following the quick, vicious thrust of the big line, went five and six yards at a time, the plays ending in a quick-settling swirl of dust as the Giant line, swept back in a flashing surge of white Colt uniforms, then slipped the blocks to make the belated tackles. Unitas passed twice to Berry, the second time for 15 yards and the second Colt touchdown. The Giants, now 11 points behind, looked well-whipped.

The feeling of the game changed suddenly and dramatically late in the third quarter on the one accomplishment which most often reverses the trend in a football game—the denial of a sure touchdown. The Colts had moved almost contemptuously to the Giant three-yard line. After the half the Baltimore team, which had manhandled the New York defense to gain on the ground for most of the first half, switched to passing. Unitas, given marvelous blocking by the Colt offensive line, picked apart the Giant defensive secondary with his wonderful passes, thrown so accurately that often Colt receivers snatched the ball from between two Giant defenders who were only a half step out of position. When this irresistible passing attack carried them to the Giant three-yard line, first down and goal to go, even the most optimistic Giant fans in the stands must have given up.

But the Giant defense, which, more than anything else, brought this team to the championship game, again coped with crisis and stopped Baltimore cold.

Now, for the rest of this quarter and most of the fourth, the Colts were surprisingly limp. The Giant stand keyed their collapse, but an odd play which set up the first Giant touchdown underlined it and so demoralized the Baltimore team that for some time it was nearly ineffectual. Conerly, quick to capitalize on the letdown, sent Kyle Rote, who usually spends his afternoon catching short passes, rocketing far downfield. Rote, starting down the left sideline, cut sharply to his right, and Conerly's pass intersected his course at the Colt 40. Rote carried on down to the 25 and ran into a two-man tackle which made him fumble. There was a paralyzed second when a little group of Colt and Giant players watched the ball bounding free without making a move, then the still life broke into violent motion and Giant Halfback Alex Webster picked up the fumble and carried it to the Colt one-yard line. Mel Triplett hurdled in for a touchdown and the Giants, fans and all, were back in the game. The crowd, which had been desperately yelling, "Goooo, Giants," roared as if the Giants had taken the lead. And the Giants did, quickly.

The Colt offense, until now clean and quick and precise, began to dodder. The protection which had allowed Unitas to wait and wait and wait before he threw, broke down, and Robustelli and Dick Modzelewski ran through weak blocks to dump the Colt quarterback for long losses. The Giants, on the other hand, were operating with the assurance of experience and a long intimacy with the uses of adversity.

They took the lead on the second play of the fourth quarter. Conerly, who had been throwing to Rote and Gifford, suddenly switched targets. He zeroed in on End Bob Schnelker once for 17 yards and repeated on the next play for 46 more and a first down on the Baltimore 15. Then he befuddled the Colt secondary with Schnelker and threw to Gifford on the right sideline, and Gifford ran through a spaghetti-arm tackle on the five to score, sending the Giants into a 17–14 lead.

The Colts now seemed as thoroughly beaten as the Giants had been at the half. Unitas' protection, so solid early in the game, leaked woefully. Only a Giant fumble slowed the New York attack, and when the Giants punted to the Colts with barely two minutes left in the game, not even the most optimistic of the 20-odd thousand Colt fans who came from Baltimore would have bet on victory.

Baltimore started from its 14, and the hero of this sequence was, of all the fine players on the field this warm winter day, the most unlikely. He has a bad back and one leg is shorter than the other so that he wears mud cleats on that shoe to equalize them. His eyes are so bad that he must wear contact lenses when he plays. He is not very fast and, although he was a good college end, he was far from a great one. On this march, he caught three passes in a row for a total of 62 yards, the last one for 22 yards to the New York 13-yard line. His name is Ray Berry, and he has the surest hands in professional football. He caught the three passes with two Giant defenders guarding him each time. He caught 12 passes for 178 yards in this football game, and without him the Colts would surely have lost.

After Berry had picked the ball out of the hands of two Giant defenders on the New York 13-yard line, Steve Myhra kicked a 20-yard field goal with seven seconds left to play for a 17–17 tie which sent the game into the sudden-death overtime period. The teams rested for three minutes, flipped a coin to see which would kick and which receive, and the Giants won and took the kickoff.

The tremendous tension held the crowd in massing

excitement. But the Giants, the fine fervor of their rally gone, could not respond to this last challenge. They were forced to punt, and the Colts took over on their own 20. Unitas, mixing runs and passes carefully and throwing the ball wonderfully true under this pressure, moved them downfield surely. The big maneuver sent Ameche up the middle on a trap play which broke him through the overanxious Giant line for 23 yards to the Giant 20. From there Unitas threw to the ubiquitous Berry for a first down on the New York eight, and three plays later Baltimore scored to end the game. Just before the touchdown a deliriously happy Baltimore football fan raced onto the field during a time-out and sailed 80 yards, bound for the Baltimore huddle, before the police secondary intercepted him and hauled him to the sideline. He was grinning with idiot glee, and the whole city of Baltimore sympathized with him. One Baltimore fan, listening on his auto radio, ran into a telephone pole when Myhra kicked the tying field goal, and 30,000 others waited to greet the returning heroes.

Berry, a thin, tired-looking youngster still dazed with the victory, seemed to speak for the team and for fans everywhere after the game.

"It's the greatest thing that ever happened," he said.

Dallas Feels the Steeler Crunch

BY   DAN   JENKINS

FEW SUPER BOWLS HAVE LIVED UP TO THE PRE-GAME HOOPLA
THE WAY THIS ONE BETWEEN THE PITTSBURGH STEELERS AND
DALLAS COWBOYS DID. DAN JENKINS RECORDED THE
PYROTECHNICS AS THE STEELER DEFENSE CONTROLLED THE
GROUND AND LYNN SWANN SOARED THROUGH THE AIR.

For all of those gaudy things that happened throughout the
afternoon, memories of the 1976 Super Bowl will keep going
back to the Pittsburgh Steelers' Lynn Swann climbing into
the air like the boy in the Indian rope trick, and coming
down with the football. He didn't come down with very
many passes last Sunday, really, only four, but he caught the
ones that truly mattered. That is why it will seem that he
spent the day way up there in the crisp sky, a thousand feet
above Miami's Orange Bowl, where neither the Dallas Cowboys nor even a squadron of fighter planes could do anything
to stop him. When it was all over Lynn Swann and the Steelers had won 21–17 and had repeated as the champions of
professional madness.

The thinking beforehand was that Pittsburgh could win this
game only if Franco Harris trampled over and through a

thing called the flex defense of the intellectual Cowboys who, in the meantime, on offense, would do enough weird things to the hard-hat Steelers to capture the day and write a perfect finish to their storybook season. Essentially Dallas stopped Harris, however, and the winning of Super Bowl X was left up to Swann and the indomitable Terry Bradshaw, who seems to collect concussions and championship rings with equal facility. Just for good measure there also was a defense that could probably take apart an attacking tank battalion if it had to. But mainly it was Swann, keeping Pittsburgh in a game that looked to be swaying, early on, toward the underdog Cowboys. It was Swann, soaring above the Cowboys' Mark Washington at the sideline, who fielded a Bradshaw pass of 32 yards and *made* the drive that put Pittsburgh back in the contest late in the first quarter. Until then Dallas had done everything but cause the Orange Bowl floats to disappear.

And in the fourth quarter it was Swann who would make the biggest catch of the day, a 64-yard touchdown heave from Bradshaw, who didn't realize until much later, after his head stopped rattling, that he had passed for a touchdown. This was the play that put the Steelers safely ahead 21–10. Only a few impossible last-minute deeds by the Cowboys could have changed the outcome of Super Bowl X, and though they were dead game and scored one more touchdown they just were not quite a good enough football team to pull it off.

The last catch of Swann's has to be dwelled on, for it had Super Bowl trophy and $15,000 to each Steeler written all over it. There was so much to the play—so much that could have happened, and so much that did. It ended with Swann catching a rocket from Bradshaw that traveled at least 70 yards in the air, Swann jumping and taking it on the Dallas five-yard line and gliding in for the touchdown, and Bradshaw barely conscious on the ground after being decked by Cliff Harris on a safety blitz. For those who collect trivia, the name of the play was a "69 Maximum Flanker Post."

The play began with the Steelers trying to protect a lead of 15–10 with just over three minutes left in the game. It was third down and four to go at the Steeler 36, and Dallas wanted the football badly. There was still plenty of time for Roger Staubach and Drew Pearson to conjure up some of that witchcraft they used on the Minnesota Vikings.

Perhaps we'll never know what possessed Bradshaw to call 69 Maximum Flanker Post when the world had a right to expect Pittsburgh to try only for the first down, the percentage move to keep the ball. It may be that Bradshaw is not as dumb as it has become numbingly popular for his critics to suggest. One could certainly say he remembered Swann at just the right time.

So instead of giving the ball to Franco Harris, Bradshaw faded back to throw the long one—a wild gamble, it appeared. Alas, Dallas had figured it properly; the blitz was on, and D.D. Lewis came storming at Bradshaw from his blind side, with Cliff Harris right behind him. For a fleeting instant it seemed that Lewis would reach the quarterback before he could release the ball, causing either a sack or a fumble. But Bradshaw, possibly just *sensing* Lewis, took a step to his right. Lewis missed him by a hair. That gave Bradshaw enough time to unload the pass.

In the next instant Cliff Harris destroyed Bradshaw with a whack the 80,197 in the stadium might have heard if their attention had not been turned to the flight of the ball and the blur of Swann's footrace with the Cowboys' Mark Washington. Washington will have to live with the knowledge that he covered Swann as well as anyone could have but could not leap as high or as deftly at the right time.

Finally, it was a beautifully thrown ball, a perfectly run pass route and a marvelous catch, all three at the most splendid moment—for Pittsburgh—of a rather important football game.

Players who are involved in such heroics seldom have much to say afterwards that would give them more meaning. Swann said, "All I did was run under the ball." He thought for a moment and figured there must be more to it than that. He remembered that earlier, referring to another pass, Cliff Harris had told him, "You're lucky you didn't come back on that ball because I'm gonna take a shot at you. You better watch your head."

Intimidation. The Cowboys had planned to be intimidating in this game, something the Steelers are famous for. And the

Cowboys *were* at first, not just with their tricks and execution but with enough hard hitting that they led 10–7 through three full quarters of play.

Swann's head was as much a factor as his hands and speedy legs. It was not even known whether he would be able to play in the Super Bowl because of a mild concussion he had suffered in the American Conference title game against Oakland. "I honestly didn't know until a couple of minutes before the kickoff whether I'd play," he said. "I felt fine and I wanted to, but I wasn't sure I would." Coach Chuck Noll was sure, just as sure as he was that the Steelers could not beat the Cowboys without throwing.

As for Bradshaw, he could only try to recall what reality was like. "I got hit right here," he said, pointing to his left cheek. "They were coming. I could feel them coming. I don't know how I got the ball off. I was hearing bells or something on the ground."

Bradshaw did not know what he had wrought. People bent over him as he lay there, but he wasn't hearing them. They told him when they led him to the sideline. They told him when they sat him down, and a couple of minutes later they were telling him again that he had done this terrific thing as they walked him toward the dressing room.

"I was in the locker room and the game was about over when I understood it," said Bradshaw.

There were enough bizarre events throughout the game to daze the most ardent fan. Dallas took a 7–0 lead, the touchdown resulting from a blunder on the part of Bobby Walden, the Steelers' punter. He had a good snap from center and he simply dropped it. The Cowboys' rush blanketed him and it was Dallas' ball at the Steeler 29. In one play the Cowboys scored, and the way they did it suggested that Coach Tom Landry had something very sinister in store for the Steelers for the rest of the afternoon. Drew Pearson ran a crossing pattern over the middle and was wide open. Staubach laid the ball in beautifully and it was six points. The Steelers' safety, Mike Wagner, who claimed the fault was his because he misread the play, would have his revenge later.

Pittsburgh tied it up 7–7, with Bradshaw starting on his 33 and giving the ball to Harris and Rocky Bleier, who nibbled away to the Dallas 48. Then came a 32-yard pass to Swann down the right sideline, on which he made his first award-winning catch of the day, one more carry each by Bleier and Harris to the Dallas seven, and finally a scoring pass to Tight End Randy Grossman.

Dallas came back with a field goal by Toni Fritsch to go into the lead 10–7. It could have been 10–10 at the half, but Pittsburgh's Roy Gerela missed a field goal that wasted Swann's next sensational performance, a tumbling, juggling catch of a 53-yard Bradshaw bomb.

It was not until the fourth quarter that either team scored again. This time it was two points for Pittsburgh as Reggie Harrison flashed in to block Mitch Hoopes' punt, slamming the ball out of the end zone for a safety. Dallas 10, Pittsburgh 9. The Steelers finally went ahead when Gerela, who by then had missed another field goal, knocked one through from the 26-yard line.

So it was a 12–10 game, with less than half of the final quarter left, when Wagner got his revenge. Staubach dropped back from his 15 to try the same type of pass Drew Pearson had caught for the touchdown. Wagner reacted as if he and Staubach had concocted the play together. He lurked just out of Pearson's sight and when the ball arrived Wagner slipped in front of him, picked it off and went screaming down to the Dallas seven. To the credit of the Dallas defense, it held the Steelers to Gerela's second field goal but Pittsburgh was now ahead 15–10 and never lost the lead. Next came Swann's dramatic touchdown catch to make it 21–10, followed by a Staubach to Percy Howard pass of 34 yards, which concluded the scoring at 21–17.

As for all that mischief in the waning moments of the game, it started when the Steelers decided to use up time by running on fourth down instead of punting. But the clock stopped when Dallas took over near midfield, leaving 1:22 to play and giving Staubach and Drew Pearson an excellent chance to produce their own miracle. The Steelers' weird decision may best be explained by a little scene that was taking place in a booth upstairs. A frantic Pittsburgh assistant coach began hollering at Art McNally, the NFL's Supervisor of Officials. From the opposite side of a plexiglass divider covered with brown paper he shouted something on the order of, "The clock stopped, McNally! Hey, McNally, they're not running the clock!"

To which McNally calmly replied, "The clock always stops when the ball changes hands." Evidently the Steeler brain trust was so pleased that Dallas had used up all of its time-outs on defense that they had forgotten the rule, and now they could only be aghast at their folly. And that is really what gave Dallas its last chance to take the game back from Lynn Swann.

Even without the excitement on the field, there were enough trappings to make the game memorable—for one thing, it was surely the first time a press box ever had Raquel Welch hanging around in it. But the Cowboys, apparently determined to start things off with a flair, had the audacity to run a reverse on the opening kickoff. Preston Pearson handed the ball off to Tom Henderson, an ebullient special-team rookie, and after Henderson had galloped 48 yards right past the Steelers' bench, everyone knew this was going to break the mold of those Super Bowls of the past.

Dallas started right off doing things that enraged the Steelers' emotional leader, Middle Linebacker Jack Lambert. "They mess up your head too much," Lambert had said before the game. "If they beat you, you feel like you've been tricked instead of whipped. I hate teams like that."

For most of the afternoon Lambert looked as if he hated everybody in white. The Steelers didn't draw a penalty the entire game, but it was not because Lambert didn't try, particularly on one very visible occasion. Gerela had missed a field goal in the second quarter and Dallas' Cliff Harris was so pleased by this development that he slapped Lambert on the helmet and then said thank you to Gerela. No one could tell whether it was a playful pat on Lambert's helmet, but they did see Lambert grab Harris and throw him down.

Referee Norm Schachter stepped in and began moving Lambert backwards, warning him that he had better cool off. "I smiled," Lambert said, thereby revealing a facet of his character hitherto well masked. This was the same Lambert who earned the reputation of being the best and meanest of the game's linebackers, and it is the same Lambert who mentioned he did not like the place where the Steelers were headquartered in Miami, as compared to where the Cowboys were staying, which was at a beach-front hotel in Fort Lauderdale. "I hope the sharks eat Staubach," he said.

In the end it wasn't the sharks that got Roger Staubach but the Pittsburgh defense. Some of the old heroes of their front four, like L.C. Greenwood and Dwight White, led the assault that sacked Staubach seven times. That happened to be a Super Bowl record as was the 161 yards that Swann accumulated on his four pass receptions. Just as important, Staubach was harrassed considerably on a few other occasions and could not move his team as successfully as he had been able to in the early going.

It was somewhat in character for the Cowboys not to realize what a spectacle the game had been. They reacted to the loss with a humor and graciousness that reflects Landry's control of the squad.

"I don't care what kind of catch a guy makes if he beats me," Mark Washington said. "Swann just beat me one time too many."

Staubach said, "We had our chances. Overall, Pittsburgh is the best, but it was a good season."

"Was it exciting?" Jean Fugett said. "I guess it was. I guess maybe we can't play a dull game."

Neither can Lynn Swann. And the combination of Dallas being there and Swann rising to the occasion—up, up and away—made it something for everybody in Miami to take home to think about until next year. Who said the Super Bowl is dull?

A Game No One
Should Have Lost

BY   JOHN   UNDERWOOD

DAN FOUTS COMPLETED 33 PASSES FOR 433 YARDS IN THE SAN
DIEGO CHARGERS' THRILLING OVERTIME DEFEAT OF THE MIAMI
DOLPHINS. BUT THE IRONY OF GAMES LIKE THIS, ACCORDING
TO JOHN UNDERWOOD, IS THAT ALMOST ALWAYS THEY ARE
DECIDED BY GUYS LIKE ROLF BENIRSCHKE.

It is the one great irony of professional football that magnificent games such as San Diego's wonderful, woeful 41–38
overtime AFC playoff victory over Miami are almost always
decided by the wrong guys. Decided not by heroic, bloodied
men who play themselves to exhaustion and perform breath-
taking feats, but by men in clean jerseys. With names you
cannot spell, and the remnants of European accents, and slen-
der bodies and mystical ways. Men who cannot be coached,
only traded. Men whose main objective in life, more often
than not, is to avoid the crushing embarrassment of a
shanked field goal in the last 30 seconds.

There, at the end, in a moist, numbed Orange Bowl still
jammed with disbelievers after 74 minutes and 1,030 yards
and 79 points of what San Diego Coach Don Coryell called
"probably the most exciting game in the history of pro

football," was Dan Fouts. Heroic, bloodied Fouts, the non-pareil Charger quarterback. His black beard and white jersey crusted with dirt. His skinny legs so tired they could barely carry him off the field after he had thrown, how many? A playoff record 53 passes? And completed, how many? A play-off-record 33? For a playoff-record 433 yards? And three touchdowns?

Ah, Fouts. The real Smilin' Jack of Air Coryell. The guy Otto Graham says activates "the greatest offense" in pro football history. (Outrageous comparisons are a dime a dozen around the Chargers these days.) Smilin' Dan takes his offensive linemen—Billy Shields, Doug Wilkerson, Don Macek, *et al.*—to dinner after a no-sack day and sets NFL passing records with every breath. If he'd only pay his union dues, what a terrific fellow Fouts would be. Fouts should have decided the game.

Or Kellen Winslow. There, at the end, his magnificent athlete's body battered and blued by a relentless—if not altogether cohesive—Miami defense. Winslow *had* to be carried off. Time after time during the game he was helped to the sidelines, and then, finally, all the way to the dressing room, the last man to make the postgame celebration. Staggering, sore-shouldered, one-more-play-and-let-me-lie-down Winslow, looking as if he might die any minute (the only sure way he could have been stopped), catching, how many? A playoff-record 16 passes? For a playoff-record 166 yards?

Winslow is listed as the tight end in the San Diego offense. The Dolphins know better. Like the 800-pound gorilla, Winslow plays just about wherever Winslow wants to play: tight end, wide receiver, fullback, wingback, slotback. Even on defense, as Miami discovered when he blocked what would have been the winning field goal and thereby spoiled what Dolphin Guard Ed Newman called—another drum roll, please—"the greatest comeback in the history of professional football." Winslow should have decided this game.

Or there, on the other side. Don Strock, the gutty, heroic, 6' 5" Miami relief pitcher. Strock coming in with the Dolphins submerged at 0—24 and not only matching Smilin' Dan pass for pass, but doing him better than that for so long a stretch that it looked for sure the Dolphins would pull it out.

Throwing (42 times, 28 completions) for 397 yards and *four* touchdowns, and getting Miami ahead and into position to win at 38–31, and then at the threshold of victory twice again at 38–38.

Strock was raised in Pennsylvania where he watched the immortal (more or less) King Corcoran quarterback the Pottstown Firebirds ("I learned by watching King Corcoran that you can't learn anything by watching King Corcoran," he says), and he used to be quite the mad bomber. He is called "Stroke" for the artful way he can cut an angle with his long, precise passes. But now he's 31, a golden oldie amid Don Shula's miraculous youth movement, and in his 10th year as a Dolphin it is his business to bail out 23-year-old child star David Woodley, the youngest playoff quarterback- starter ever. He did so again Saturday when Woodley suffered a first-quarter malaise—sacks, misfires, interceptions—right out of Edgar Allan Poe. In the end, breakdowns not of his doing cost Strock exactly what Newman said it would have been—the greatest playoff comeback in the NFL's history. "Strock," said Fouts, "was awesome." Strock should have decided this game.

Fittingly, all of the above helped make it what Fouts himself called "the greatest game I ever played in." (See? It's catching.) But, typically, none of them had even a bit part in the final scene. Overtime games almost always come to that because in overtime the objective shifts to a totally conservative aim: The first team close enough tries a field goal. Be cool, play it straight, pop it in. Thus, after a day-into-night parade of exquisite offensive plots and ploys—including a spectacular fleaflicker Shula called from the bench, Strock throwing 15 yards downfield to a button-hooking, well-covered Duriel Harris, who quickly lateraled to Tony Nathan for a 40-yard scoring play that ended the first half to bedlam noise—the final blow was a comparative feather duster, struck by a former 123-pound weakling in a dry, spotless uniform. After the haymakers that had kept the old bowl rocking for almost four hours, it was a finishing jab that buckled the Dolphins. A tidy little 29-yard love tap that Rolf Benirschke put slightly right of center, 13 minutes and 52 seconds into overtime.

Two years ago Benirschke, son of a German-born animal pathologist, almost died from the effects of an intestinal illness known as Crohn's Disease. He lost 50 pounds, and his courageous comeback after two operations, which left his stomach zippered with a massive scar, has been well chronicled. He is a placekicker (soccer-style, of course). It takes nothing away from him, however, to say that the denouement last Saturday evening was more negative than positive, not a question of which team would deliver the knockout punch, but which team's kicker would not miss one more easy field goal.

Six minutes into the overtime Benirschke missed a 27-yarder that would have won it then and there. "I must have rushed to set up," he was to say later, "but that's no excuse." After the overtime kickoff Fouts had driven the Chargers 79 yards in 12 plays to the Miami eight, and Benirschke went in and duck-hooked the kick to the left. "Fortunately," he said, "I got a second chance." The Dolphins' Uwe von Schamann (who was born in West Berlin) had two chances, too. He missed both.

From doing everything wrong at the start to doing everything right for almost three quarters, Miami had lost its touch again when ahead 38–31 with less than five minutes to play in regulation time. Strock had just put together the kind of drive Shula had schemed up beforehand (before, that is, the shock of 0–24 and the need to dust off Strock and such gaudy acts as the fleaflicker that Coryell hadn't seen "since high school")—a 13-play expedition that consumed seven minutes and had the Dolphins on the San Diego 21, in good shape for some clinching points. But there Fullback Andra Franklin was stripped of the ball by Defensive Tackle Gary Johnson and Linebacker Linden King, fumbling it away, and Fouts quickly charged his team 82 yards to the tying touchdown—a nine-yard pass to Tailback James Brooks.

Back came Miami, driving all the way to the San Diego 25 in less than a minute. Stopping the clock with four seconds to play, Shula sent in von Schamann to try a 43-yarder. Uwe is no stranger to pressure. Four times this year, under like circumstances, he has rammed through game-winners. The snap was high, but Strock got it down in good order. Apparently, however, von Schamann kicked too far up on the ball and it did not rise quickly enough. Winslow, a defensive ringer, a padded Wilt Chamberlain lurking at linebacker, leaped and batted it away.

Von Schamann went down to the far end of the Dolphin bench, away from everybody, and meditated as the overtime started. After Benirschke's life-giving miss, he got his second chance. A weak San Diego punt and a 21-yard Strock pass to Jimmy Cefalo got Miami into field-goal range once more.

On fourth down at the Charger 17, in went von Schamann. The snap was true, the hold good—but in his eagerness to get under the ball, von Schamann dipped his left side a little too much and his right foot, sweeping across, scraped the ground behind the ball. Von Schamann turned away disgustedly almost as soon as he finished his follow-through. Dolphin Tackle Eric Laakso said such kicks have a "distinctive sound," and even though you don't see them the sound "gives you a sick feeling." The ball disappeared into a sea of dirty white shirts.

Afterward, von Schamann said that although he knew he would "find the answers" for his failures, he had none now. He was appropriately philosophical. The irony is that such crucial games are so often decided by such a disproportionately small number of specialized plays and players: that the field-goal kicker's importance is so exaggerated at those times. Doubly ironic for the Dolphins was that, almost 10 years ago to the day, they had *won* such a game: the longest game in playoff history, a double-overtimer in which Kansas City's Jan Stenerud missed, and then Miami's Garo Yepremian made, the winning field goal.

It is also true that Miami—that is to say, *other* players making *other* mistakes—had dug itself into a ghastly hole to begin with, one 10 placekickers could not have dug them out of. Sipping coffee in his office on the eve of the playoffs, Shula had said the Dolphins could not afford to let San Diego "have anything quick, anything cheap." Which is exactly what they did, with a comedy of errors that even included the failure to cover a kickoff. The kick, wind buffeted, dropped between two lines of Miami receivers and the Chargers recovered it, setting up a touchdown.

Miami had gone off a three-point favorite, more a reflection of Shula's reputation, said one league man, than anything else. On paper, Miami seemed weakest where San Diego was strongest, most especially in the passing game. Air Coryell had Fouts; Miami had a suspect secondary that one local columnist at mid-season had given, en masse, "the turkeys of the year award." A high-scoring game did not augur well for the Dolphins; they had gotten 24 points or more only seven times in 16 games. San Diego had turned the trick 11 times.

But always, figures are relative. Two croutons make little impact on a Caesar salad. Two wives are an overabundance. From early on Shula had seen "something special" about this Miami team, and despite having failed again to advance in the playoffs (the Dolphins have not won a playoff game since the 1973 season), and despite so heartbreaking a finish, the defeat was "something we'll be able to handle," he said, because obviously his is a team on the come.

For San Diego, on the other hand, the future would appear to be now. It has been a year of wrenching acrimony and thrilling vindication for Coryell. He has lost star players (John Jefferson, Fred Dean) and suffered withering criticism. A man with a rival club said that San Diego lacked "the one thing Miami has—character." Coryell himself had seemed beaten down by the implications. He told a San Diego writer the week of the game how tough it had been, losing four out of the five playoff games he had coached; how it took "two or three months" to "get over the depression." As the Dolphins went ahead in the fourth quarter, he could be seen hunched over, hands on knees, his eyes looking despairingly at the scoreboard, as if a new depression had already begun.

But as Fouts said later, this is a "more mature" San Diego team that "seems to get better with adversity." The drive to the winning field goal over Miami was as good an indication as any of what Air Coryell is now capable of, and it was all the more impressive because it came at a time when Miami was apparently the stronger team.

In that 74-yard advance from the Chargers' 16-yard line, a semblance of order returned to San Diego's attack. "We ended the game as we began it," said Fouts, noting key catches and the fact that he had almost unlimited time to work his will on the reeling Dolphin defense. Fouts's linemen picked up the Miami stunts and moved the Dolphins around like pinballs, caroming them from one blocker to another.

The field-goal setup was a beauty. Wide Receiver Charlie Joiner, in motion, cut across the field at the snap and saw that Miami had switched from a three-deep to a two-deep zone. He broke his pattern and split the defense up the middle. Fouts looked right, then left, then saw Joiner—"and I had all the time in the world to get it to him." The play covered 39 yards to the Miami 10, and Coryell immediately sent in Benirschke. Lights out, Miami.

Struggling off the field afterward, the redoubtable Winslow grasped Charger Publicist Rick Smith and whispered, "I feel like I've been to the mountain top."

"You're there, Kellen, you're there," said Smith.

"No," said Winslow, barely audible. "Not yet. Not quite."

Off on the Wrong Foot

BY   PAUL   ZIMMERMAN

JOE MONTANA TO DWIGHT CLARK. FEW PLAYS IN THE HISTORY
OF SPORTS ARE AS FAMOUS AS CLARK'S TOUCHDOWN CATCH
AGAINST THE DALLAS COWBOYS IN THE 1982 NFC TITLE GAME.
PAUL ZIMMERMAN WAS THERE AND RETURNED WITH THIS
MEMORABLE REPRISE OF A SAN FRANCISCO TREAT.

It will be part of San Francisco's history; it will become a
legend of this city, right up there with the Great Earthquake
of 1906. The Drive. Eighty-nine yards to the Super Bowl, 89
yards at the end of a day that seemed hopeless. The Drive. In
10 years at least half a million people will claim to have been
in Candlestick Park the day the 49ers drove the length of the
field in 13 plays to beat Dallas 28–27 and win a trip to Supe
XVI. In 20 years the number of people who were there will
be more than a million.

"Were you in Candlestick that day, Grandpa?"

"Damn right I was."

"Tell me about it?"

"Well, you see, there were less than five minutes left and it
looked bad for us, boy, real bad...."

Eddie DeBartolo, the team's owner, didn't see The Drive.

He had threaded his way through the crowd to get down near the 49er locker room so he could tell his players how proud he was of them in defeat. "Before that, I'd been out on the deck outside our box leading cheers," he said, "but now it looked hopeless. Just hopeless. I wanted to get in the locker room to commiserate with them."

It hadn't been the 49ers' day. They had turned the ball over only 25 times in 16 regular season games, but they had coughed it up six times against the Cowboys, two of the turnovers leading to touchdowns. Two interference penalties against their brilliant rookie cornerback, Ronnie Lott (one of them on a very questionable call by Side Judge Dean Look), had led to 10 more points. A tough game. The lead had already changed hands five times, with neither team ever leading by more than a touchdown. The 49ers had moved smartly up and down the field and outgained the Cowboys, but Dallas had a historical hook into them in playoff action— the Cowboys had knocked them out of their last three play-offs—and as the 49ers took the ball on their own 11-yard line down 27–21 with 4:54 left, a deep gloom settled over the Candlestick fans.

"I didn't feel gloomy. I felt like we were going to win," said John Brodie, who'd been the 49ers' playoff quarterback in the 1970s. "I knew we were the better team. I'm so sick of Dallas saying, 'Well, those weren't the real Cowboys out there.' They said it when we beat 'em this year and when the Giants beat 'em. How many guys do they carry on their roster anyway?"

"I looked down the field and I saw that patch of grass between our huddle and their goal posts," San Francisco Center Fred Quillan said, "and I thought, 'That's it. That one patch of grass between us and the Super Bowl.'"

Bill Walsh, the 49er coach, gave Quarterback Joe Montana the first two plays to call, sent him out and adjusted his head set. He checked his phone hookup with Line Coach Bobb McKittrick, 10 yards upfield, and Quarterback Coach Sam Wyche, in the press box. He looked up at the clock.

"Almost five minutes left and all our time-outs," Walsh would say. "I liked our chances. If we got as far as the 35, we'd go for it on fourth down, no matter what. If we got stopped before that, we'd probably punt."

The Cowboys were in their nickel defense—four linemen, one linebacker, Champ Dickerson, and six backs. On the first play, Montana threw low on a little dump-off pass to Lenvil Elliot, his halfback. Elliott is 30 years old, a Cincinnati castoff. The speed is gone from his legs, but San Francisco activated him the previous week because he knows Walsh's passing scheme. Misfire, second and 10. A draw play to Elliott picked up six. "I cut-blocked Dickerson, and he went flying through the air and landed on his head," Quillan said. "I don't think he expected that. I think the run surprised them a little."

Walsh signaled a sideline pass to Flanker Freddie Solomon. He grabbed the ball just above his knees for a six-yard gain and a first down on the 23.

"Bob-18," McKittrick said into his head phones—Elliott sweeping right and both guards, John Ayers and Randy Cross, pulling. "Our best running play for the last three years," McKittrick calls it. It picked up 11 yards. First down on the 49er 34.

"Let's run it the other way," Wyche called down from the press box. "You got it," Walsh said. Bob-19, Elliott sweeping left, good for seven yards. Ayers, who'd thrown the springing block, picked himself up slowly. He looked over at Dallas' Randy White, who'd been battling him all day. White was still down. "We were both laying there," Ayers said, "but he didn't get up right away." White left the game for Bruce Thornton. Leg and chest cramps.

"Before our last drive," Cross said, "Walt Downing, our reserve center, came up to me and said, 'Wait till you see the films of Ayers vs. Randy White. They've been flailing and kicking and screaming all day.'"

On second and three Montana misfired to Elliott. Thornton was called offside on the next play, and the 49ers had a first down on the 46. White came back in, the 49ers completed a five-yard curl pass to Fullback Earl Cooper, and the two-minute warning sounded. Cross, who'd been battling the flu, along with a dozen other 49ers, dropped to one knee and got sick on the field.

"I'd thrown up on the sidelines twice before that," he said. "This time I couldn't make it over there. A couple of guys in

32

the huddle got annoyed. They said, 'What the hell did you want to do that here for?' I said, 'Sorry, I couldn't help it.'"

On the sidelines Walsh asked Montana, "What do you think of Freddie Solomon on a reverse left?" "I'm not sure," Montana said. Then he said, "O.K., I'll block the defensive end," who was Harvey Martin. "I aim for the knees," Montana said later. "The great equalizer. Actually, Harvey went upfield, and I sort of collided with Randy White, chest high. I remember last game I did that once and he just started laughing."

The reverse gained 14 yards to the Cowboy 35, then Montana drilled Split End Dwight Clark on an out pattern, right, for 10 more, a very risky, low-percentage pass into the teeth of double coverage by Everson Walls, who'd already intercepted two, and Nickel Back Benny Barnes. "Walls actually got a hand on it," Clark said. "then the ball hit me in the chest." "I thought it would be a knockdown for Walls," Montana said.

A minute and a half left now. Montana hit Solomon on an underneath pattern for 12, down to the 13-yard line, and the 49ers called time with 1:15 showing. Clark slowly sank to the ground. Hal Wyatt, the co-trainer, went out to him. "You O.K.?" he asked. "Water, gimme some water," Clark said. Half a dozen Cowboys were on one knee, heads down, chests heaving. "I looked over at them," Cross said. "They had, well, I don't want to say, a beaten look, but I saw on their faces the same look Thomas Hearns had when Sugar Ray hit him a few times. They had had us backed up, but now they were no longer the aggressors. They were fighting for their lives."

The 49er coaches had taken off their head sets. Walsh talked to McKittrick. They conferred with Montana. The play would be 29-Scissors, the big banana, Solomon dipping inside and then breaking for the left corner, behind a semi-pick by Mike Wilson, who'd replaced Clark. A TD play. Solomon got clear, but the ball sailed wide. Walsh, who seldom shows emotion, let out a yell and leaped high in the air.

"I jumped as high as I've ever jumped in my life," he said. "I thought that was the championship right there. We were never going to get that open again. It had worked perfectly to get Solomon free in the end zone, and we missed it."

"The timing on it was a little off," Montana said. "Yeah, I did happen to see Coach Walsh's reaction. He looked pretty disgusted."

Second and 10 from the 13. "Eighteen or 19-Bob," McKittrick told Walsh. "Pick one." He picked 19, sweep left. It gained seven yards, down to the Cowboy six. "I wasn't thinking TD in that situation," Elliott said. "I was thinking, 'Hold on to the ball, get as much as you can, try to get out of bounds.' "

"They were executing with guys that I didn't even know who they were," Cowboy Strong Safety Charlie Waters said. "I mean who is No. 35? [Elliott]. Who was that No. 30 [Bill Ring] who was in there? I don't mean to be demeaning, but they're not exactly Tony Dorsetts."

"I felt like running out on the field and tackling somebody," said Cowboy Quarterback Danny White.

The 49ers called time with 58 seconds showing. The Cowboys got out of their nickel defense and put three linebackers back in. "Bob-18," McKittrick told Walsh. Sweep right. Walsh shook his head. "We'll pass," he said. "Sprint right option." In the press box Wyche smiled. It was the play that had given the 49ers their first touchdown, Solomon slotted inside Clark on the right side and breaking to the corner after Clark had cleared out underneath in a semi-pick. But it was Step Two of the play that Wyche really enjoyed. Step Two, if Solomon were covered, involved Clark's cutting across the end zone, right to left, doing an about face and braking back right. Montana, rolling to his right, had to find him.

Clark, 6' 4" and 210 pounds, is one of the NFL's greatest possession receivers. The 49ers drafted him out of Clemson in the 10th round in 1979 when they'd gone there to scout Steve Fuller, the quarterback. They had liked the way Clark worked with him in practice. The stop and reverse move is something Clark and Montana have going together. They'll work on it on their own time in practice. "We practiced it from Day One in training camp in Sierra College in Rocklin, California," Wyche said.

"Surround Joe," Quillan told the linemen in that final

huddle. "Give him time." The Cowboys gathered themselves for one last rush. Montana scrambled right. Solomon was covered. Too Tall Jones and Larry Bethea and a blitzing D.D. Lewis were closing in, forcing Montana to the sidelines. "I wasn't going to take the sack," he said. "I couldn't see Dwight open. I knew he had to be at the back of the end zone. I let the ball go. I got hit and wound up on my back. I rolled over. I saw Dwight's feet hit the ground. I heard the crowd screaming."

They were screaming partly from the memory of another great 49er combination, Y.A. Tittle to R.C. Owens, the famous Alley Oop, only this time it was Clark who climbed the sky wire and came down with six points with 51 seconds left. "It was over my head," Clark said. "I thought, 'Oh oh, I can't go that high.' Something got me up there. It must have been God or something."

Walls had lost coverage on Clark. The supposed double coverage never came.

"They're so good at it," Waters said. "It's kind of like sand-lot football, but they're the best I've ever seen at it in the NFL. It's like Fran Tarkenton football, maybe even better than Tarkenton."

The game now stood tied, but, almost anticlimactically, Ray Wersching's extra point resolved the issue. One thrill was left for the record crowd of 60,525. The Cowboys had one last gasp, a 31-yard pass from White to Drew Pearson that carried to the 49er 44-yard line and was halted only because Cornerback Eric Wright got a hand on Pearson's collar and yanked backward. Ten or 15 yards more and Dallas would have had a shot at a winning field goal. It was lights out on the next play, though, when Tackle Larry Pillers shot up the middle, sacked White into a fumble, and End Jim Stuckey recovered.

"The center had pulled out to help on Fred Dean," Pillers said. "I grabbed the center's jersey and hung on for the ride. He pulled me right up to the quarterback and gave me the extra momentum."

Later on, Dallas Coach Tom Landry was asked what was the key to the 49er victory. "Montana has to be the key," he said. "There really is nothing else there except the quarterback."

Well, Cincinnati will find out in the Silverdome. Even now the Cowboys don't seem to be fully convinced, but they're still suffering from shock. The shock of The Drive.

Driven

BY RICK REILLY

WHEN YOUR BACK IS TO THE WALL, WHO YOU GONNA CALL?
WELL, IF YOU ARE THE DENVER BRONCOS AND YOU NEED TO
GO 98 YARDS IN A LITTLE OVER TWO MINUTES, YOU GO TO
JOHN ELWAY. AS RICK REILLY WAS EMINENTLY ABLE TO TESTIFY,
ELWAY TOOK HIS TEAMMATES FOR QUITE A RIDE.

Nobody likes to look into the valley of death and spit as
much as John Elway. Nobody is better when the dogs are at
his cuffs, the barn is burning and the rent hasn't been paid.
No wonder Elway owns three car dealerships in the greater
Denver area. Who runs a better year-end closeout drive than
he? Eighteen times in his nine-year career he had gathered up
his outrageous nerve, magic cleats and nuclear right arm and
taken the Denver Broncos from behind in the fourth quarter
to win. But surely not this time. Not again.

For one thing, the Houston Oilers had just punted the
Broncos into a cozy little corner at their own two-yard line.
For another, there was only 2:07 left in regulation, and Houston's murderous and underrated defense was going to blitz
everybody but the Gatorade boy. There were 98 yards to go,
no timeouts to go it in, and Elway was ready to be fitted for

37

a stretcher. At one point in the fourth quarter of this semifinal playoff game in Denver, he was so out of breath that one of his linemen told Elway that his teammates were having difficulty understanding him in the huddle. Yeah, he had pulled off The Drive, the 98-yard wonder in Cleveland in the 1986 AFC Championship Game, but this situation here was downright unthinkable. One thing about miracles: They don't Xerox well.

Mile High Stadium was a giant woofer. On the Denver sideline, Bronco backup quarterback Gary Kubiak was resigning himself to a permanent goathood. He had bobbled a perfectly good snap and ruined an extra-point attempt in the first quarter. Now, as the minutes ticked down, Denver was behind by that one botched hold, 24–23. "I was standing there thinking, I've got to live all year knowing I messed up that PAT," Kubiak said.

As Elway got ready to drag himself back onto the field one more time, Kubiak yanked on his arm. "Pick me up, Wood," Kubiak said. In sportsese, "pick me up" means "save my bacon." Wood is what Kubiak calls Elway, Wood being short for Elwood, Kubiak's handle for Elway. To Elway, Kubiak was always Koob. Drafted the same year—Elway the shiny first pick in '83, Kubiak the 197th—Kubiak always knew what the score was in Denver. He would sweep up after Elway's parade. Still, they became roommates and best friends. In Elway's first tumultuous years in Denver, the years when he felt hounded, confused and ready to quit, nobody dealt out more hang-in-theres than the Texas farm kid, Kubiak.

But there was more than just bacon to be saved this time, and they both knew it. Elway knew that Kubiak was going to retire after the season. Maybe nobody but Elway cared about the retirement of a lifetime understudy. Here was a guy who had spent his best years behind one of the most durable and celebrated quarterbacks in history, with not a hope of starting, hardly a hope of playing. And yet Koob had never bitched, sniped, complained or even short-sheeted anybody.

"As I was walking out there," Elway said, "I was thinking, We can't let Koob end his career on that bobbled snap."

Some great things are done for history. Some for glory. Some for country, family, God, self. But once in a while, in the dark of a chill January afternoon, great things are done in the name of a roomie.

Not that Elway didn't have a few career pressures on the line himself. He is the one man nobody wants at his Super Bowl party. Three appearances in the Big Bowl so far and three train wrecks. A bad blond joke. Unfortunately, Elway has this annoying habit of not taking a hint. He knows that for all his greatness—he is the NFL's winningest quarterback from 1984 to '91—nothing seems to stick in people's memories quite like the flash of a world championship ring.

"I have a vision of getting a perfect team and winning a Super Bowl," Elway was saying one day before the game against Houston. "Us going in against a team we should beat, and winning big." And if it means he has to "go 10 times" and "get beat 10 times," he says he will. "I just want another chance to win it."

Of course, all of that looked dead now at the feet of the Oilers. All day Elway had been trying to match Houston quarterback Warren Moon missile for missile. Moon started out blazing, three touchdown passes in his first three drives for a 21–6 lead. Elway and his tiny receivers led the Broncos back, picking and begging and running for their lives during a second-quarter 88-yard drive to pull within eight, 21–13. Kicker David Treadwell's field goal—a clothesline 49-yarder in the third—made it 21–16, but Moon was a vision. Of the three dozen passes he threw on this remarkable Saturday, only nine weren't caught, and three of those were drops. One, by Haywood Jeffires in the end zone, would have been a touchdown. At one point, Moon saved a sure sack with a preposterous lefthanded flip to Lorenzo White not six inches before the quarterback landed face-first on the turf. It set up a 25-yard field goal by Al Del Greco and another eight-point lead, 24–16.

Still, as any Cleveland Browns fan will tell you, Elway is like a magazine salesman—he's hard to keep off your doorstep. Back Denver came on an 80-yard fourth-quarter touchdown drive, this one featuring 1) a fumbled snap that Elway scooped up and fired for a first down, 2) a converted fourth-and-four that went for 26 yards and 3) innumerable fingernails and shoestrings that somehow slipped through

Houston's gasping defenders. At one point, Houston defensive end William Fuller was so frustrated that he sat down in the middle of the field and didn't get up for two minutes. Now Denver trailed by one.

Finally, and for once, Denver's defense held. Now came Greg Montgomery's first punt of the afternoon. Now the plea by Kubiak. Who better to answer it than Elway? "Nobody," said Moon later.

The first play was planned, a .22-caliber bullet to wideout Michael Young for 22 yards, but the rest "were all John improvising," marveled Denver center Dave Widell. And almost nothing worked. On first down from the 24-yard line, Elway threw an incompletion. The Broncos then went nowhere on second and third, and Elway faced a fourth-and-six at the 28. He set up, abandoned that setup and set out for a very bright orange first-down marker on the east sideline. If he got there before Houston's disagreeable linebacker, Lamar Lathon, Denver's season could go on. If he didn't, it was over. He got there. Nervy.

Again, on first, second and third downs, Denver was stifled. Now it was fourth-and-10, still 65 yards from a touchdown, only 59 ticks to go, Denver's third fourth-and-the-season down of the day. Coronary specialists turned on their beepers. Every alley Elway looked down, there was a guy standing with a gun. The crowd at Mile High Stadium was beside itself. On the scoreboard, in 15-foot high letters read a simple comment: THIS IS TENSE.

But who is better in a furnace than Elway? He took the shotgun snap, stepped up in the pocket, eluded the fingers of poor Mr. Fuller and darted forward as if he might run. Ahead of him were two Johnsons. The one in orange was Denver receiver Vance. The one in blue was Houston cornerback Richard. One knew what Elway would do. One didn't. Richard ran toward Elway, refusing to give up another maddening first-down scramble. Vance took off madly toward the sideline. Elway tossed the ball on the run. "Not my prettiest pass," he said, "but it got there." When it did, Vance turned upfield and saw a very pretty sight—open pasture. Forty-four yards later, Denver had a first down at the Houston 21.

"I was soooo close," said Fuller. "Then all of a sudden,

boom, he gets the ball over there. Basically, that was all she wrote." Widell was as giddy as a schoolboy. "Who else in this league makes that play on a fourth-and-10?" he giggled. "Who else?"

One play later, Treadwell trotted onto the field for a 28-yard field goal try with 16 seconds remaining that could make Son of The Drive a legend. Off came Wood. On came Koob to hold. Unfortunately, as the snap came toward Kubiak, it was low, dangerously low. It's funny how sports can be so wonderfully symmetrical. A guy asking to be bailed out can suddenly bail himself out. Kubiak did not catch it so much as he smothered it, trapped it. As Treadwell started forward with his right leg, Kubiak somehow righted the ball. Treadwell double-clutched, Kubiak spun the laces, and the ball went screaming off, obviously unhappy but nonetheless above the crossbar and through the uprights. Somebody call Sotheby's. Works of art *can* be copied. Denver 26, Houston 24.

Wood and Koob approached each other on the sideline. They grinned and hugged the way good friends will, forehead-to-forehead, each with his right hand on the back of the other's neck. Roomies don't need many words.

On the other sideline, the Oilers—five straight years in the playoffs and still only two wins—looked like they had been marbled. "We knew Elway would take it upon himself to run all over the park," a still disbelieving Houston coach Jack Pardee said following the game. "We expected it. And he *still* outran us." Then there was Moon, who could not have played better in a hundred Saturdays. "He's done this time and time before," Moon said, droop-faced. "But to have it done to you, it's really a shock."

Across the way, the demolition engineer was indulging himself a little. "I don't know of a better feeling for a quarterback to have," Elway said. "If there is one, I'd like to feel it. Maybe I will.... in a couple of weeks." First, it's Buffalo on Sunday for Elway's fourth AFC title game in six seasons. Count him out if you want, but he hasn't lost one yet.

Later, in his press conference, Elway had Kubiak on his mind: "I don't know if you guys know this, but Koob's planning on retiring this year."

Surprise hushed the room. Elway looked plaintively at the

Broncos' public relations director, Jim Saccomano, who looked back at Elway as surprised as everybody else. "You mean it hasn't been announced?" Elway asked.

Uh, no, it hasn't. "Uh-oh," Elway said.

Boy, backups never get to do *anything*.

PLAYERS

◆ ◆ ◆

They All Go Bang! At Bambi

BY   EDWIN   SHRAKE

ONE OF THE STARS OF THE AFL WHO LATER ATTRACTED A SUB-
STANTIAL FOLLOWING IN THE POST-MERGER NFL WAS LANCE
ALWORTH, THE SPEEDY AND ELUSIVE WIDE RECEIVER FOR THE
SAN DIEGO CHARGERS. IN 1965 EDWIN SHRAKE WROTE THIS
PROFILE OF THE MAN MOST KNEW SIMPLY AS BAMBI.

Putting a nickname on an athlete is a trickier business than
one might suppose. The idea is to pick out some distinction of
appearance or behavior and symbolize it. Often the best and
simplest symbols are animals, since animals have qualities that
are universal. A fox wherever encountered is a fox, and when
a receiver like Bill Howton is called The Red Fox one knows
at once not only the color of his hair but something of how
Howton used to run pass patterns. In professional football
there are a badger, a hog, a snake, a skunk, an alligator, a
weasel, a tiger, a bull, a hare—a menagerie of symbols. What
makes symbol-selecting difficult is that the nickname must be
precise and easily recognizable, whether it is an animal symbol
or not, and it must be comfortable on the tongue. One could
hardly walk up to Red Grange and say, "Hah yew, Galloping
Ghost?" Nor could one approach Vince Lombardi, who played

on a Fordham line called the Seven Blocks of Granite, and inquire, "What's new, Block?" However, one could address Clyde Turner as Bulldog or Alan Ameche as Horse or, in the quasi-amateur aspect of the game, Paul Bryant as Bear and not feel awkward about it. And in all of sports there has never been a more apt or more accurate nickname than the one borne by Lance Alworth of the San Diego Chargers. It does not please him, as is frequently the case with nicknames, but the image it evokes is of Lance Alworth running, jumping, dodging, all with incredible grace, and that style is Lance Alworth.

They call him Bambi.

Bambi was a deer pursued by wicked hunters with guns that went bang! in a child's tale written by Felix Salten. Maybe children no longer read Bambi but, as it is a cruel and sentimental story, it was perfect material for a Walt Disney movie of 15 or 20 years ago and everybody knew Bambi then, when the current pro football players were of an age to appreciate him. In 1962, when Lance Alworth—a pretty evocative name in itself—was a rookie with the Chargers, he came off the field one afternoon to find Charlie Flowers, a former Mississippi All-America, staring at him with the expression Bob Kane must have had when he woke up with the inspiration for Batman.

"You're Bambi," said Flowers.

"What for?" Alworth asked.

"For your big brown eyes and the way you move," said Flowers.

And he was Bambi. Alworth has tried growing his hair long and dyeing it red to change the impression. He has neglected shaving and gone about scowling, but that merely made him look like Bambi at a masquerade. The only time he escaped the symbol was when a few of the Chargers began calling him Governor Faubus after an Arkansas political campaign in which Lance made speeches in behalf of his friend Orval Faubus. The nickname, besides being a joke, was artificial and could not endure. Nobody can say exactly what class is but everybody is aware of it when in its presence, and Lance has too much class to be called Governor Faubus for long. He is the best spread receiver in professional football and is the classiest-looking at his job. If Alworth played for the New York Giants or Jets—in

that city where all a second-string quarterback named Earl
Morrall had to do was show up to get a network radio program—he would earn $100,000 a year in salaries and endorse-
ments. Alworth is not on relief in San Diego, a sunny, palm-
rustling town in a pocket between the Pacific to the west, the
Cuyamaca Mountains to the east, Los Angeles to the north
and the Mexican border outpost of Tijuana to the south but,
being from the provinces and the generally underestimated
American Football League, Alworth does not have the star status he deserves.

An exception is the state of Arkansas, where Alworth was an
All-America halfback at the university in Fayetteville. It would
not be enough to say that the people of Arkansas have affection for Alworth. They have passion for him. At one pro exhibition game in Little Rock the stands were jammed with people who had come to see Lance. On the second play of the
game Alworth was knocked out. He was carried off the field
by Ernie Ladd and Ernie Wright, which made an interesting
photograph in the Little Rock papers the next day, since Ladd
and Wright are Negroes. Lance returned at the half to wave at
the crowd and assure them that he was all right, and he
appeared twice on television, but his coach, Sid Gillman, did
not put him back into the game. The people were not there to
see the Chargers or their opponents, the Houston Oilers, but
to see Alworth, and club officials expected a noisy protest
from the stands. There was none. The people simply loved
Bambi too much to want him to risk getting hurt.

At the College All-Star Game in the sumer of 1962, Alworth
was trying to explain to a Big Ten tackle the emotion
Arkansas has for its football players. "When I go home they
don't recognize me," said the tackle. The All-Stars were on a
bus driving through Evanston, a Chicago suburb, and the tackle pointed out the window to a car with Arkansas plates. "See
if they recognize you," the tackle said. As the bus passed the
car Lance leaned out the window and did what they refer to in
Arkansas as calling the pig—yelling, "Whoooo, pig, sooey!" the
Arkansas battle cry. From the car came shouts of "Whoooo,
pig, sooey!" and "Hey, Lance!" The tackle was convinced.
The tackle did not know that the people in the car were University of Arkansas Publicist Bob Cheyne and his family, but it

is not likely that it would have made any difference who was in the car. Anybody in a vehicle with Arkansas plates would have known Lance Alworth.

Alworth led the nation in punt returns at Arkansas in 1960 and 1961 and the Razorbacks won 25 of 31 games during his career, but his ground-gaining was unimpressive. Arkansas played the wing T, and Lance was used as an outside running threat. Forced to cover Alworth, the opposition allowed the Arkansas quarterbacks to cut back against the flow of pursuit for good yardage. Alworth was seldom employed as a pass receiver, although he did score on a 67-yard pass against SMU in 1961. He was a run-pass-kick athlete who could do anything better than anybody else, and by merely stepping onto the field he helped Arkansas win or tie three straight Southwest Conference championships when the Razorbacks were not that strong.

Lance went to Arkansas through a combination of Frank Broyles's charm and Johnny Vaught's rules. Born in Houston, Alworth grew up in Brookhaven, Miss., where he won 12 high school athletic letters. He had learned football in the oil camps of Mississippi and Louisiana among college football players working at summer jobs. "They called the game roughhouse," he says. "I was in the second grade and played with the big boys on a hard, graveled lot. One boy would kick off and 15 or 20 of us would go after the ball. The one who got it ran as far as he could. When he was downed he'd throw the ball over his head and somebody else would get it and start again until somebody took it across the goal. When we finished, our faces would be scraped to shreds, but it was fun."

Ole Miss signed Alworth after his senior year in high school, but Coach Vaught had rules against married players and Lance, at 17, had married 15-year-old Betty Allen. While Vaught was thinking up some exceptions to his rules, Arkansas Coach Broyles and his wife, Barbara, entered the situation, and soon the young Alworths were en route to Fayetteville. "If you're a high school kid and Frank talks to your parents, you're going to Arkansas," Lance says. "He comes on with that solid, Christian, considerate, engaging manner of his, telling them how he's going to take care of their boy, and you're gone." Alworth is still consumed by devotion for Arkansas. His Charger roommate, All-AFL Fullback Keith Lincoln, sat with Lance, watching the Arkansas-Texas game on television this year. "Lance got blue in the face from yelling, and first thing I knew I was standing on the bed yelling for him," says Lincoln.

Alworth lives with Betty and their two children in a two-story house in a fashionable section of Little Rock, where he has recently retired from the advertising business because, he says, "I worked from 8 in the morning until 11 at night and was mentally and physically exhausted as I've never been before. I won't do that again. I like to play golf and fish too much." He considers himself a citizen of Arkansas, and as such worked for Faubus. (He believes the man was misunderstood during the Little Rock integration trouble in 1956.) Lance went out and shook hands for Faubus, but he also shakes hands with every Charger before every game. He accepted with grace the kidding his teammates gave him when he returned from the Faubus campaign. Crosses were burned above Alworth's dressing cubicle in San Diego. Negro Halfback Paul Lowe, who was born and brought up in the Watts district of Los Angeles, led Freedom Marches and made civil rights speeches in front of Alworth in the locker room. On Lance's first day back from the Faubus campaign, white Linebacker Paul Maguire, since traded to Buffalo, stepped into a huddle and said, "What's going on here? I thought this was a segregated scrimmage." The Negroes laughed, and so did Alworth. "In my honest opinion, the southern players get along with Negroes better than most players from other parts of the country," says Lance. "Maybe we try harder because of where we're from, but as far as I'm concerned we're all the same. There are no racial factions of this team. We have the speeches and Freedom Marches in the locker room only when everybody is feeling good. There's nothing bitter about it."

Lance was signed for the Chargers by Al Davis, now the coach and general manager at Oakland, and it was a con job of rare smoothness. Alworth had been the first draft choice of the San Francisco 49ers of the National Football League but did not discuss salary with them. "Davis had me sold on San Diego," Lance says, "and when I met Red Hickey [then coach of the 49ers] I asked for a no-cut contract. Red is from

Arkansas, but I don't know him well. He spent 10 minutes telling me why I couldn't have a no-cut contract. I told him I had a no-cut offer from the other league, and he said, O. K., he guessed I could have one from San Francisco. I didn't much like that attitude. I didn't care which league I went to, except Davis had promised I could play sooner at San Diego and that was what I wanted."

Alworth's career with the Chargers began off-key. Several players were kicking 40-yard field goals for fun in practice when Line Coach Joe Madro shouted for them to stop before someone got hurt. Alworth, who had absorbed a number of beatings as a college football hero and had soaked up a skinful of buckshot while leaping a fence with a watermelon under his arm, could not imagine getting hurt kicking a field goal. As he kicked one last time, another player pushed him. Lance's foot hit the top of the ball and flew up with a tremendous snap. A muscle in his right thigh, above the knee, popped and rolled up like a window shade. Alworth was put into a cast and warned by a doctor not to straighten his leg for two weeks, but the Charger trainer (who has been replaced by efficient young Jim Van Deusen) ordered Lance out of the cast and told him to run his leg into shape. Later, two men held Alworth on a table while the trainer tried to massage what he insisted was a "blood pocket" out of Lance's leg. "I could feel that muscle squibbling around. He'd mash it down and get the blood to bulge up and then the muscle would squibble loose again. I had tears in my eyes when I finally made them let me up. I figured, well, it was all the same in football from high school on. Nobody would believe you were hurt. They'd say for you to come on and get at it when you couldn't walk, and they'd lug you off the field like a sack. But last year when I had a bad knee, Jimmy Van Deusen asked me three days before the championship game if I could run on it and I told him no and he believed me. I appreciated that."

Alworth—as Bambi, the gifted, the quick, the graceful—survived that first experience and played four games as a rookie, catching 10 passes and scoring three touchdowns. His statistics since then have been remarkable. In the three following seasons, including this one, Lance has had an average of more than 20 yards per catch and, carrying out the primary mission of a deep receiver, which is to score, has made a touchdown once every five receptions. And that is not on a small number of catches. In 1963 he caught 61 passes for 1,206 yards and 11 touchdowns. Last year it was 61 catches for 1,235 yards and 13 touchdowns. So far this year Lance has 62 catches for 1,428 yards and 12 touchdowns—picking up 147 yards and two touchdowns just last Saturday against the Jets. In his first two seasons Alworth was not working against defenses as tough as he would have faced in the NFL, but in the past two seasons there has not been that much difference between the leagues. And Alworth has not had a Johnny Unitas throwing to him. He did have Tobin Rote, but in a fading period, and now he has John Hadl, who has become a clever quarterback but never will be chosen to illustrate a picture book of classic passers.

Alworth, moreover, managed his accomplishments of 1963 and 1964, both All-AFL years, without learning the moves that are to a pass receiver what feints are to a basketball player. He got by on 9.6 speed and his sure hands. This year has been different. Lance has faced so much double coverage that he has been forced to resort to foolery. "The move gets me away from the first man," he says. "If there's a linebacker out there with me and he crowds me and hits me, he can knock me off the pattern. But if he stands back a couple of yards he doesn't have a chance, because the only linebacker quick enough to do that and stay with me is Bobby Bell of Kansas City. I saw Bobby Bell almost catch Paul Lowe from behind once, and if he can do that to Lowe he can do it to me. Usually I can use a move to get away from the linebacker and then worry about the corner back. If there are two backs on me, John [Hadl] will spot it and throw to somebody who has single coverage. It's funny how I used to think a move was just a head fake. I'd run a square-out pattern and not even do a square-out, just kind of circle around, but the backs played me so loose I was open anyway. After studying films, I know better. Charlie Hennigan [of Houston] has the best moves in either league. Every step, he's doing something."

The receiver's most important task, obviously, is to catch the ball when it arrives. That requires concentration as well as touch. Alworth's only flaw is that he tends to become careless, which he admits, and not watch the ball into his hands or run out his patterns when he is not the primary receiver. Now Lance tries to catch a number of slant-in patterns early in the season. "If you catch those, when people are all around you, it means you're concentrating," he says. "I'm aware of the defensive backs, especially in practice, but if I can catch a slant-in and tuck the ball away it means I have a good grip on the ball. There's nearly always something there with a slant-in, an opening between the linebackers or the deep men, and you're running when you get the ball. For a while this year I was dropping the ball—more balls than I've dropped in my whole life—and I was afraid I'd lost it, like a golfer loses it, but it came back. An outside receiver needs quickness and hands. Lots of people have one or the other. I've been lucky."

Although he is devoting more care to his moves, Alworth does not run patterns as they are drawn on the board, and Gillman does not expect him to. The Chargers often throw the ball to a "breaking point"—a specific location on the field—and allow the receiver to arrive there however he thinks best. When the receiver is Alworth, he is frequently seen several feet off the ground, seemingly hanging in the air in a high, balletish leap, while the defensive backs who went up with him are falling back to earth. That leap, that uncanny ability to hang, is as characteristic of Alworth as his grace or his speed. It is a knack that puzzles him. "I can't really jump very high when I try," he says. "In high school as a basketball player I could never cram the ball into the basket. But I have pictures of myself going up for rebounds with my hands above the rim. If I'm concentrating on the ball I don't realize how high up I've gone. A couple of us had a kicking contest with Sam Snead the other day and Snead kicked the top of a seven-foot door. He's 50 something, isn't he? I'm 24 and I couldn't kick anywhere near as high as he could."

Of course, there was no football at the top of that door. Going for a football, Alworth is magic. "Sometimes I jump when I don't need to, I guess," says Lance, "but one reason I jump is to get my body into the ball so it can't be knocked away, especially on third down. And when you're up in the air you don't get hit so hard. They sort of push you. If you're on the ground when you catch it, they pulverize you." Alworth flanks either right or left, usually to the strong side but occasionally to the weak. As a play begins he sometimes stands upright, hands on hips, right knee slightly bent and right foot back a few inches, head turned toward Hadl to hear the snap count and the audible, if there is one. Then he does a little dance step as he starts toward his rendezvous with the ball. But Alworth uses the upright stance only when the footing is uncertain. He prefers to move out from a sprinter's stance, digging hard off his right foot for acceleration, particularly on short patterns. He and Hadl have learned to anticipate each other by now, and their mutual respect has increased. "Lance is the best receiver I ever saw. He makes the clutch catches," says Hadl. "Football," Alworth says, "is recognition, and John can read defenses as well as the coaches can. He spends from four to six hours a day looking at films. He complains about it some. All of us complain about having so many meetings. We meet more than any team I ever heard of, but when the game comes every man knows what he is supposed to do, even though we don't always play like it. Sid Gillman is a fantastic person, with a brilliant mind, and he has taught John a lot. Early this year in a scrimmage, John walked up to the line, spotted a blitz that the defense wasn't supposed to have yet, and called time-out. Last year we'd have run the play anyway and wondered what went wrong. Sid can make anybody a great football player who listens to him. The fans and writers were asking if we could win this year with Hadl, now that Rote had retired. Hadl put us into the championship game last year, which people don't seem to realize. But the fans act like they're trying to boo him out of here the way they booed Jack Kemp out of here. I don't know what they expect."

Hadl calls a San Diego running game which moves well with Lowe, the league's leading rusher, rookie Gene Foster and Lincoln. One factor in its success is that Alworth blocks, a rarity for a spread receiver. "Art Powell [the Oakland end] keeps telling me wide receivers shouldn't have to block," Lance says, "but he doesn't have Sid Gillman harping at him about it. If I block, it helps the passing game and the running game and it helps me. When I go up to a defensive back he can't be sure whether I'm there to block him or catch a pass. All I have to do is get in somebody's way and any of our backs can go the distance. The backs help me by blocking on blitzes to give me more time to get open, so why shouldn't I help them? I've scored two or three times catching the option pass when the defense thought I was blocking and hurried up to meet the run. Besides, blocking feels good."

It was an Alworth block, stubbornly maintained, that freed Lincoln on a 66-yard run with a flare pass in the second game against Buffalo this season, and several times in that same game Lance knocked the safety man off his feet on sweeps. The memory of those blocks must frighten Gillman as he sits meditating at his mountaintop retreat, with orange trees, a swimming pool and a view of the ocean and Tijuana, but nevertheless he insists that Alworth hit the blocking dummies in practice and not spare himself heavy duty in the game. At 6 feet and 185 pounds, Lance is large enough to damage a corner back with a block and clever enough to slip past the man with a touchdown pass. Against Kansas City this year, the Chargers had fourth and one at their own 49 and Hadl threw a quick out-pattern to Alworth. The play was designed for short yardage, but Lance spun by Fred Williamson and went 51 yards to score. "Only Alworth could have made that play to beat as good a corner man as Williamson," says Gillman.

In his double role as coach and general manager, Gillman has had many contract disputes and this summer several Chargers were near mutiny. The San Diego defense is at the top of the AFL in statistics, and the anchor of that defense, 300-pound Tackle Ernie Ladd, is playing out his option, as is Defensive End Earl Faison. Ladd probably will sign a new contract, but Faison maintains he will leave the club. Gillman is as dedicated to winning as he is to bow ties, but he is not an easy man to deal with. ("In Sid Gillman, the milk of human kindness has turned to yogurt," says Sonny Werblin of the New York Jets.) Alworth also was among the late signers, but not because of Gillman. Lance had been advised that the two pro leagues were about to merge and that he should wait and see what happened. There was no merger and Alworth signed, but he still has a yearning to play against NFL defenses—although with an AFL team.

"Any athlete with pride wants to compete against the ones

who are supposed to be the best," Lance says. "The fact is, I don't believe the NFL is the best. I watch plenty of NFL films. Their defenses are not as complex and advanced as ours have become in the AFL. Most NFL teams use the old 4-3 defense, with red dogs coming off of it. Hardly anybody ever does anything that simple in our league anymore, which is why our games don't have as much scoring as theirs. And their corner backs are just people. The only edge the NFL has over us is their experienced quarterbacks—Johnny Unitas, Frank Ryan and Sonny Jurgensen. Our top four teams and the NFL's top seven are not far apart. I hope we get to play against them someday and shut them up."

It is a shame that Alworth's someday seems so far off. A look at him bounding with his long, high stride through an NFL secondary would pleasure the country as much as the fact would satisfy Alworth. And it will take that sort of competition to get Bambi recognized for what he is—the finest spread receiver in the game—before the hunters finally catch him.

The Sweet Life of Swinging Joe

BY DAN JENKINS

IN 1966, WHEN DAN JENKINS WROTE THIS FEATURE ON JOE
NAMATH, THE JETS' QUARTERBACK WAS IN HIS HEADIEST HEY-
DAY. BOLD, BRASH, EXPRESSIVE OF HIS ERA, NAMATH WAS
YOUTH PERSONIFIED. RARELY HAS SUCH A MOMENT IN A LIFE—
AND IN A CULTURE—BEEN MORE VIVIDLY CHRONICLED.

Stoop-shouldered and sinisterly handsome, he slouches against
the wall of the saloon, a filter cigarette in his teeth, collar
open, perfectly happy and self-assured, gazing through the
uneven darkness to sort out the winners from the losers. As
the girls come by wearing their miniskirts, net stockings, big
false eyelashes, long pressed hair and soulless expressions, he
grins approvingly and says, "Hey, hold it, man—foxes." It is
Joe Willie Namath at play. Relaxing. Nighttiming. The boss
mover studying the defensive tendencies of New York's off-
duty secretaries, stewardesses, dancers, nurses, bunnies,
actresses, shopgirls—all of the people who make life stimulat-
ing for a bachelor who can throw one of the best passes in
pro football. He poses a question for us all: Would you rather
be young, single, rich, famous, talented, energetic and
happy—or President?

Joe Willie Namath is not to be fully understood by most of us, of course. We are ancient, being over 23, and perhaps a bit arthritic, seeing as how we can't do the Duck. We aren't comfortably tuned in to the Mamas and the Uncles—or whatever their names are. We have cuffs on our trousers and, freakiest of all, we have pockets we can get our hands into. But Joe is not pleading to be understood. He is youth, success, the clothes, the car, the penthouse, the big town, the girls, the autographs and the games on Sundays. He simply *is*, man. The best we can do is catch a slight glimpse of him as he speeds by us in this life, and hope that he will in some way help prepare us for the day when we elect public officials who wear beanies and have term themes to write.

Right now, this moment, whatever Joe means to himself behind his wisecracks, his dark, rugged good looks, and his flashy tailoring, he is mostly one thing—a big celebrity in a celebrity-conscious town. This adds up to a lot of things, some desirable, some not. It means a stack of autographs everywhere he goes ("Hey, Joe, for a friend of mine who's a priest, a little somethin' on the napkin, huh?"), a lot of TV and radio stuff, a lot of photography stills for ads and news and continual interviews with the press. Such things he handles with beautiful nonchalance, friendliness—and lip.

Then comes the good part. It means he gets to sit at one of those key tables in Toots Shor's—1 and 1A, the joke goes—the ones just beyond the partition from the big circular bar where everyone from Des Moines can watch him eat his prime rib. It means when he hits P. J. Clarke's the maître d' in the crowded back room, Frankie Ribando, will always find a place for him, while, out front, Waiter Tommy Joyce, one of New York's best celebrity-spotters, will tell everyone, "Joe's inside." It means he can crawl into the Pussy Cat during the late hours when the Copa girls and the bunnies are there having their after-work snacks, even though the line at the door may stretch from Second Avenue to the Triborough Bridge. It means he can get in just as easily at two of his other predawn haunts, Mister Laffs and Dudes 'n Dolls, places long ago ruled impenetrable by earth people, or non-members of the Youth Cult.

Easing into the clubs and restaurants that he frequents, Joe

Willie handles his role well. "Don't overdo it, man," he says. "I can hang around till 3 or 4 and still grab my seven or eight." He sits, he eats, he sips, he smokes, he talks, he looks, and maybe he scares up a female companion and maybe he doesn't. "I don't like to date so much as I just like to kind of, you know, run into somethin', man," he says.

Namath is unlike all of the super sports celebrities who came before him in New York—Babe Ruth, Joe DiMaggio and Sugar Ray Robinson, to name three of the more obvious. They were *grown men* when they achieved the status he now enjoys. Might even be wearing hats. They were less hip to their times and more or less aloof from the crowd. Joe thrusts himself into the middle of it. Their fame came more slowly—with the years of earning it. Joe Willie Namath was a happening.

He happened first when he was a sophomore passing whiz who made Alabama Coach Bear Bryant change his offense. He happened again as a junior when he proved to be such an away-from-the-field mover that Bryant had to kick him off the team for drinking and carousing before the last two games of the season. He happened again when he returned to take Alabama to the 1964 national championship on a gimpy leg. Then Sonny Werblin, the owner of the New York Jets, made him *really* happen when he gave him that $400,000 contract on the second day of 1965. No football player in history had ever been worth half that much. But this wasn't all. He quickly had to undergo an operation on his knee to have a torn cartilage removed and a loose ligament tied. And, thanks to those splendid satirists, Robert Benton and David Newman, the hip line in New York became, "Sorry I can't make your party, Sybil, but I'm going to the tapping of Joe Namath's knee."

He was already a celebrity then, but his image grew throughout 1965 when a certain amount of suspense built as to whether he would be drafted, or whether his knee would allow him to play any football at all for Werblin's $400,000. During it all, the wisecracks flowed like cocktails.

"I'd rather go to Vietnam than get married," he said as the draft board in his home town of Beaver Falls, Pa. requested that he appear for his physical.

Then after he flunked it and a lot of superpatriots bristled, as they did at Cassius Clay's attitude, Joe said with brutal honesty, "How can I win, man? If I say I'm glad, I'm a traitor, and if I say I'm sorry, I'm a fool."

Once when he was asked to point out the difference between Bear Bryant and Jet Coach Weeb Ewbank, Joe grinned and unwisely said, "Coach Bryant was always thinking about winning. Weeb is mainly concerned over what kind of publicity you get."

When a writer tried to tease him about his classes at Alabama, asking if he majored in basket-weaving, Joe Willie said, "Naw, man, journalism—it was easier."

When he was asked to explain the origin of the white shoes that he wore—and still wears—during a game (and now endorses commercially), he shot back, "Weeb ordered 'em. He thought it would save tape."

But all of this was a year ago. Now in this season as he goes about the business of proving that he is worth every cent of his contract (he has thrown nine touchdown passes and put the Jets in first place in the American Football League's Eastern Division through five games), he is becoming the quarterback that Werblin gambled he would be—a throwing artist who may eventually rank with the best—and he is still a swinger. Namath may be Johnny Unitas and Paul Hornung rolled into one; he may, in fact, be pro football's very own Beatle.

He lives in a penthouse on New York's upper East Side, one that features a huge white llama-skin rug, an Italian marble bar, an elaborate stereo hookup, an oval bed that seems to increase in size with each glance, a terrace, and a couple of roommates—Joe Hirsch, a writer for *The Morning Telegraph*, and Jet Defensive Back Ray Abruzzese, whom he knew at Alabama.

Of Hirsch, Joe Willie says, "I got my own handicapper." Of Abruzzese, he says, "I got my own bartender," referring to Abruzzese's onetime summer job tending bar at Dudes 'n Dolls. And of his apartment, he says proudly, "I had the same decorator that Sinatra had for his pad."

He whirls around the city in his gray Lincoln Continental convertible, the radio blaring, parking by fireplugs whenever

58

possible, wearing tailor-made suits with tight pants and loud print linings, grabbing checks, laughing, enjoying life, spending maybe $25,000 a year ("On nuthin', man") and wondering why anyone should be offended.

"I believe in letting a guy live the way he wants to if he doesn't hurt anyone. I feel that everything I do is O.K. for me, and doesn't affect anybody else, including the girls I go out with," he says. "Look man, I live and let live. I like everybody. I don't care what a man is as long as he treats me right. He can be a gambler, a hustler, someone everybody else thinks is obnoxious, I don't care so long as he's straight with me and our dealings are fair. I like Cassius Clay, Bill Hartack, Doug Sanders and Hornung, all the controversial guys. They're too much. They're colorful, man. If I couldn't play football, I'd like to be a pro golfer. But I like everybody." Joe's eyes sparkle, as if he is getting ready to make a joke, and he says, "Why, I even like Howard Cosell."

Joe Willie's philosophy is more easily grasped when one realizes what he lifted himself up from in Beaver Falls. It is a picturesque but poor town in the hills about 30 miles outside of Pittsburgh. He was the youngest of five children, and his parents were divorced when he was in the sixth grade. His father was a mill worker. He lived with his mother, and there was little money, so Joe hustled. He shot pool, he shined shoes, he ran messages for bookies, he hustled; he got by. "Where I come from," he says today, "ain't nobody gonna hustle *me*, man."

As he prepared for his senior year of high school the idea of going to college was remote. An older brother, John, was a career man in the Army, a warrant officer now in Vietnam. Joe was set on joining the Air Force and making it a career. What stopped him was a lot of touchdown passes and offers from precisely 52 universities, including Notre Dame—but not Alabama.

"I wanted to go to Maryland because I was stupid enough to think it was down South," he says. "I didn't know from outside Pittsburgh, man. All I knew was that I wanted to go South. I think a lot of kids from the East and Midwest do because of the climate."

Namath took the college board exams and failed them at

Maryland. "You needed 750 and I scored 745, right? They wanted me to take it again, but I said to hell with it." He thought next of Penn State, but Maryland had to play Penn State the next few seasons and didn't want to face Namath. Maryland's coaches promptly called Bear Bryant at Alabama, whom the Terps would not play, and Bear welcomed, "the greatest athlete I've ever coached."

Despite his dismissal for the last two games of his junior season, Namath worships Alabama and his experiences and successes there. Bryant is the greatest man he has ever known, Joe even has the hint of a southern accent, his closest friends are from Alabama, and if there is anything that makes him mad today, it is the eastern press, which he calls "the northern press."

"There's only three things I'm touchy about," says Joe Willie, who naturally got that name down South. "No. 1, the northern press and how it ignores southern football when I'll guarantee you that a team like Louisiana Tech can beat about 80 of these lousy schools up here. Two is the publicity that Notre Dame gets. And three is a joke about a Hungarian."

One other tiny thing bothered him when he first went to the Jets after taking Alabama to three bowl games with seasons of 10–1, 9–2 and 10–1. He read a statement by a pro player who suggested that Joe might not want to "pay the price" with his big salary. "Can you believe that?" he said. "Why, you can't play for Bryant for four years and not know how to *pay the price* for what you get out of life."

Considering that the most money Joe ever had at one time before he signed the Jet contract was $600, which he got for peddling some Alabama game tickets, he might have been justifed in blowing the whole stack on a car, a blonde and a diamond ring. He had a shrewd business consultant, however, in a Birmingham lawyer named Mike Bite. At Bite's bidding he learned to spread the money out as he would an evening on the town. He takes only $25,000 a year in salary, and will through 1968. He has $200,000 in bonuses working for him over the next 100 years or something like that. And he was generous enough to let members of his family in on the loot. Two brothers and a brother-in-law are on the Jets' scouting payroll at $10,000 a year.

Contrary to popular notion, Joe did give the St. Louis Cardinals, who drafted him in the NFL, some serious consideration. "And they weren't that far off in money," he says. "But they had it laid out wrong, like I had to do a radio show for part of my salary. I couldn't believe that. I said, man, I'm just a football player, and what I make will be for football only." He did guess that the Cardinals, who had an established passer in Charley Johnson, might be dealing for him in behalf of the New York Giants, who had nothing, and, one way or another, he wanted to "get to this town." Bear Bryant's only comment was that Ewbank had won a couple of championships at Baltimore and, if Joe was still interested in winning, he might give that some consideration.

He wasn't a winner right off, of course. The Jets' 5-8-1 record last season made New York the worst team Joe had ever played on. Admittedly, he didn't know the first thing about quarterbacking a pro team. He had the quickest delivery anyone had ever seen, and he got back into the Jets' exceedingly secure passing pocket, formed by Sherman Plunkett, Dave Herman, Sam DeLuca, and Winston Hill—his "bodyguards"—so fast that Kansas City's All-AFL lineman, Jerry Mays, said, "He makes the rush obsolete." But there was so much he had to learn.

At Alabama he had raced back only five yards and released the ball in approximately 1.3 seconds. Ewbank, however, demanded that he get eight yards deep and go 3.2 seconds before throwing. His firmly braced knee prevented him from using the threat of the run, which he had done so well for two and a half seasons in Tuscaloosa.

He had to learn how to read defenses, how to look for tips among the defensive backs, how to hit his receivers on the break, how to set up when he threw, how to call audibles and how to convince his Jet teammates that he could lead them.

"Last year," says Defensive End Gerry Philbin, "there was an undercurrent of resentment—nothing you could pinpoint, but it was there—about Joe's money and his publicity. That was at first. It disappeared when everybody found out what a great guy he is."

Curley Johnson, the punter, says, "Mainly we wanted to see how good he was. He really didn't throw the ball that damn well for a long time. Now, we know how good he is—the best."

Says the ace receiver, Don Maynard, "At first he'd knock us over on short patterns. Now he's slacked off. His timing is great, and he adjusts to situations like a veteran." To this, George Sauer Jr., another top Jet receiver, adds, "He never knew how to throw on the break last season. The ball was always early or late. Now it's there."

Not according to Joe Willie, though. "I haven't thrown well since Alabama," he says. "Maybe it's my leg. I don't know. If I knew, I'd throw better. You hear a lot about getting the ball up here by your ear, but that's junk. It doesn't matter how you deliver as long as the ball goes where you aim it and gets there when it's supposed to. I don't know *how* I throw the ball, and I don't remember anybody ever teaching me to throw it. But there's a lot I *have* found out."

For one thing, Joe says, the quarterback who has to call a pile of audibles (changing plays at the line of scrimmage) is a dumb one. "You're supposed to know what the defense will be when you're in the huddle. I'll only call five or six audibles a game now. Last year it was more. That's funny, too, because the public thinks it's a big deal if a quarterback can switch plays a lot at the scrimmage line. They think it makes him brainy. Man, most of the time it means he's stupid."

A simple thing it took Joe all last season to learn was that backs key on the mannerisms of a quarterback and cover their areas accordingly.

"For example," he says, "about 80% of the time when the quarterback takes the snap, turns and races back to set up with his back to the defense, he'll throw to the right. That's because it's easier, more natural, to plant your feet when you start that way. On the other hand, it's easier to throw left when you drop straight back, without turning around. There are defensive backs who'll play you for this and, of course, you have to cross 'em up."

Among the defenders that have Namath's highest respect are Oakland's speedy Dave Grayson and Miami's Jim Warren, who was with San Diego a year ago. "All you can say about 'em is they play you tight and cover you. To beat 'em, you have to run what we call progressive patterns, you know, something that goes out, slant, down and in. The whole game is trying to get the defensive man's feet turned wrong."

Strangely enough, Joe finds that the ball has a tendency to turn wrong on his home turf of Shea Stadim. "It's my unfavorite place to play," says he. "Somehow, the wind swirls in there, and I don't like what it does to the balls I throw. It could be some kind of fixation, I don't know. Like I have about throwing a night football. It's different, man, I swear. The coaches and sporting-goods salesmen say it's the same ball, but it isn't. It goes different. So does the ball in Shea."

It certainly went differently in Namath's first home game of 1966. He passed for five touchdowns as the Jets humiliated the Houston Oilers 52–13. Joe's hottest streak of all so far came in the fourth quarter of a game at Boston, where he had to hit 14 of 23 passes for 205 yards and two touchdowns so the Jets could salvage a 24–24 tie. This sent the Jets into pure ecstasy. "He brought us back from a bad day in a real clutch situation," said Ewbank. And Publicity Man Frank Ramos, with his usual sharp eye on statistics, pointed out, "The papers are raving about Terry Hanratty at Notre Dame, but do you realize Joe hit as many passes in *one quarter* as Hanratty hit against Northwestern all day long? I think that's interesting."

The supertest for both Namath and the Jets came last Saturday night, however, and they were more than up to it. While Shea Stadium shook from the noise of 63,497 New Yorkers—an all-time AFL record crowd—who had come to cheer their town's only winning team against unbeaten San Diego, Joe Willie's arm was right when it had to be. He threw a touchdown pass to Matt Snell early that gave the Jets a 10–9 lead, which they carried into the last 10 minutes. Then, after San Diego pulled ahead 16–10, Namath rapidly fired three straight completions and whirled his team 66 yards to the winning touchdown and the final 17–16 score. He had shown once more that he could deliver in the clutch, and the Jets had the only defeatless record (4-0-1) in the AFL as proof.

If there is a single myth that Joe Willie would like to have destroyed about pro football, it is the widely held belief that the game's quarterbacks are pampered by opposing defensive linemen; that they are not "shot at," particularly himself because of his bad knee and what his drawing power means to the AFL.

"O.K.," he says. "How about the Houston exhibition in Birmingham in August? Don Floyd comes at me after the whistle, and I move to miss a shot and reinjure my knee. What's that? Of course, Don didn't mean to. He says he didn't hear the whistle, and I believe him. But he was comin' at me and I kind of think he'd of hit me if he could have. What about the Denver game? I still got the wrist bandage and a sore back from that one. Johnny Bramlett, one of their linebackers, is a buddy of mine—he played for Memphis State—and he had me over to dinner the night before the game. His wife cooked an Italian feast, plenty good, too. But the next day he was after me like a tiger, and he'd cuss me when he missed. He wanted to win, man. That's the way it is. I don't think any of our opponents are too interested in my health."

If he stays healthy, Joe Willie may achieve his deepest ambition, which is "to become known as a good quarterback, not a rich one." He may even become what Boston Owner Billy Sullivan says he is now: "The biggest thing is New York since Babe Ruth." Slowly, because trying to fathom youth is always a slow process, you get the impression that Joe is quite serious about it and, despite his hip ways, is working hard to make it. Beneath the gaudy surface there somehow beams through a genuine, considerate, sincere, wonderfully friendly and likeable young man. But he's going to be himself. He's going to do it his way, and nobody else's.

The Blood and Thunder Boys

BY   JOHN   UNDERWOOD

IN THE SUMMER OF 1972, THE MIAMI DOLPHINS WERE POISED
TO BEGIN AN UNFORGETTABLE UNDEFEATED SEASON THAT
WOULD CULMINATE IN A 14–7 VICTORY OVER THE WASHING-
TON REDSKINS IN SUPER BOWL VII. THE TEAM WAS POWERED
BY AN IRREVERENT PAIR OF BACKS NAMED CSONKA AND KIICK.

Don Shula says he would appreciate Larry Csonka even if
Csonka weren't Hungarian. Csonka is unmoved by his filia-
tion. He refers to his father, a former Akron movie-theater
bouncer who once spiraled a chap through a plate-glass door,
and to Shula, his coach, as "those crazy Hungarians," as if he
were somehow exempt. When Edwin Pope, the Miami
columnist, was chided by Shula for slipping out of a Dolphin
press conference to talk to Csonka, Csonka commiserated
with him in a voice just loud enough for Shula to hear:
"Don't worry about it, Edwin, you heard one Honky, you
heard 'em all."

By the same token, Shula says he would appreciate Jim
Kiick even if Kiick were not loath to participate in Shula's
tough practices. Kiick says he hates to practice. ("He's
putting you on," says Shula hopefully.) Kiick particularly

hates Shula's annual 12-minute run. For days beforehand friends and relatives are subjected to his discontent. Two days before this year's run, Kiick announced, "I'm going to tell him that if I wanted to run cross-country I would have gone out for it in high school." He told Shula exactly that, and then ran the 12 minutes ("Another clutch performance by Kiick," an observer noted), bringing up the rear in lockstep with his faithful Hungarian companion Csonka. Shula said the two are so close they even get tired together.

Shula puts up with these insubordinations because he knows some things about Kiick and Csonka. He knows, to begin with, that they have become the best pair of running backs in the NFL, both in accumulative effect—the Dolphins rush for more yards, with a higher average, than any other team—and in all-around intimidation. They run, do Kiick and Csonka, not fancily but with overwhelming finality, like a cave-in. If foot-pounds at impact were measurable in football, it could well prove out that at 233 pounds Csonka hits harder than any back ever hit. Consider this: he once drew a personal foul while running with the ball, having come close to removing the head of a defensive back with his forearm.

Kiick is cuter ("I like to run where there's holes; Larry likes to run where there's people"), but no less resolute. They both block brilliantly. They catch passes. Kiick on third down is as sure-handed as any receiver. And they play hurt, do not blow assignments and never fumble. Well, hardly ever. One fumble apiece in 448 carries last year.

"Kiick and Csonka. You can't spell 'em but you can't stop 'em," says a rival coach, to which Shula would add that you can't trade for 'em, either, because he laughs at those who try. Shula admits it: Kiick and Csonka have come to represent the identity of his team. The successful football coach adapts to his talent, and more than anything else the blood and thunder image of the Dolphins under Shula is an adaptation to Kiick and Csonka. The components necessarily include the team's more spectacular players, Paul Warfield, the gifted wide receiver, and Quarterback Bob Griese, the AFC's leading passer, who shake things up, but the end product is ball control—80-yard drives consuming nine or 10 minutes at a time—and the image of that is Kiick and Csonka.

"Heavy heads," the Buffalo coach called them after the two had rushed for more than 100 yards apiece in a game last year. They were to repeat the pleasure a month later against the Jets. "Throwbacks," Shula calls them. They are two manifestly uncomplicated football players who love the game for the simple things it can do to a man. Dirty his shirt. Bloody his chin. Satisfy his inhibitions. Relieve his tensions. Says Csonka, "It gives a man great satisfaction to do something people are trying to stop him from doing. You don't get ulcers playing football."

Shula does not "send" Kiick and Csonka to play, he "turns them loose." He does not take them out of a game, he calls them off. Kiick sulks when Shula spells him. "It's my way," Kiick says. "Larry is more likely to say something. 'Let me back in, coach.' I never say anything. I sulk." Alice Kiick says her husband's sulks are very outspoken.

Shula has a favorite scene, one he considers typical of the pair, although it involves only Csonka. It was captured for posterity in the highlight film of the preposterously successful 1971 Dolphins, who did not quit kiicking and csonking until they were in the Super Bowl, where they were stopped at last by the Dallas Cowboys. The scene shows Larry Csonka arriving in the end zone. "The image of manhood," Shula says. Csonka's mustache is dripping mud. His face and uniform are slathered with it. His helmet is twisted grotesquely on his head. His expression is impassive: the stoic marine atop Suribachi, vaguely aware that the battle must have been won but certain that the war is not over. In the final frame, Csonka turns and nonchalantly flips the ball over his shoulder. "A picture I love," says Shula.

There are other pictures, not all recorded or authenticated, but still parts of the growing saga of Kiick and Csonka, or "Butch" and "The Kid" as they are called by their worshipful fans. The president of a woman's club in Washington strode into the Redskins' office to buy 5,000 tickets to an exhibition game the other day, and when asked which one she wanted to see, replied, "I want to see Butch Casssidy and the Sundance Kid!" The association with the movie heroes, though tiresome, has been profitable. At least 2,000 posters of them in Western costume were sold in the off-season and a TV film has been made of their exploits, featuring them on horseback, riding into the sunset at the close of another tough day on the trail (actually hotel row on Miami Beach).

But that is make-believe. The true-life adventures are more revealing. The time, for example, when Kiick was seen biting the arm of a New York Jet. Why did you do that, Jim? he was asked. "Because he was twisting my leg." Did you bite him hard? "Hard enough to make him stop twisting my leg." Or the time the two drove 20 hours straight to deliver a new car to Csonka's dad in Ohio. They had just returned from defeat at the hands of Oakland in the 1970 divisional playoffs, and all the way from Miami to Ohio they talked of football and of retribution, and how they must allow nothing to stop them in 1971 short of a broken limb or a concussion, and they got so excited over the prospect that Kiick nearly demolished the dashboard with his fists.

Kiick-Csonka episodes proliferate like hangers in a closet. In the ones involving Csonka a description of his nose is usually included. It has been "laid on the side of his cheek" (one side or the other) nine times. When he was a farm boy in Ohio, it was kicked out of line by a steer. In a high school wrestling match, it led the way to the mat under an opponent Csonka had draped around his neck, only to lose control of. Last season he got up from a nose-to-elbow collision with a Buffalo Bill, streaming blood. Gauging the flow to be unfatal, he returned to the huddle. As he leaned over, the blood dripped audibly on the shoes of Marv Fleming, the Miami tight end. Csonka said Fleming's eyes got wider and wider. His face turned, well, white. Fleming ordinarily is black. "So I leaned the other way to bleed on Kiick, " said Csonka. "He loves it. It makes him think he's been in a game."

Dr. Herbert Virgin, the Dolphin team physician, has found Csonka to be "an extremely stubborn individual." In return for his advice Dr. Virgin has learned to expect such rejoinders as "I'll get over it" (broken nose, sprained knee, etc.) or "I ain't going to the hospital, and that's final." In 1968 Csonka suffered a concussion in a collision with a Bengal linebacker. For weeks afterward he suffered severe headaches. His career was thought to be in jeopardy. A neurosurgeon suggested he reevaluate his occupation. Knocked unconscious again in a game at Miami, Csonka came to on the sidelines to find Dr. Virgin hovering over him and a photographer standing on his hand. He told the photographer to get the hell off. Dr. Virgin called for a stretcher and an ambulance. Csonka got to his feet. "I'm going out the way I came in or I'm not going." Dr. Virgin threw up his hands and followed Csonka to the dressing room.

Csonka wore a special helmet after that, with liquid and air compartments to absorb shock, but he eventually discarded it. The headaches went away. "I had absolutely no doubt I'd be all right," says Csonka. He now runs with greater intelligence, using his head more by learning how to use it less, and he wears his old helmet in a fashion peculiarly his own: the suspension shifted so that it sits forward and down over his head. Willie Lanier, the Kansas City linebacker, tells Csonka it looks as though his helmet's empty. "All I can see is your mustache," he says. "Good," says Csonka. "I'd just as soon you didn't know which hole I'm looking at."

As is often the case with conspicuously physical people, the wreckage on Csonka's face and that which he causes does not in any real sense expose his true character. It is, in fact, a contradiction to it. It is true, for example, that Csonka was an avid hunter, but he can no longer bring himself to kill. He speaks, rather, of the majesty of the moose he has seen in the wilds of Canada and of the cunning of the beavers who built a dam he fell off of last winter.

Csonka actively, vigorously objects to the notion that a brutish football player is necessarily a brute. Last year he was critical of President Nixon for putting himself into the pro football picture, but Csonka says his message was lost in translation.

"I have no hassle with Mr. Nixon," he says. "Who am I to knock a fan? What I object to is that when it comes from him, from the President, it's as if he has sanctioned *all* of football, that football is just naturally wonderful for everyone. Parents start pushing a kid toward the game without realizing the dangers in it. You see it in these Little Leagues. Poor equipment, poor coaching. Some 25-year-old frustrated jock making kids run 8,000 laps. And *gassers!* A kid gets his nose broke, and the coach yells at him and calls him a coward and shames him. Hey, kids listen to adults, especially if he is a coach. They start to believe. Maybe a kid believes he can't compete, that he *is* a coward. If a kid's not ready to hit or be hit, he shouldn't have to."

Csonka explains, in part, his close friendship with Kiick as being a matter of relaxing in each other's company. "No competition for attention," he says. One rainy night before a game in Boston they retired to their room to relax with non-competitive but expensive bottles of bourbon. The game the next day was played on a field barely visible under a sheet of water, and on one particularly untidy run Kiick slid 30 feet in the clutches of a Patriot tackler. He almost drowned, says Csonka. He came back to the huddle looking like a section of the field. Just as signals were called Csonka said, "Don't swallow, Kiick, or you'll spoil all that good bourbon."

Dolphin Trainer Bob Lundy says Kiick and Csonka make him look good because he never has to report them *hors de combat,* and he no longer worries whether they have a high or low threshold of pain because he doubts they feel pain at all. Kiick once played with a broken toe, a broken finger, a hip pointer and a badly bruised elbow. Lundy put a cast on the elbow, and during the game kept asking Kiick how it felt. "Fine, fine," said Kiick. Afterward Lundy unwrapped the elbow to find it swollen twice its normal size, and knew it had to be extremely painful. He asked Kiick how he stood it. "Hell, I'm paid to play," said Kiick.

Last March, in a basketball game at a Miami high school, Kiick fractured his left ankle. While he was at it, the doctor X-rayed both ankles and found the right one had been broken, too, at an earlier time, and was actually in worse shape than the left. "No kidding?" said Kiick incredulously. A couple of weeks later he wore out the bottom of his cast playing basketball.

Medical records and love of football aside, for two men who appear to be so much alike, Jim Kiick and Larry Csonka are nothing alike.

James Forrest Kiick is a Jersey dude who went to the University of Wyoming because his grades weren't good enough to get him in school back East. His mother Alice objects to his candor on the subject; a delightfully prepossessing

gray-haired woman, as well as a first-grade teacher in Lincoln
Park, N.J., she wishes Kiick would say that only Wyoming
had the sense to recognize his ability.

At Laramie, Kiick was both a star and an iconoclast. His
teammates called him Nicky Newark. He wore pointed
shoes, Italian knit shirts, fluorescent pants. "All my clothes
were monogrammed, even my underwear. I always liked wild
clothes. Shirts with girls' pictures on them. I'm also a shoe
freak. In high school my mother would send me down to get
a pair of pants and a shirt, and I'd come back with four pairs
of shoes."

If Wyoming never saw anything like Kiick, Kiick never
expected anything like Wyoming. "Flying in, I couldn't
believe it. Hundreds of miles of nothing. If I'd gone out
there to visit first, I'd never have gone back. The fans were
great, and we had good teams, but nobody back East knew
we were playing except when we went to the Sugar Bowl in
1967. My mother used to complain to *The New York Times*
about its coverage of our games. A line score on Monday
mornings. I had to call her at two a.m. after a Saturday night
game to give her the play-by-play."

Kiick's life as a Wyoming undergraduate was not encum-
bered by serious study. Pushed into phys ed courses that
bored him, he would, of a morning, start for class and make
it as far as the pool table in the student center, where he
financed his dates and phone bills. Except for the love of
Alice, who played hard to get, a tactic that baffled him ("I
thought, 'How can she turn me down?' "), Kiick was not
won by the West. He rode a horse for three hours, and was
cured of the desire for a lifetime. When the team went to
New York to play Army, all the players wore cowboy hats.
Except Kiick. He held his under his arm. "I was afraid some
of the guys from Jersey might see me. When I signed with
the Dolpins I was written up as a 'cowboy from Wyoming.'
They all laughed at that one. I was a pool shark from Jersey."

In Lincoln Park, says Kiick, "We have the oldest kids in
the world. Thirty-five, 40-year-old kids who have found a
way to do nothing in life. Just hang around, play some basketball, drink some beer, relax. That's the way I'll be. I have
the opportunity now to do it in the off-season. I don't have

to preplan my day. I do what I want. I can play basketball for hours, even by myself. Maybe go sit in a bar and relax. I'd like to have my own bar. I'd like to be able to walk in and say, 'Buy that guy a drink.'

"Alice doesn't go for those ideas much. She wants something permanent. She'd like me to have a job in the off-season. Nine to five. Get me out of the house. I look around to please her. I go out and shoot baskets, and maybe have a few beers, and come back and tell her, 'Nothing today, honey.' I guess you'd call that irresponsible. That's how my mother describes me."

Kiick's Pennsylvania Dutch father George played two years for the Pittsburgh Steelers in the 1940s, but he did not push Jim into athletics. Mother Alice did that. While George reminded him of his errors, Alice threw the football to him and led the cheers. He was good at everything—football, basketball, baseball—but he was told he had a bad attitude. "I've always been what you might call lackadaisical. It makes for a bad appearance. For example, I hate exercise. I hate sit-ups. Larry thrives on hard work. Raised on a farm, up at 5:30, milking cows, getting the work done. I was lazy. Or looked lazy. Shula yells at me for the way I do exercises. I just like to loosen up. I don't worry much about form. I don't knock myself out on the unnecessary stuff. Why run back to the huddle? Conserve your energy. Pick your spots. Pete Rose draws a walk and he sprints to first base. Why? It'll wait.

"I was better in basketball than football. I always wanted to be 6' 5" [he is 5' 11"]. If I was 6' 5" I'd be playing basketball now instead of football. And I was better at baseball than anything. The coach and I didn't see eye to eye. He bought me a new glove. Mine was old and floppy, but it had character. A nice pocket. This new $40 glove was beautiful, but it was flat and hard. I wouldn't wear it. We argued. One game I forgot my hat. He made me sit in the bus the whole game."

Unlike Csonka, Kiick is a natural athlete. Put a golf club in his hands, says Shula, and he'd probably break par. The finer points of a game, however, do not fascinate him as they do Csonka. "I'm not a student of anything," says Kiick. "I stopped growing mentally at 17. I know absolutely nothing about football. I don't know how to read a defense. I'm always afraid they'll quiz me on something I'm supposed to know."

Success would seem to have left Jim Kiick totally unspoiled. Only the wrapping has changed: to Levi's and tie-dyed shirts, hair that hangs around his ears and a mustache. The new shoe styles delight him. He now wears clogs and red and white string-ups with two-inch heels, and is "tall at last." He also has gone along with the fashion for "different" names ("Jim gets old after a while") by calling his firstborn, now 16 months old, Brandon. "I'll tell you a name I used to like," he says. "There was a shotputter named Dallas Long. Remember him? I used to think that was a great name. Dallas."

He pauses, reflecting on the irony. "The letdown came after the Super Bowl," he says. "Not on the next day, but later. Dallas wasn't that much better, but football is momentum. We lost it in the first quarter when we fumbled and they scored, and we never got it back. The letdown came when you realized how much it took to get there. How many things had to be right, or went wrong, that allowed us to get there. Luck. Injuries. More luck. How many times is Jan Stenerud going to miss a 24-yard field goal [as he did in The Longest Game at Kansas City]? So those things work for you, and when you get there, you've got to get the job done, because you might not get back there for a while."

Jim Kiick believes, as a friend once told him, that "you are fortunate in life if you have one or two good friends." He found Larry Csonka at the College All-Star camp in Evanston, Ill. in 1968. Kiick was a fifth-round draft choice of the Dolphins, appreciated mainly by his mother. Csonka was a consensus All-America from Syracuse, the Dolphins' No. 1 pick with a $100,000 bonus. Csonka was to be, in that All-Star Game, the Most Valuable Player. Kiick never got in the game. Norm Van Brocklin, the All-Star coach, said he was too fat, too slow and had a bad attitude. "I did, too," says Kiick, "when I realized he could say all that without ever having seen me play." Csonka obviously saw things in Kiick that Van Brocklin didn't. He introduced Kiick to Miami sportswriters as "a guy you better get to know. Maybe you never heard of him, but he's going to be a hell of a player."

Thrown together as roommates then, they have been room-mates by choice ever since. "Two things can happen in a case like that," says Csonka. "Either you communicate and get along or you wind up hating each other. If you don't get along, it's pretty obvious. Show me the game films of a team and I'll tell you whether the running backs get along. When Jim and I run a sweep I can sense exactly what he's going to do, how he'll react to the defensive end or the cornerback. We don't have anything in common except friendship, but that makes it work."

Kiick was awed by Csonka. "He was huge," he says. "I was embarrassed to be around him. He was taller. He was stronger. I measured my thighs and thought, boy, 28 inches. His were bigger. We kidded him every time he ran a pass pattern: 'Lineman down field!' We were nothing alike, but we hit it off. Larry likes to fish. I hate the outdoors. But I could enjoy it with him. I like to play basketball or shoot pool. He doesn't give a damn, but he'll come watch."

Lawrence Richard Csonka was raised on an 18-acre farm in Stow, Ohio. His father Joseph worked at Goodyear in Akron besides doing a little bouncing on the side. Larry remembers that his father made him hoe beans "until I want-ed to hit him with the hoe," and as punishment kneel on corncobs, and that he and his brother slept in a rough board attic where it was so cold "I could watch my breath go the length of the room. I had a runny nose the first 10 years of my life.

"I hated that farm until I was old enough to know better," he says. "Now I think how rewarding it was—growing things, having animals. Hey, there was a creek and about 20 dogs running around, and we chased woodchucks and climbed trees to get baby crows for pets. Think how ironic it is. My dad didn't have much money, and here I am with two boys [Doug, 5 and Paul, 3] who are rich kids by comparison, and I'm trying to get enough to afford to give them the life my dad gave me."

The Csonkas—uncles, cousins and so forth—were known around Stow as a physical bunch. "If my father liked you, he hit you on the arm." If he didn't like you, he was liable to hit you. "He was always in great shape," says Larry. He's 53 now, and he's still got a 34-inch waist. And can hit you quicker that you can think about it."

Larry weighed 150 when he was 12, and by the time he was a high school junior, he had tried every position, including quarterback. "There was something about throwing the ball. I didn't want to turn it loose." His high school games in Stow were memorable as much for the fights in the stands as they were for the play on the field.

Csonka's wife Pam was his high school sweetheart and joined him at Syracuse his junior year. The year before, Coach Ben Schwartzwalder had converted him from fullback to middle linebacker. "Biggest mistake I ever made," said Schwartzwalder. Csonka was converted back to fullback. "Smartest move I ever made," said Schwartzwalder. A Syracuse tackle named Gary Bugenhagen had told Csonka that he should strengthen his forearms by banging them into things. Csonka was envious of the size of Bugenhagen's forearms. That summer Schwartzwalder got a call from Mr. Csonka. He said to please get Larry out of his house because he was "knocking down the walls."

"Actually," says Csonka, "it was only one wall, and it was coming down anyway. I used to leave a couple hundred pounds of weights on my bed. My mother would raise hell. She couldn't lift them off to make the bed."

Csonka broke all the Syracuse rushing records, surpassing the feats of Jim Brown, Ernie Davis, Jim Nance and Floyd Little. "I'm not really in their class," he says. "I just carried the ball more." When he broke the last of Little's records, they stopped play to give him the ball. Csonka flipped it to the sidelines. "I didn't know what they were doing," he says. "I thought it was defective or something."

Rookie camp with the Dolphins was a special hell for Csonka. George Wilson was the Miami coach then, and he was a traditionalist who believed that rookies were made to suffer. Csonka was the biggest target. He suffered most. The veterans called him "the Lawnmower" for his peculiar lock-kneed, low-to-the ground running style. They not only made him sing his school song, they made him sing *every* school song. They sent him out for sandwiches at two in the morning. They did not get him drunk one night, as is the custom, but took him out and tanked him up 10 nights in a row. "One time they had us drink a gallon of white lightning," Csonka says. "Kiick sat there, motionless. Sometimes he does that, just sits there, so I wasn't concerned. He looked sober. Then he said, 'We gotta go.' We made it back to the room, and he was sicker than I've ever seen a man. The next day we had to run the ropes, and we got tangled so bad you wouldn't believe it."

It was, harassment notwithstanding, a foregone conclusion that Csonka would be Miami's regular fullback from the beginning. Kiick soon joined him, by default. Injuries—a pinched nerve in the neck of Jack Harper, appendicitis for Stan Mitchell—eliminated the competition. "I had a no-cut contract," says Kiick. "They had to try me."

The rest, of course, is history, or getting there. As his head cleared and the games rolled by, Csonka became easier to spell ("'C as in Carl, S as in Sam'... I've heard him tell it to the operator 100 times," says Kiick) and tougher to defense. Last year he went over 1,000 yards, and Shula, having recognized an astonishing thing—Csonka is fast enough to run outside—has given him more latitude. Weak-side sweeps, quick pitches. ("I always wanted to run outside just to prove I could," says Csonka.) The advantage he has out there, says Shula, is that "even if he's not as fast as some backs, he's bigger." (Pause) "Bigger than *most* backs." (Pause) "Bigger than *all* backs." And Kiick, of course, continues to get his 1,000-yards-plus rushing and receiving and to remind people of such alltime all-purpose backs as Paul Hornung and Tom Matte. Shula says nobody makes the third-down play—the tough two yards, the clutch reception—more consistently than Kiick.

The Kiick-Csonka dimension grows. Their affairs are now handled by Mark McCormack (Arnold Palmer, Rod Laver, Jackie Stewart), and that means endorsements. Last year they even held out on their contracts together.

It is very easy to be with these two. One need only watch them limp into the training room on Monday morning. "It's a pitiful sight," says a regular. "Able to walk, but barely. Dr. Virgin comes in and just shakes his head."

Csonka, the Sundance Kid, takes up the oral banner for the

two on this most tender of subjects. "No matter what your style, you have to take a beating," he says. "If you're small and quick, it might catch up to you all at once, or if you're like me you might prefer to get it in regular doses, but sooner or later the bill collector comes.

"It's all in the game. I'm no masochist, but I wouldn't want it any other way. I want to be physically involved. I don't want to be in a game where all you've done is throw the ball and don't feel a thing on Monday. Maybe it's a way of letting off steam, I don't know, but afterwards Kiick and I can relax better than anybody. We can relax at a party till five a.m., just sitting in a corner. Kiick with that look on his face, not saying anything. But hey, I *like* people. I present the image of being a brute, of knuckles dragging. I've had people hesitate to come up to me because they weren't sure what I'd do. I hate that. They don't know me.

"I love the game, that's all. I bitch, but I love the whole thing, the total experience. Mind and body. And the result is right there at the end. Running backs figure to last four to six years. The lucky ones last eight or 10. I'd like to go 15. And the only thing that troubles me is that I won't be able to play forever."

It is barely coincidental, perhaps, but worthwhile telling anyway, if only for the fun of it: Pam Csonka was out on the tennis court when little Paul Csonka came crying for attention over a slightly bloody mouth. Pam took a quick look and said, "Just dab it with something," since she was busy. "In this family," she says, "you learn to live with pain."

Gettin' Nowhere Fast

BY ROBERT F. JONES

IN 1977, JUST A FEW MONTHS AFTER OAKLAND'S SUPER BOWL VICTORY, ROBERT F. JONES SPENT SOME TIME WITH QUARTERBACK KENNY STABLER. DURING THE VISIT, JONES ACCOMPANIED STABLER TO A FEW OF HIS FAVORITE HAUNTS DOWN HOME IN ALABAMA. THE RESULT WAS THIS MEMORABLE STORY.

The black Chevy Silverado pickup burbles down main street. Past the sun-faded feed and grain store, where less elegant trucks stand scarred and dusty while their owners dip snoose in the shade, comparing notes on drought damage. Past the sporting-goods store with its display of heavy handguns and shiny fishing lures. Past the church, the high school and the obligatory but somehow anachronistic shopping center, where young housewives in curlers and short shorts stride purposefully through the heat with a baby on one hip and a bag of groceries on the other. The driver of the Silverado studies the scene closely. As if feeling his eyes on them, some of the townsfolk turn and stare at the truck. After a moment, their faces inevitably break into wide country grins.

"Hey there, Kenny!"

"Hoo boy, Snake!"

The driver acknowledges them with a wave of his free hand. Actually the hand is not fully free. The big knuckles bulge around a beaded can of beer, second of the morning though it is scarcely 9 a.m. "This is home," says Kenny Stabler. "I'll die here."

The flat tone of the statement, issuing as it does from a face masked by a grizzled brown beard and mirrored sunglasses, raises questions. Does the premier quarterback of the NFL, the 1976 Most Valuable Player, the star of Super Bowl XI, whose deft passes and clever calls eviscerated the Minnesota Vikings, mean that he's outgrown his hometown? That the rustic pleasures of Foley, Ala. (pop. 4,000)—farming corn and soybeans; hunting doves, quail, woodcock, snipe and ducks in the nearby fields and sloughs; fishing bream and bass and speckled sea trout; eating boiled shrimp and fried oysters and smoked mullet; drinking more beer a day than any four Milwaukeeans; boogieing late into the night in roadhouses; racing boats and trucks, and anything else that moves, with other good old boys—is beginning to pall? That he would die of boredom if he had to live here year-round?

Not a bit of it.

"I love the place," says Stabler, gunning the motor as he hits the edge of town. "It's got everything I'll ever need. Come on, let's get some beer and go for a boat ride."

The week shot by like a long wet blur. Through it ran the sounds of Stablerian pleasure: the steady gurgle of upturned beer bottles, the clack and thunk of pool balls, the snarl of outboard motors, the whiny cadences of country music. At the end of it, anyone following in Stabler's wake would be ready for a body transplant: liver and lights, heart and kidneys, eardrums—maybe even a few new teeth.

Since it is virtually impossible to catch Stabler at rest, any portrait of him must convey his nonstop motion. To that extent he epitomizes his nickname: "Snake." Try to get, say, a blue racer in repose for an interview. All you'll come away with is an impression of flickering tongue and a sapphirine slithering through the weeds.

It began in Memphis, where Stabler was expected to perform in the pro-am of the Danny Thomas–Memphis Classic. Stabler was waiting at the airport. He was, of course, in the bar. He had been there since noon. It was now close to 5 p.m. Surrounded by reeling pals, beautiful girls and an array of empty or partially drained glassware—beer bottles, Bloody Marys, Salty Dogs, Seven and Sevens—he grinned at a newcomer. "You're late," he exulted. "Thank God. Here"—he unwrapped his thick left arm from a petite blonde, who emerged like a bauble from the shadow of his armpit—"meet Wanda." She smiled demurely, then stuck out her tongue.

The next morning a caravan of Continental Mark Vs wound erratically through southeastern Memphis. "Where the hayull is the golf course?" snarled a Southern voice. "Danged if *Ah* know," answered another. "Turn on the goldurned *ayer* conditioner," gasped a third. "It's runnin' full blast, you knucklehead!" was the response.

"Wayull, shore," continued Bear Bryant, as if he hadn't been interrupted. "Ah remember that boy. He looked like a good 'un but he always left his football game in some parked car the night before we played. Ah remember that Auburn game in...." Bryant, Stabler's coach during his college All-America days at Alabama, was paired with Stabler for the pro-am. His deep, hoarse, mellifluous voice, eroded by hard living and the football wars of a quarter of a century, filled the car with meaningless magic, reminiscence. It was the only alleviant to the nightmare of the ride. Stabler giggled like a schoolboy at the great man's mots.

Later, under a scorching sun, Stabler quit short of nine holes. A tremendous roar had gone up moments before his retirement from the golf match. Ex-President Gerald Ford had just shot a hole in one. Playing behind him, Stabler stopped. His own shots were snaking into the rough. He pleaded "migraine."

"Hayull," grumped Bear in mock chagrin as Kenny was departing for the clubhouse. "Ah was gonna pull that one myself but you beat me to it."

The ride back to the motel is a montage of hysterical blasphemies and hollow pauses while people catch their wind. One of the passengers, a fat man named "Philadelphia Phil," pours sweat and outrageous jokes in equal profusion. During one of the lulls, Stabler turns and eyes his entourage. "Let's

blow this pop stand," he says. "We'll clear out of here tonight
and head back home. We've had three days in Las Vegas and
now this. Too much. I want to just lay back and maybe drive
my boat some. I'm one of your clean-living NFL quarterbacks
and I need to replenish my physical *ree*sources."

"Sure you are," says Henry Pitts, Stabler's lawyer and good
buddy from Selma, Ala. "Sure you do. I'll have you out of
here and home by midnight. But meanwhile let's stop and
grab us a six-pack."

Shortly after midnight, emerging from the airport at Pensacola, Fla. on his way home, Stabler is haled to the curb by a traffic cop. He's just made a left turn, the cop informs him, on a
red light. Stabler produces his license with decorum—no
protest, no mention of who he is or what he'd done to
become it. The cop writes him up. Now take care, heah?" the
cop says, unsmiling.

"Shore," says Kenny. Then he smiles into the dark. "Win a
few, lose a few."

Stabler is eating a fried-oyster sandwich in the Pink Pony Pub.
A pitcher of draft beer sweats on the table before him. Both
sandwich and beer are disappearing at a remarkable rate. He is
clad in a red T shirt with a silvery cobra silk-screened on the
chest, its hood opening and closing to his swallows, white
shorts and a pair of battered flip-flops. This is the uniform of
the day when he's at home. The Pink Pony Pub dominates the
beachfront of Gulf Shores, Ala., a resort-cum-fishing community south of Foley. A rickety string-pier extends into the Gulf of
Mexico. Milky blue water laps the dunes of the offshore
islands between Mobile Bay and Pensacola. Girls in bikinis
bake on the beach, turning slowly, voluptuously. Stabler never
misses a move.

Twice divorced and now living just up the coast from Gulf
Shores with the blonde girl named Wanda—"Wickedly Wonderful Wanda," as she styles herself, but more prosaically,
Wanda Blalock, age 23, from Robertsdale—he eschews the married state or any demanding facsimile thereof. He likes to
watch girls. But now his anatomical studies are interrupted by
a lean, middle-aged man who plunks himself down at the table
to chat. Denzil Hollis was Stabler's baseball, basketball, track

and football coach in junior high. "That was when I gave him the nickname 'Snake,' " says Denzil. "Back in the eighth or ninth grade. He'd run 200 yards to score from 20 yards out." He slaps Stabler's thick gut. "Skinny as a snake too, back then. Straight up from top to bottom, and when he turned sideways, he weren't no thicker than a airmail letter."

Even in 1968, when Stabler first appeared on the Oakland Raiders' roster, he was snake-slim—6' 3" by 185 pounds. Now he weighs 215. "I've been working with weights," he says. "You can't play quarterback in the league at anything under 200 these days. The stronger you are, the more muscle you got around those joints, the less likely you are to get hurt."

In high school, Stabler actually achieved greater renown as a baseball player than for his football skills. He was a smoking southpaw pitcher who, with a mediocre squad, won nine games in his senior year, racking up 125 strikeouts and five shutouts on speed alone. The only loss that Don Sutton of Clio, Ala. ever suffered in high school was a 1–0 game to Stabler and Foley, with Stabler striking out 16 and Sutton 14. "When I was 17," Stabler says, flatly, not boasting, "the Pittsburgh Pirates offered me $50,000 to sign. But by then I'd gotten to like football. And I wanted to play for Coach Bryant. If it hadn't been for sports, I wouldn't have gone to college. My dad was a mechanic in a garage up to Foley, and I'd have followed him, I'm sure. I went to college to play football, not for education. That may have been wrong, but that's the way it was. I always wanted to play pro ball, and I've done it." He finished up the pitcher of beer. "Come on, let's get out on the water."

En route to the Bear Point Marina, where Stabler motors his V-hulled, 150-hp outboard racing boat, *Boogie*, he pulls to a stop beside a dank, reed-grown tarn. A chain-link fence surrounds the pond, and a neatly lettered white sign proclaims CHARLIE.

"Charlie's a 12-foot alligator, something of a local celebrity," says Stabler. "We'll see if he's home." He rattles the fence and hoots a few times, but the big 'gator doesn't appear. "Maybe he's taken a stroll into town for a Big Mac," says Stabler. All that moves in the black water is a soft-shelled turtle the size of a manhole cover. As Stabler is about to climb back into the truck, a police cruiser brakes to a stop behind him. Out jumps Chief James E. Maples of the Gulf Shores heat—the headquarters is located just beside the 'gator pond. Maples, stout and bouncy, insists on showing Stabler his latest set of pictures.

Inside the office, he produces a sheaf of Polaroids depicting Maples in a soldier suit, armed with an M-16 and various other weaponry, standing before what appear to be blazing bales of hay. "We got 17 tons of grass off that cabin cruiser yesterday," he says. "Buncha damn hippies runnin' it up from Mesko, I do believe. Hayull, I stood right in the middle of it when it was burnin' and didn't feel a thang." As he flashes the photos like a new parent with baby pictures, one wonders what got him so high.

"Shucks, the Chief jest gets high on work," says Stabler as he drives away. "He's a dedicated man, Chief Maples is." There's a wry twinkle in the blue eyes, crows' feet at the corners of the broad, bearded face.

The Intracoastal Waterway, rimming the Gulf from Texas clear around to the Florida Keys, affords Stabler and his boating buddies with an all-weather playground. Even when gales are blowing outside the barrier islands that protect the Waterway from the Gulf, the seas inside are flat enough to run wide open at 70 mph. It's hazardous sport, what with the mile-long strings of barges being threaded by their tugs through the serpentine, buoy-marked channels, but Stabler loves nothing better than jumping the wakes of the barges or running flat out beside them and making commerce look like it's standing still. He's doing it right now.

"Here he comes," says Bobby Holk, a young, pale-haired engineering grad from Auburn and—despite the rivalry between his school and Stabler's alma mater—a good boating buddy. Roger's gonna whip him, though, you watch." The two racing boats appear from behind a barge train. Stabler in the lead and Roger Tyndal coming up fast behind him. Roger is a farmer—corn, mainly—but with the spring drought working havoc in the Deep South he has little to do. His corn tassled out at knee height. No ears. Hardly worth saving for silage. So Tyndal might as well spend the day racing.

The boats close rapidly, hulls angled up clear of the water, screws lashing the channel. The sound comes on like a swarm of giant killer bees. Just as Holk had predicted, Tyndal's boat—with an added 50 hp—snaps Stabler's up as soon as they reach flat water beyond the barge wake. Stabler shakes a fist in mock frustration, then the two leap one another's wakes as they head for the next marina.

"That's how we do it," Stabler says after he ties up at the Shelter Cove Marina. "We race around on the Waterway and stop at all the marinas. There's about 10 or 12 of 'em between where I live and the end of the line, down there below Gulf Shores. Good way to travel, gettin' nowhere fast."

The marina is equipped in the uniform fashion of the region: air conditioner, bar, pool table, juke box. The bare essentials, in precisely that order. Tyndal and Holk order a bottle of Tickled Pink flavored wine while Stabler feeds the juke box and racks the balls. As Waylon Jennings extols the virtues of "Luckenbach, Texas," Stabler proceeds to whip his buddies in a game of 8-ball. He wins a free beer, of course, and thus must play them another game so they can get revenge. Before they chalk the cues for the last time, Stabler and his partner (a middling player at best) have won all five games. Stabler picks up a tab from a beer can on the way out and slips it over his finger. "Looky here, Bobby," he says to Holk. "This is a Auburn class ring. See, it's got a built-in nose picker."

Stabler is now dining at a Gulf Shores squat-'n'-gobble, Wanda at his side, before him his third Scotch of the meal and a heaping plate of scampi in garlic sauce. "Scotch and scampi," he crows between chomps, "I love 'em. Johnnie Walker Red. Namath drinks it. Sonny Jurgensen is a Scotch drinker, too. Maybe all the great quarterbacks drink Scotch. And I love seafood, particularly these babies." (Munch, crunch, gulp.) "I told Pete Banaszak last season, just after we beat Pittsburgh in the opening game, that I'd eat scampi for 14 weeks in a row if it would guarantee us winning all our games." Like Proust's madeleine, the jumbo shrimp provoke a remembrance of the season past.

"They were all tough games—that's true in any season—but the only one that was really bad was the Patriots. And that's the only one we lost. New England kicked our butts good and proper, 48–17. I guess we should have been wary when we went up against them again in the first playoff game. But I wasn't. That was stupid. They damn near ended our playoff bid right there. In fact, at the start of the fourth quarter, with them leading 21–10, I got to thinking that maybe they had us, maybe all that work earlier in the year was going down the tube. But then we put one on the board and it was 21–17. That's when the controversial stuff started.

"They got down to our 32 and then, thank God, missed that field goal. When we got the ball back, I told the guys that this was it, this might be the last time we'd have the ball until next season. I figured we had to throw on every down to do it, and I hit four out of five. That put us in good shape on their 18. But then one of their tackles—I think it was Mel Lunsford—nailed me good for a nine-yard loss, and I missed the next pass. So there we were, third and 18, and we could only win on a touchdown. And only a minute to go.

"I called a sideline pass to Carl Garrett, but they had him covered like gangbusters. I threw anyway. Just as I cut loose, Ray Hamilton smacked me across the chops with his forearm. He'd been going for the ball, but I'd got it past him and he hit me with the momentum. They called roughing the passer. Salvation! We had a first down on their 13. I hit Dave Casper for five and Clarence Davis picked up four more on a run. Then Banaszak got a yard. It was going to be a close measurement, but one of the Pats started yelling at the officials and they called unsportsmanlike conduct. We had first and goal from the one.

"Banaszak tried to poke it in but they stopped him. Fourteen seconds left. I called an option play that we'd worked on Cincinnati—a roll-out to the left. I either throw to Casper or run. Gene Upshaw was in front of me, and he flattened the only guy in my way, and there we were—24–21."

The waiter brings another plate of scampi, another drink.

"Then we give Pittsburgh a whuppin'—24–7. That felt good. Don't let no one tell you that the Pittsburgh-Oakland rivalry is a press hype. We hate them; they hate us. Beating them that bad in the playoffs was sweet indeed. People who'd been saying we couldn't win the big ones had to eat crow. And Pittsburgh couldn't say we'd been lucky—the way they were in '72 when Franco picked up that ricochet and won in the final seconds. No, we blew them away."

Wanda, bored, utters a pussycat yawn. Stabler chucks her under the chin.

"The thing is, we really didn't know what to expect from the Vikings in the Super Bowl. We knew they were an experienced team, disciplined, and well coached at all levels, a no-nonsense bunch of guys, straight up, older than us but not necessarily wiser. We didn't think they'd add any new wrinkles for the Super Bowl, and we didn't plan to, either. We'd stick with what had worked, what got us there. Some of our guys got up so high that they vomited before the game. I remember Freddie Biletnikoff was tying his shoes over and over again. He'll do it maybe 50 times before a regular-season game, but that day Freddie must have hit 1,000.

"After the game was over, for the first time I felt real happy for myself. I remember thinking that there are only about six quarterbacks who have ever won the Super Bowl, and now I'm one of them. A great feeling, a great release, an ego balloon. Freddie was crying and Coach Madden was all red and grinning and guys were hugging each other like a bunch of fruits and pouring champagne over each other and then I suddenly had this tremendous urge for a great big plate of scampi and a bottle of Johnnie Red."

On Friday night, the mayor of Foley is hosting a barbecue in Stabler's honor—a build-up of sorts for the big festivities of the night to follow. On Saturday, Stabler will submit to a "roast" in the civic auditorium. There, for $12.50 a plate, the local citizenry can watch their favorite son get insulted, maligned, slandered, humiliated and otherwise dumped upon by a panel of experts. The roast is for a good cause, though: a new field house for the Foley Lions high school teams. Anyone with the scratch can attend the roast, but the mayor's barbecue is by invitation only. The mayor of Foley is Arthur Holk, a sprightly slat of a man, an inveterate fisherman and boatman who owns much of the prime real estate in adjacent Gulf Shores. Mayor Holk is the cousin of Bobby Holk, Stabler's boating and 8-ball buddy.

The guests circulate under Japanese lanterns and electric bugzappers on the spacious grounds of the mayor's house, wreathed in the smoke from sizzling steaks, munching freshly boiled jumbo shrimp and corn on the cob. It's an odd contrast in groups: on the one hand, the Foley upper crust, matronly, Rotarian, with cash-register eyeballs; on the other, the Stabler gang, raffish, sunburnt, hard of hand and piratical of glance. Two new arrivals add another element to the scene. Pete Banaszak and Tony Cline, a defensive end who played six seasons with the Raiders before being traded across the Bay to San Francisco, have showed up for the roast, and they plan to accompany Stabler to his week-long football camp near Selma. Banaszak and Cline are clearly on their best behavior. They've been in the air most of the day, flying in from the Coast, and are much the worse for wear. "We started drinking before we got on the plane," laments Cline, "and then we had to wait two hours in the Pensacola airport before Kenny remembered to send someone to pick us up. Where's that steak?"

Stabler, too, is the model of decorum. Freshly showered and deodorized, wearing crisply pressed slacks and a shiny open-necked shirt of many colors, he "Ma'ams" the ladies and "Sirs" the gents with the utmost deference. His voice is mild, an octave or so higher than when he's shooting pool. The smile is tentative, almost shy. But the bad-boy twinkle, though a bit disguised, still lights his eyes whenever he gets off a double entendre at the expense of the stuffed shirts. Wickedly Wonderful Wanda clings to his arm with dutiful, downcast eyes. Every now and then she looks up and winks knowingly behind his back at one or another of the Stabler entourage.

Stabler's house, just over the Alabama line at the tail end of the Florida Panhandle, and half an hour's drive from Foley or Gulf Shores, was stripped to the bare minimum of furnishings by his most recent divorce. A painting of a tiger glares from the wall of the empty dining room. A lone couch adorns the living room. The refrigerator is stocked mainly with beer and white wine (the latter for the Wickedly Wonderful one). In the den, things are a bit homier. Team photographs depict him as a Foley Lion, a 'Bama Crimson Tidester and a young, beardless Oakland Raider. In all of them, he is wearing his "barbecue face," and, thinking back, one realizes that all the photos of

Stabler except the candids show him as shy and self-effacing. They do not capture the driven playfulness of the man.

The garage and the yard, though, tell a different story. In the garage are fishing rods, tackle boxes laden with lures, leaders and hooks; a bench rest for the barbells with which he works out three days a week; a Honda MR-250 Elsinore dirt bike; a glossily flaked dune buggy; his four-wheel-drive pickup truck. Out on the Bermuda-grass lawn, resting in its cradled trailer, the *Boogie* looks like it's still moving at 70 mph. And down at the Bear Point Marina, not yet ready for the water, is his latest acquisition: a tunnel-hulled racing boat that should leave the V-hulled *Boogie* gasping in its wake—and Roger Tyndal's boat as well. "I picked up the tunnel-hull cheap from a boy over near Mobile," Stabler says, his voice firing with eagerness. "I'm going to fix her up—needs a little glass work here and there—and paint her real nifty, and then hang a big Merc on her. I reckon she'll go 80 plus."

If a man can be assessed by his possessions, and particularly his attitude toward them, then Ken Stabler is a man in motion. Furious, violent motion. Exultant motion.

"Gettin' nowhere fast," he says. "I like it. As philosophies go, it's as good as any. What counts isn't so much where you're going—I mean, we all end up in the same place—but what counts is the getting there. Kind of simple-minded, maybe, but it's fun."

You hear the roadhouse before you see it—the amplified four-four beat of country music pounding like surf through the woods, silencing the bullfrogs, setting the beards of Spanish moss dancing on the trees that fringe the two-lane blacktop. The parking lot is jammed with pickups, most of them costly 4-WDs with customized paint jobs. Men reel and glare and slosh beer on themselves as they stagger around the veranda—skinny, sunburnt men in Levi's and workshirts, with scuffed cowboy boots and baseball caps cocked back on their foreheads to reveal the badge of the farmer: that blanched expanse of skin where the cap has shaded the face, babyhood pallor above the sun-blackened snoose-bulging jaws. Half shot with drink, they wear the faces of Confederate dead in Mathew Brady photographs.

Stabler and Wanda disappear into the musical melee. A pair of Stabler's friends, J.B. and Glen Campbell (distantly related to the singer, says Glen), belly up to the bar. They are joined by Henry Pitts, Stabler's attorney, who flew in from Selma for the barbecue and roast, and Henry's wife Sister. Pitts is the paragon of Southern hospitality, a witty, well-read man in his late 30s who, from his small country-lawyer office in the heart of the Cotton Belt, handles all the arrangements for Stabler's travel, endorsements and guest appearances—no easy task with a subject as whimsically peripatetic as Stabler. It's always amusing to watch Pitts introducing his wife to a stranger. "This is mah wife, Sistah." "Your wife's sister?" "No, mah wife—Sistah!" ("It always draws a double take when we check into a motel," he says.) Her real name is Mary Rose.

Foley's Kenny Stabler roast is well attended. The spacious new civic auditorium is nearly full in anticpation of seeing the local hero who has made it nation-wide get his verbal comeuppance. Mayor Holk and Dr. John E. Foster, the master of ceremonies and long-time physician to Foley's athletic teams, are everywhere, planting suggestions for sharp jibes with the forgathered roasters. The most interesting contrast of the evening is between Stabler and Scott Hunter, the Atlanta Falcons' quarterback and Stabler's successor at 'Bama who has journeyed down to Foley to deliver the invocation. Stabler is massive, bearded, almost bearlike in his heavy-shouldered carriage; Hunter, active in the Fellowship of Christian Athletes, is dapper, clean-shaven, very sincere. He could be the president of the Jaycees. Stabler could be a fugitive from a chain gang.

Seated in a high-backed, throne-like chair in front of the stage, Stabler takes the roasters' best shots, wincing with mock outrage at the repeated references to his dubious intellectuality, his unconventional training habits ("Eight beers and two hours' sleep a night," says Banaszak, "that's the way to stardom as an NFL quarterback"), his penchant for monogamy ("He's a one-woman man—one woman a night").

"The other day," says Tony Cline, "my son asked me, 'Daddy, when are they going to roast *you?*' 'When I get overweight and overpaid,' I told him."

Terry Henley, a former Auburn football player, embroiders

on the theme of Stabler's womanizing. "Up at 'Bama, Kenny had a girl friend who was so ugly that when she went to the school psychiatrist he made her lie face down on the couch. Why, she was so ugly that Kenny couldn't bring himself to take her out to dinner. Instead he'd put her in a corner and feed her with a slingshot."

The digs are harsh, hard, biting close to the marrow. The fans love it. Stabler gives as good as he gets. When all the roasters have had their say, he delivers a brief rebuttal. His voice is once again his public voice, shading to the higher registers, tentative, almost boyish. But in a few words he rips everyone who savaged him, and then some. The good people of Baldwin County, Ala. leave the hall sated with rubber chicken and ribaldry.

"Good folks," Stabler says later, driving back toward Gulf Shores. "Yeah, I'll die here. I really haven't given much thought to what I'm going to do when I'm done with football. Something competitive, though. It has to be something with a hard challenge to it. Maybe racing boats, or racing cars. I really get off on high speed, keeping to the edge of control. If I was to coach, as a lot of people have suggested, I wouldn't want to coach anything above the high school level. Not college football and certainly not the pros. But my life-style is too rough—too much booze and babes and cigarettes—to be a high school coach. I'd hardly be a shining example to the young athletes of the future. The quarterbacks I admire most are Bobby Layne and Billy Kilmer—tough, hard-living guys who don't know how to quit. We've got a lot of that spirit on the Raiders. For the past five or six years we've been the best team, overall, in the game, and yet, until last season, we never quite made it all the way. But we kept on a-truckin', never quitting, never doubting our ability to do it. Al Davis is tough and it rubs off on the rest of us, all the way down the line.

"But Al can be generous, too. Look at this Super Bowl ring—it's got to be the most expensive one any owner has ever given to his team." The crest of the ring glints in the humid darkness—16 small diamonds, one for each of the Raiders' 1976 victories, encircling a large stone that represents the Super Bowl triumph. "The only thing that's missing is a little chip of coal on the bottom of the ring, to represent the shellacking New England gave us early in the season."

Stabler cruises down the main drag of Gulf Shores. A light surf is sloshing in off the Gulf, lit by a fat, white moon. From the Pink Pony Pub come the sounds of revelry—war whoops and rebel yells, the clink of beer pitchers and the whine of the juke box. Kenny Rogers' voice grates through the cooling, wet air, bitter with salt. "You picked a fine time to leave me, Lucille, with four hungry children and crops in the field...."

"Sure hope it rains," says Stabler. "The farmers are losing their shirts. Anyway," getting back to his point of departure, "I'll never end up in coaching. Maybe I'll open up a honky-tonk here in Gulf Shores. Or maybe a little marina with a pool table and a juke box and tanks full of live bait. Honky-tonks and marinas—that's where I spend most of the good time anyway. But whatever it is, I'll die here." He turns the truck toward the sound of the music. "Hell, I'm falling behind in my clean-living campaign. Let's grab us a beer."

The Roots of Greatness

BY   BRUCE   NEWMAN

THE SAGA OF EARL CAMPBELL IS ONE OF THE NFL'S GREAT HOR-
ATIO ALGER STORIES. BORN INTO POVERTY, CAMPBELL MADE IT
TO THE PINNACLE OF THE PROFESSIONAL RANKS BY DINT OF
PERSEVERANCE, HARD WORK AND AN IRRESISTIBLE TALENT.
BRUCE NEWMAN TOLD THE TALE IN THIS POIGNANT PORTRAIT.

Here is what we know about the state of poverty: its bound-
aries do not appear on any map; it has no flag or official
song, but once you are there it is difficult to get your zip
code changed; as a character-building experience it is over-
rated by the rich and overpopulated by the poor; and it's a
place where nobody goes for the weekend.

Earl Campbell has never given much thought to being
poor, had never really realized how deprived his family had
been, until—in the space of a single year—he won the Heisman Trophy, signed a contract worth $1.4 million to play for
the Houston Oilers and became the hottest thing to hit the
NFL since *Monday Night Football*. When the full weight of
his family's privation hit him, Campbell decided to take
some of his NFL greenbacks and build a spacious new house
for his mother and then turn the rundown plank shack

where he had grown up into a museum where other under-privileged kids could come see firsthand that the NFL was, indeed, the land of opportunity.

And so, as Campbell's fortunes soared on football fields across America last season, his mama's new house went up. And lest the contrast between his past and his present would be too subtle to grasp, Campbell had the new house built about 25 feet from the old one, with only a large gray septic tank between them.

If anyone ever deserved to have a shrine of his very own after only one year in the NFL, that person surely is Earl Campbell. Last year as a rookie he rushed for 1,450 yards—more than O.J., more than Walter Payton, more than Tony Dorsett, more that any other running back in the entire league—and he led the Oilers, who had had an 8–6 season in 1977, to the AFC championship game against the Pittsburgh Steelers, who then put an end to Campbell's spectacular season.

The Steelers, who had lost a game to the Oilers in Pittsburgh during the regular season when Campbell ran for three touchdowns, were glad to have seen the last of Campbell. "He can inflict more damage on a team than any back I know of," says Mean Joe Greene. "O.J. did it with speed, Campbell does it with power. He's a punishing runner. He hurts you. There are very few tacklers in the league who will bring Earl Campbell down one-on-one. When we're preparing for the Oilers, we emphasize the importance of gang-tackling Campbell. We work on it."

For Campbell, there was no period of transition as there had been for Simpson, no bow to the depth chart as Dorsett had been obliged to make with the Cowboys the year before. From the moment Campbell touched the ball for Houston, the Oilers were the Earlers. On his third professional carry he took a pitchout and thundered 73 yards for a touchdown against the Atlanta Falcons. Campbell became the first rookie to lead the NFL in rushing since Jim Brown did it in 1957, and he led the Oilers to a 10–6 record—and their first playoff berth in 12 seasons.

"Houston could always move the ball with the passing game and the quick screens and the gimmicks," says Coach

Don Shula of the Miami Dolphins, who lost to the Oilers in the Astrodome in a game in which Campbell scored four touchdowns and rushed for 199 yards, and then lost a play-off game to the Oilers in Miami. "When the Oilers got Campbell it made Dan Pastorini that much more effective at all the things he's been doing through the years. I don't think it's any coincidence that Pastorini came into his own as an NFL quarterback at the same time the Oilers got Campbell. He's the guy Pastorini was always looking for and never had."

Among the 29 awards Campbell won were NFL Rookie of the Year and NFL Player of the Year. Bum Phillips, the Oilers' coach and maybe the only clipboard toter in the league who refuses to take himself seriously, says of Campbell that no one in the past 20 years had a greater impact on the NFL in his first season "except Pete Rozelle."

The Oilers had gone 9–33 for the previous three years when Phillips, wearing his lizard-skin, zircon-encrusted, needle-nosed cowboy boots, took over in 1975. In those days you could fire a cannon into the Astrodome's stands without hitting anybody and fire the same cannon at the Oilers with only a 50-50 chance of hitting a real football player. Bum had a 10–4 record in 1975, a 5–9 season in 1976, the 8–6 record in 1977, and the big juicy No. 1 pick in May of 1978.

Soon Houstonians took to saying, "Since Earl came...." Well, for one thing, since Earl came, the Oilers have played to sellout crowds in the Astrodome; average attendance rose to a capacity 51,573 in 1978, and all tickets for this season's 10 games, including exhibitions, were sold out last March.

Elvin Bethea, Houston's standout defensive end the last 11 years, recalls the grim pre-Campbell days. "Before Earl came along," Bethea says, "this was just a stopover for a lot of players. We'd show up on Sunday and give the other team a good fight, but we knew all along what the outcome was going to be. Earl put us at the watering hole; now we're going to drink with everybody else."

Until Campbell arrived, the quarterback had long been the Oilers' most visible player. Dante Pastorini had earned a reputation as a hell-raiser by racing jet dragboats and crashing cars, and it seemed that if anyone was likely to have a personality clash with Campbell, a Baptist Bible-thumper, it would be the infernal Dante. Instead, Campbell and Pastorini soon came to hold one another in a kind of awe. Pastorini can't get over Campbell's attitude. "It would be easy for a guy coming into the game with all those accolades and all that publicity to be cocky or arrogant," says Pastorini, "but Earl's not that way. He does his job, and if he hasn't got something good to say, he doesn't say anything. You hear a lot of backbiting in this league, but I've never heard anyone say a bad word about Earl."

When Phillips talks about Campbell you could swear those tiny hairs on top of the coach's great granite head are standing straight up, out of sheer excitement. "Earl has gotten nine million compliments without letting them swell his head," Phillips says. "I said if he got by last year without changing, he'd survive. I don't believe he'll ever change now. Earl's mama did a heck of a job raising him."

There may be no greater tribute one Texan can pay another than telling him he must have a wonderful mama. Nowhere are mamas held in greater esteem, and nowhere are the things that mama don't 'low held in lower repute. When Campbell was going through the hazing that veterans traditionally inflict upon rookies in training camp, he was required to stand up during one meal and sing a song from soup to nuts. Campbell sang *Mamas Don't Let Your Babies Grow Up To Be Cowboys*, a country-and-western anthem to the Texas matriarchy that was made popular by his good friends Willie Nelson and Waylon Jennings.

Like all but three of his 10 brothers and sisters, Earl Christian Campbell was born at home in the same bed where he was conceived. From the time she was pregnant with Earl until he was a sophomore at the University of Texas, Ann Campbell worked as a cleaning lady for some of the wealthiest families in Tyler, Texas. She did floors, polished other people's silver for their fine parties, and at Christmas she gratefully accepted the hams they gave her. When her famous son signed with the Oilers, Ann Campbell didn't do cartwheels. "All this money don't make me nervous," she said. "I was always in fine places, beautiful homes. They may not have been mine, but I could enjoy them just the same."

There is a prevailing roundness about Mama (it is no use calling her Ann, this being among the things that Mama most assuredly don't 'low), a pleasing full-bodiedness that makes her seem to be built implausibly close to the ground. Mama's face is expressive but doesn't give away anything she isn't ready for you to know. One of her front teeth has a gold jacket, giving a certain unassailable value to just about everything she says.

Ann and Burk Campbell were married in June 1942, soon after the U.S. entered World War II, and she spent the war years living with her parents and his uncle while he served in the Army in France. After five years of marriage they inherited a 14-acre plot in Tyler, on which they began to grow peas and corn, and eventually roses.

Now and then Willie Nelson sings *Stardust,* which contains this lyric:

The nightingale tells his fairy tale
Of paradise where roses grew.

Tyler grows more than half of the rosebushes sold in the U.S., as many as 20 million bushes a year. There are small wooden roadside stands all over Tyler at which a dozen roses sell for a dollar, and there are 2,000 people who depend upon the Tyler rose industry for their living. Though the Campbells couldn't hope to compete with the larger nurseries, they scratched out a living.

"I've been on this corner for 32 years," Mama said the other day, "and all my life I never had to file an income tax return, never had no money in the bank. What little we made on the roses we spent right here. We had to take a lot of our clothes from the Salvation Army, stuff we could get for 25¢ or so. My kids were never crazy, though. They never refused to wear other people's old clothes. We grew all the food we needed. In the spring I'd slaughter a calf or a hog and we'd have our beef and pork for the year."

As the Campbell family grew in numbers, its members in size, more spacious quarters were needed. When Earl was 10 years old, the family moved a few hundred feet to another house on the same property. Mama recalls that the family completed the move just in time to celebrate Christmas of 1965 in their new house. "But the whole time we were moving, my husband was always complaining he didn't feel right," she says. "We'd only been in the new house for four months when he died of a heart attack."

The house that was so new and full of promise in 1965 now is abandoned. Perhaps because it is raised on concrete blocks, it has something of the look of an old jalopy. In fact, there is the front seat of a car on its porch.

On summer days the tar on County Road 492 blisters where it passes these two Texas monuments, and small bubbles percolate to the surface. At noon on sunny days, trees strain themselves to produce a few feet of shade. All around the Campbell house the wind holds its breath, and the sky is the purest blue. The new house is made of brick and seems to catch the full brunt of the sunlight; the old house gets the same light, but its gray, weatherbeaten pallor makes it look like the big house's shadow.

Last spring when the new house was finished, Earl Campbell's mama couldn't shed the old shack that had been like a second skin to her for 13½ years, so she asked Earl to leave it standing. That is when he began to consider the idea of turning the old place into a museum.

"When they told me I could start moving everything into the new house," Mama says, "I was kind of sad about it, you know. It took me quite a while to get everything moved in, and I kept my bed in the old house for a long time. One day my daughter asked me why I did that, and I just told her I wanted to take my time. If I was moving and night was to catch me in the old house, why I'd just spend the night there. And if it caught me in the new house, I'd sleep there. I wasn't particular."

When Earl was growing up, he shared a room as well as a bed in the old plank house with his brothers Herbert and Alfred Ray. It was the first room you saw when you opened the front door.

The Campbells in residence varied from one year to the next, depending upon the intercession of natural disasters. When Ann Campbell's mother and sister lost their home in a fire, they packed up three children and moved in, temporarily swelling the ranks to 15. The air above the peeling linoleum floorboards always was close and clammy during the long Texas summers. In the winter the family sometimes used space heaters to keep warm, but the body heat of several Campbells to a bed usually provided warmth enough even on the coldest nights.

Ann Campbell always told her children, "If you want to be someplace safe, be in church." And every Sunday from the time he was christened until he went away to college, that is where Earl was, front and center at the Hopewell Baptist No. 1. For four years he sang in the church choir.

"I never paid a fine for any of my children and never bailed any of them out of jail," Mama says proudly. "We always had a lot of love, and I think that's why they all turned out so well. We worked together in the fields during the day, and we all slept together at night."

It seems odd, given his extreme rectitude now, that Earl was his mama's only real problem child, the one who came the closest to real trouble with the law. When Earl was in the sixth grade at Griffin Elementary School, he began smoking a pack and a half of cigarettes a day, a habit he maintained for three years. "I used to be a thug from about the time I was in the sixth grade until I went into high school," Earl says. "I lived the street life for a while. I gambled and stole, and I used to make a pretty good living shooting pool. I did just about everything there was except get mixed up with drugs."

Naturally, this type of behavior didn't win him his mama's gratitude. "She's the onlyest person in life I would steal for, or lie for, or kill for," Campbell says now. "She's a great lady, but she's a terrible person to be on the bad side of. I'm her son and it took me a *long* time to get on her good side."

The ascent to grace didn't occur until Campbell was nearly 14. One evening, as he set out upon the road to one of Tyler's iniquitous downtown street corners, probably for a crap game, Earl abruptly decided to change his ways. "I never really liked the country life when I was growing up," he says. "I was always searching for something else. Then that day out on the black tar road that passed by where we lived, I said, 'Lord, lift me up.'"

Once set upon the path of righteousness, Campbell found football. He was so strong and so gifted that in his senior year at John Tyler High School he scored 28 touchdowns, leading his team to a 15–0 season and the state 4A title.

"You just knew every time he got the ball he was going to get you three or four yards, even if there was no blocking at all," says Miami Dolphin rookie Tight End Ron Lee, a teammate of Campbell's at John Tyler. "And at each level he's advanced—and made it look easy. I guess you could say that Earl's just a person who was born to be great."

After Campbell had scored two touchdowns in the state championship game, the coach of the losing team said, "I always thought Superman was white and wore and 'S,' but now I know he's black and wears No. 20."

When Campbell left home for the first time in his life, to attend the University of Texas, 200 miles away in Austin, he became so homesick that, as former Longhorn Coach Darrell Royal recalls, he "would sit on the curb and face in the direction of Tyler."

In college Campbell took every opportunity to spread the credit for his rushing feats among his teammates. "If it were up to Earl," wrote David Casstevens in *The Houston Post*, "he would probably change the name of the 'I' formation to the 'We.'"

Last year, after Billy Sims of Oklahoma had won the Heisman Trophy that Campbell had won the year before, Sooner Coach Barry Switzer offered this comparison between Campbell and his own star running back: "Earl Campbell is the greatest player who ever suited up. He's the greatest football player I've ever seen. Billy Sims is human. Campbell isn't."

When the Oilers, desperate for both a quality football player and a box office attraction, acquired the No. 1 pick in the 1978 draft from Tampa Bay and then used it to select Campbell, former Texas Assistant Coach Pat Patterson warned Bum Phillips what to expect. "When you meet Earl," Patterson said, "you're not going to believe anybody can be that honest and sincere. So you're going to be waiting for him to make a slip, for his true temperament to show through. But you can stop waiting because it's not going to happen. Earl is exactly what he seems to be, one of the nicest people you'll ever meet."

In college Campbell never shied away from hard work, and, when pressed, he wasn't diffident about assessing his own worth. Worth, as it happens, is a concept dear to his heart. Once, when someone implied that Earl would be picking up easy money when he signed with the pros, the 5' 11" Campbell drew himself up to his full height and said coolly, "There isn't a check big enough to pay me back."

As Campbell has discovered, it's much easier to leave the state of poverty than it is to get rid of the poor man's state of mind. When he purchased a comfortable three-bedroom house on Houston's southwest side last year, he asked a contract landscaper to quote him a price for cutting, weeding and trimming the lawn. When the contractor told him it would be $150 a month, which he could easily afford, Campbell whistled softly and thanked the man for his time. Then he went out and bought himself a power mower. "Earl isn't going to waste any money," says Oiler Offensive Backfield Coach Andy Bourgeois. "He's a most frugal young man."

Campbell dislikes signing autographs probably because he finds the attention embarrassing. Whatever his reasons, he avoids such situations. Yet when he ran out of candy last Halloween, rather than go out and buy more, he gave each kid who came to his door an autograph. A heartwarming instance of generosity, or just plain old tightfistedness?

Consider this. Shortly before the Oilers' training camp opened in July, Campbell threw a small party for a few of his close friends in Houston. When he stopped by a liquor store near his home, he was amazed and somewhat horrified to learn that it would cost him $60 or $70 to stock his bar for the evening's roistering. Rather than cough up that kind of money, Campbell identified himself to the owner of the store, and then proceeded to talk the man into supplying the liquor for the party in exchange for four autographed pictures. When Campbell tells this story, he does so without irony, trying to make a point about the high cost of hooch.

None of this is meant to imply that Earl Campbell is

cheap. His thriftiness is punctuated by occasional bursts of generosity, or in the case of his Earl Campbell Crusade for Kids, a long-standing commitment to making life a little more pleasant for underprivileged children in the Houston area. This summer he went on local television in Houston and asked the community to donate old books, school supplies and toys to the crusade. Campbell's fans came through with a truckload of gifts, and Earl kicked in with some lunch boxes and notebooks of his own, then handed the swag out to kids in several Houston parks.

Though he doesn't own an expensive car, Campbell recently bought a $34,000 Mercedes 450 SEL for Reuna Smith, his girl friend of the past 10 years, "just for putting up with me all that time." As training camp got under way at San Angelo State, Campbell gathered his offensive linemen around him and gave each of them a gold money clip in the shape of a spur, engraved with the words 1,000 YARDS. An act of simple gratitude, or a rite of self-preservation? "If I took all the credit all the time," Campbell says, "maybe someday our offensive linemen and Pastorini will say, 'O.K., this time we're going to let Earl *really* do it alone.' I'm nothing without them."

And, he might truthfully add, they without him. He has the speed and quickness of a great running back, as well as a marvelous sense of invention that can turn a routine off-tackle play into a big gainer. The power he generates by his enormous thighs and prodigious backside makes it nearly impossible for a single tackler to bring Campbell down.

Toni Fritsch, the Oilers' placekicker, was at Campbell's home recently when, without warning, he grabbed his host around the thighs—"ties," as Fritsch calls them in his Austrian-accented English—and began imploring Campbell to protect his massive assets. Fritsch is 5' 7", weighs 200 pounds and is balding; he looks more like a cabdriver than a pro football player. But he has Super Bowl rings on both his hands, thanks to five years' employment with the Dallas Cowboys, and they give his monologues a lift they might otherwise lack. Fritsch looked up into Campbell's face and shouted, "Watch out, please, Mr. Oohl. These are your capital. You can buy a new house, a new car but, excuse me, please, these you cannot get back."

It seems that all of Campbell's teammates are protective of him. Last season Pastorini passed for more touchdowns and yardage than he ever had before and also had the second-best completion percentage in his eight-year career—hats off, he says, to Campbell. "Earl made us the best play-action team in football," Pastorini says. "We were on the verge of becoming a good team even without him. Earl can make us great."

Freezing onrushing linemen dead in their tracks by faking to Campbell, Pastorini has time to wait for his receivers to get open. The quarterback had often been booed in Houston, especially on the several occasions he had publicly requested to be traded, but with Campbell alongside him, he suddenly was being called a "field general." Campbell's presence also seemed to have a tonic effect on Bethea, who had grown tired of Houston. "Nobody had worked harder than Elvin," says Pastorini, "but he had lost some of his enthusiasm for playing in a losing situation year after year. When you're losing, you wonder when it's going to end and where your career is headed."

Says Bethea, "It's hard to go out and play when you lack the confidence that the offense is going to do anything with the ball when you get it for them. With Earl, the defense isn't constantly on the field. A thing like that makes a big difference."

The Oilers gave the ball to the Tyler Rose an average of 19 times a game in 1978, and he responded with an average gain of 4.8 yards and 13 touchdowns while fumbling only seven times. With a number of talented wide receivers—notably Ken Burrough, Rich Caster and Mike Renfro—the Oilers rarely threw to Campbell; he caught only 12 passes. But if Pastorini calls on him to run pass patterns this season, or to become a blocking back, or, for that matter, to wallpaper the Astrodome, no doubt Campbell will.

"Anything you ask him to do," says Phillips, clearly impressed, "he's going to do it. It's very important to have a player of Earl Campbell's caliber, but it's even more important to have him be the kind of kid he is."

One authority on the subject of running in the NFL

believes it is an instinct for leadership that makes Campbell such a surpassing talent. "Earl's physical talents are considerable, of course," says O.J. Simpson, "but he has inspirational quality far beyond those talents. He provides a certain lift to a team; everything will be going along normally, then all of a sudden he takes over. I tell you, I'm inspired by his kind of performance."

Campbell's running style is markedly different from the way Simpson ran when he was in his prime, though the results are often the same. More often Campbell, who carries 225 pounds, is compared to the Cleveland Browns' superstar of 1957-65, Jim Brown. But Brown's old coach, Paul Brown, and Simpson both feel the comparison is not entirely apt. "Earl jukes as many as he runs over," Juice points out. "He's a true halfback, and Jim was a fullback. I was amazed how short Earl is. He sure looks bigger on the TV."

Paul Brown is right when he says Campbell will have to put together a string of outstanding seasons before he can be meaningfully compared with Jim Brown. "Brown didn't take an intense physical pounding for his yardage," says Paul Brown. "Campbell does it the physical way. He's not as good a pass receiver as Jim was, and I don't think he has the same straightaway speed. But Brown never liked the blocking aspects of football, and I think Campbell tries to do his part. The only thing you can question about Campbell is whether his style is the type that will allow him to have a long career."

There are a few incandescent moments in any great athlete's career when muscle seems more tightly joined to bone, and when his body crackles like a summer cloud with heat lightning. When one of those moments coincides with desperate necessity, it is advisable not to stand too near, for the brilliance can be blinding.

Last November, Campbell had just such a moment—really an entire game of such moments—on a Monday night in the Astrodome against Miami on national TV, churning through and around the Dolphins, as previously noted, for four touchdowns and 199 yards. Campbell can remember thinking after his third touchdown that he couldn't move anymore, that he was so exhausted his legs felt like concrete piles—the kind that hold bridges up. Late in the fourth period the Oilers were holding a 28–23 lead and facing second-and-long at their own 19. Pastorini could see that Campbell was breathing heavily, but when he knelt down in the huddle he called, almost automatically, "Pitch 28."

"Before Pastorini tossed me the ball," says Campbell, "I would have sworn I couldn't run anymore at all. Even after I was through the hole and I saw [running mate] Tim Wilson hit his man, I didn't think I could make it to the other end of the field. Then I saw pure sideline, and I decided to keep running until somebody knocked me down."

Nobody did. Campbell swept right end, his body leaning hard to the left, and then straightened and rumbled down the sideline 81 yards to the end zone, ensuring a 35–30 Oiler victory.

"He gave them what they had to have," acknowledges Miami's Shula. "He had some head-on collisions with our players and I think he won them all. We had some people get run over that don't get run over." Dolphin Linebacker Steve Towle, a friend of Campbell's, was similarly impressed. "When he sees his spot, he's into it before the hole can be filled," Towle says. "He had two tremendous games against the Dolphins in one season, and I can't recall anybody else I could say that about."

After the Monday night game, Campbell lay wide awake until nearly dawn, just as he does after every game. The buzz in his ears wouldn't go away, and the lightning in his body he had not used up was now flashing behind his eyes. "I usually lie there in bed, tossing and turning, until about 4 a.m.," Campbell says. "Most of the time I have flashbacks from the game, mental pictures in which I can see holes forming in front of me, and then see the defensive linemen fill them up as they charge at me. But I'm never scared. It's just like in the game, fear doesn't enter into it."

Earl Campbell put down a pool cue in his game room, and his face tried to break into a smile, but his lower lip was so full of snuff he couldn't. "Waylon says cowboys are like smoky old pool rooms," he said. "You clear 'em all out in the morning."

And with that, he began to sing in an affecting falsetto:
Cowboys ain't easy to love and they're harder to hold,
They'd rather give you a song than diamonds or gold....
Mamas don't let your babies grow up to be cowboys
'Cause they'll never stay home and they're always alone,
Even with someone they love.

Sometimes the Good Die Young

BY FRANK DEFORD

THE CYNICAL SOUL OF THE TWENTIETH CENTURY HAS
LEARNED TO RESIST THE VERY NOTION OF GENUINE TRAGEDY.
IN THE STORY OF JOE DELANEY, FRANK DEFORD FOUND IT
ANEW AND THANKFULLY LET US ALL IN ON HIS DISCOVERY. AS
USUAL, DEFORD LEFT NARY A DRY EYE IN THE HOUSE.

Last Sunday, Oct. 30, Joe Delaney's team, the Kansas City
Chiefs, played the Denver Broncos. And in Shreveport,
down the road from Haughton, where Joe was reared, the
Louisiana State Fair was in its last day. The signs said: IT'S
YOUR FAIR—SO BE THERE, and for sure a goodly number of
folks came out.

Had he lived, Delaney last Sunday would have celebrated
his 25th birthday while playing against the Broncos. But on
June 29, 1983 he died, a gentleman and a hero, in Monroe,
at Chenault Park, around two in the afternoon.

There was a huge hole there, carved out of the earth
some time ago. The hole had filled with water, and three
boys waded in. They didn't know it, but a short way out
the bottom dropped off precipitously, and suddenly the boys
were in over their heads and thrashing and screaming.

There were all sorts of people around, but only Joe dashed to the pond. There was a little boy there. "Can you swim?" he asked Joe.

"I can't swim good," Joe said, "but I've got to save those kids. If I don't come up, get somebody." And he rushed into the water.

One boy fought his way back to the shallow part. The other two didn't. Neither did Joe Delaney, 24. He was hauled out a few minutes later, dead. He gave his own life trying to save three others.

God rest his soul.

Shortly thereafter, back in Haughton, JoAnn Delaney woke up from a nap. She'd had a terrible pain come over her, so she had lain down; but now, miraculously, she felt whole again. Later she found out the pain had come as Joe had approached Chenault Park in his baby blue Cougar and had departed when he'd died.

JoAnn was Joe's twin.

When they were born in Henderson, Texas on Oct. 30, 1958, JoAnn's birth was uneventful, but Joe turned blue and almost died. He had some kind of bubble over his face, his mother, Eunice, says, which made it hard for him to start breathing. The midwife was familiar with this problem. She called it a "veil," and when the crisis had passed and the baby had filled his lungs with air, she told Eunice, "Any child born with the veil will die of drowning."

Lucille, one of Joe's five sisters—he had two brothers—says, "We were mighty glad when he learned to swim." But he was never more than a rudimentary swimmer; he was scared of water any deeper than his waist. It was amazing that he would rush in after those boys.

Let us now go down the road and around the bend from Joe's house on West Madison Street in Haughton to the Galilee Baptist Church ... to listen to the people eulogize him. The words are all real, but you're going to have to imagine the scene, because when Joe died there were so many people, from far and wide, who wanted to honor him that his parish church, the Galilee, couldn't be used for the services. They had to be held in the largest building in town, the high school gym—HOME OF THE BUCCANEERS it says on one wall, over an American flag. Joe rested there in an open casket before the services.

It was July 4, Independence Day, brutally hot, and a number of mourners passed out. Many Chiefs and other NFL players came, but the local people watched Norma Hunt especially closely. She's the wife of Lamar Hunt, the owner of the Chiefs, and if the home folks were impressed that this millionaire had come to pay his respects to Joe Alton Delaney, they were moved that his wife had come.

But for the purpose of the retelling, we're not in the Hades-hot gym. Instead it's a soft Loosiana autumn night—midweek, no football games—and we're assembled at the Galilee to hear the encomiums for the late Joe Delaney.

Galilee was originally used by both races, the whites letting their slaves worship there on Sabbath afternoons. Since 1863, after Vicksburg fell and that part of the Confederacy began to crumble, the blacks have had Galilee to themselves. These days the church is located in a neat, solid red-brick chapel, and Joe spent his Sunday mornings there during the off-season. He was an usher. His spot was in the back, just to the left as you come in. A little sign there says USHER, and Joe's folded chair is still in place, leaning against the wall. Look hard: you might see him there as his friends begin to enter.

Outside, a harvest moon ducks out from behind the clouds. Inside, the Rev. W.B. James is presiding. He's a trim little man who has known the Delaneys for years. Back in the Depression he walked to the Slap Chapel school for the colored with Joe's late father, Woodrow, and Woodrow's twin—Joe had twins on both sides of his family. More than 40 years later, two of the Rev. James's sons played with Joe on the football team at what's called Northwestern Louisiana, down in Natchitoches, which is pronounced NAK-a-tish.

Now the Rev. James stands in his pulpit and bids the people talk about Joe. Scour the area and Kansas City, too, and you'll never hear a bad word about Joe Delaney. He was a hero at the last instant, but he'd been a good man all the time leading up to it.

Marv Levy, who was Joe's coach in both his years at Kansas City, speaks first. Levy had no idea how talented Delaney was when the Chiefs drafted him in the second round in '81. Joe was penciled in as a "situation back," but in 1981 he gained 1,121 yards, started in the Pro Bowl and was AFC Rookie of the Year. Levy says, "Joe was a person who was genuine and honest right to the core of his being."

He sits down, and near him A.L. Williams, who coached Joe at Northwestern Louisiana, gets up. The football people are over on one side, more or less, and the home folks are on the other, with the family up front, all save Uncle Frankie Joe, Eunice's baby brother, for whom Joe was named. Of all his nephews, Uncle Frankie Joe was especially close to Joe. The two of them and Lucille would often sing together. But Uncle Frankie Joe wouldn't go to the funeral services, hasn't visited Joe's grave yet and, when Eunice gave him first crack at Joe's belongings, he wouldn't take a thing. So he wouldn't be here at the Galilee on this night, either.

Coach Williams speaks now. He says: "The first year Joe was up in Kansas City, Les Miller, the Chiefs' director of player personnel, called me on the phone. He said, 'I want to talk to you about one of your players.' I thought something was wrong. But then he said, 'I just wanted to tell you that Joe Delaney is the finest young man and the hardest worker we've ever had here.'

"You know when Joe came to Northwestern he was a wide receiver. The night I signed him, we went and sat on the fender of my car, and I promised him he could play there because he thought his best chance to make the pros was at that position. But we had a few injuries to running backs early in his freshman year, and Joe came to me and said if we needed a running back he'd switch and play there.

"People ask me, 'How could Joe have gone in that water the way he did?' And I answer, 'Why, he never gave it a second thought, because helping people was a conditioned reflex to Joe Delaney.'"

Bobby Ray McHalffey, who coached Joe at Haughton High, stands up next. Coach McHalffey says he has had a number of better athletes down through the years, but Joe worked a whole lot harder than the other boys. Coach McHalffey finishes up: "You missed somethin' when you didn't know that young 'un—a fine American man."

That's it for the coaches. The next person to speak is

Harold Harlan, principal of Haughton High. He says, "Joe was one of those who assumed responsibility. He was one of those who had goals. He was one of those you could always count on." He pauses then and scans the crowded church. "Joe Delaney was a cut above."

Carolyn Delaney, Joe's widow, sits in the front row, nodding. She brought their three girls to the church in the baby blue Cougar. There is Tamika, who's seven, Crystal, four, and JoJo (for Joanna), who wasn't even four months old when her daddy died. They all look up as Alma Jean rises. She's Joe's oldest sister, and she has been selected to read aloud the proclamation from President Reagan that Vice President Bush had personally delivered to the family back in July.

It finishes by saying, "By this supreme example of courage and compassion, this brilliantly gifted young man left a spiritual legacy for his fellow Americans, in recognition of which Joe Delaney is hereby awarded the Presidential Citizens Award."

A lot of people—even many of the football people—are crying now. Crystal wants to leave. Her father spoiled her something awful, and she can't bear to stay in any room when people talk about him. But Lucille is going to be the final speaker. She has brought her guitar, just to strum a couple of notes on, and then in the hush she reads MR JOE D., the poem that she wrote about her brother two weeks after he died:

> *My brother Joe was a small man in size*
> *but you'd have to know him to understand*
> *and realize just how big a heart he had.*
> *He would always help others, whether good or bad.*
> *Some people said he couldn't, but Joe said,*
> *'I can! I can!'*
> *Oh, how grand, and he did...*
> *Joe earned the right to have capital MR. in front of his name,*
> *But because of his love and not just his fame...*

There are more tears, and it's now time to conclude the service. The Rev. James says, "I don't know *any*body who had a spot on their heart about Joe. People ask me, 'Reverend James, why would God take *him* away?' and I say, 'God wants something good, too. Amen.'"

From the earliest, Eunice says, "He told me he was goin' to make the pros and make me happy." Joe didn't get any encouragement at home, though. Eunice and Woodrow, a hardworking truck driver till the day he died in 1977, thought football was stuff and nonsense. That may be why there haven't been any other athletes in the family. But then, Joe was also the only one ever to make college.

Joe was born four years after the Supreme Court outlawed segregation in the schools, but he was nine years old before this message, with deliberate speed, came to Louisiana. School integration there was called "the crossover," a term borrowed from the music business, and there isn't anybody around Haughton who doesn't profess that athletics helped ease the transition. As a star black player who was as impeccable of character as he was celebrated, Joe had an impact on his community.

In Haughton, everybody knew Joe D. The tracks of the Illinois Central Gulf line cut smack through town, but that doesn't mean the white folks are all here and the black ones over yonder. Instead, there is a crazy quilt pattern. The Galilee Baptist Church, for example, is in a white enclave. "We have some worldly peoples around here," the Rev. James says. Still, Baptists and fishermen predominate—both creatures of abiding faith.

Joe was a fisherman, was he? "Called hisself one," Eunice says, chortling.

She's in her house, the old sagging place where Joe grew up, where eight people live now, where Joe's trophies are all over and the television set is on all the time. This afternoon she's caring for Joe's children. After he signed his first contract Joe made his mother stop working as a cleaning lady, and he was going to get her a better place to live.

"Muh," he said. He called her Muh. "Muh, I'm going to buy you a house in Kansas City."

"No you ain't," she said. She didn't want to leave Haughton and her family.

What Joe did instead was build a house down the street for

himself and Carolyn and the girls. Carolyn had lived in an old house on that plot. She was the girl down the street all the time Joe was growing up. The new house isn't large, but it's trim and immaculate, with plastic covers on the chairs, Joe's trophies all over and the television set on all the time. "Joe wanted to build here," Carolyn says, "We wanted to feel in place." In Kansas City, he always introduced Carolyn as a home girl, but he was a home boy, too.

If Joe had lived, there would have been a star's contract, lots more money, and then he could have moved his family into a subdivision. In that neck of the woods in Louisiana, and in a lot of places in the U.S., subdivision has come to mean what uptown once did. There may be all sorts of neighborhoods, but there are no bad subdivisions. You can be sure of one thing, though. No matter how much money Joe might have made, and no matter where he might have gone to live, his '81 baby blue Cougar would always have been parked outside.

Joe spent a lot of time over at his mother's house. Carolyn has to devote a great deal of time to her own mother, who is blind. She says she really isn't a home girl; foremost she's a family girl. She lost her father in March and her grandfather in June, just two weeks before Joe died. "Joe, all I got now is you," she had said then.

"You'll always have me," he had replied.

In the mornings, Joe would bring JoJo over to Muh's, sometimes not much past six o'clock. Then he would roust everybody, get the music going. He was almost never still. "Sit down and rest awhile, Honey," Eunice would say.

On Independence Day Joe was lowered into the earth at Hawkins Cemetery. There was a two-mile-long procession of cars from the gym to the burial ground and then a long walk down a dirt road under the worst of a July midday sun. People can remember a little black girl running after Norma Hunt and asking her about the pretty bracelet she had on.

Joe, like Uncle Frankie Joe, hated that cemetery, and far as anybody knew, he'd never been back there since his father's burial in '77. Hawkins Cemetery isn't like the white people's graveyard down in Haughton proper, which is all green and manicured. It's up in Belleview and really no more than a clearing back in the woods, where the sandy earth is still piled up from graves dug years ago. It's so far out of the way that there isn't much use putting flowers on the graves; they get stolen and given to girl friends.

Joe is amid ancient company there. Only three down from him is a great-great uncle. Moses Kennon, born in 1848, 15 years before emancipation. On a lot of the stones it says GONE BUT NOT FORGOTTEN or OVER IN THE GLORYLAND or just plain ASLEEP. *Rest awhile, Honey.*

"The sky was the limit for him," Coach Williams said the other day. "We never got to see what Joe D. would be."

After Joe signed his contract with the Chiefs, Joe Ferguson, the Buffalo quarterback, who was raised in Shreveport and knew Joe D., showed Joe how to write checks. How would Joe D. know about things like that? The first big purchase he made then was a car. He was very careful about it because he didn't want to be ostentatious and spend too much of his money on one item when there was so much the family needed.

Finally, Joe came to Coach Williams and told him he'd thought about it and had settled on a Cougar. What did Coach think of that? Well, Coach Williams thought that was a fine choice, and so straightaway he picked up the phone and called Harry Friedman, the Lincoln-Mercury dealer in Natchitoches. Friedman told Coach Williams he was delighted that Joe had selected a Cougar and he would make sure to give Joe the best possible deal because everyone loved Joe D. and he had meant a great deal to Northwestern and Natchitoches.

Truth to tell, Joe did splurge a little. He sprung for just about every option available on the '81 Cougar. When he brought the car home, he told Carolyn that he would never get rid of it, no matter how good he became or how much he made or where he lived, because it was the first fine thing he had ever been able to buy in his life. He was going to keep it and tend to it and give it to his girls many years from now, when they were old enough to drive.

Since Joe didn't live to see that faraway day, Carolyn says she will honor his intention. The baby blue Cougar is parked outside the house now, in the driveway. It has two stickers on the back, one for the NFL Players Association, the other for the Chiefs.

Crystal is playing on the front lawn by the car. JoJo is napping. Tamika is still at school. Carolyn comes out and calls for Crystal to come in, and she does, because the grown-ups inside are through talking about her daddy, a man who died a hero one hot summer's day and, before that, had never put a spot on a human heart.

Happy birthday, Joe D.

The Long
Way Up

BY   PAUL   ZIMMERMAN

IT IS HARD TO IMAGINE A MAN AS TOUGH AND AS TALENTED AS
HOWIE LONG EVER FEELING ANYTHING BUT CONFIDENT AS HE
APPROACHES HIS SPORT. BUT, AS PAUL ZIMMERMAN DISCOVERED
WHEN HE SPENT SOME TIME WITH THE RAIDERS' STAR, LONG
NEEDED A LOT OF HELP TO OVERCOME A TROUBLED PAST.

The headlights cut through the blackening gloom of the
Charlestown section of Boston, and occasionally the car
bumped a little as it ran over a patch of cobblestones or an
abandoned trolley track. Howie Long slumped low next to
the driver and watched the familiar streets slide by.

"The Neck," he said. "This part is called the Neck. It's
where the British landed the day before Bunker Hill. We
used to go down to the playground here when we were kids
and look out across the water and watch Chelsea burn. Every
two or three years Chelsea burns."

There was a pause. The car passed a series of dark, low
apartments.

"The Projects," he said. There was no further comment.
Howie Long's sister lives in the area.

It was a bleak night in February and Uncle Mike Mullan was

driving. Mike Mullan, a man as tough as his name. Bald, hard, he spoke in four- and five-word sentences, and his occasional snappers had an edge of bitterness. When he died of leukemia four months later, it hit Howie Long very hard. Uncle Mike was one of the four Mullan brothers, Long's four uncles who took charge of a maverick Charlestown street kid and turned him into a 6' 5", 275-pound All-Pro defensive end for the Los Angeles Raiders. Actually five Mullans had a hand in it.

The fifth was Long's grandmother, Elizabeth Hilton Mullan, whom everybody, including Howie, calls Ma. It was to her house, which she shared with Uncle Mike until his death, that they were driving on this winter night. Every year Long leaves his home in Redondo Beach, Calif. and comes back to Charlestown. It helps him keep things straight—where he is now, where he has been.

The car turned off Main Street onto Albion Place to No. 7, halfway up a hill that leads to a dead end. It's a two-way street with one lane. If you meet another vehicle on the way up, you back down and try again. Imitation gas streetlights provide a kind of antique touch.

Parking is no problem on Albion Place—if you live there. People don't park in front of someone else's house. An occasional stranger who makes that mistake doesn't make it again. Once, a couple of off-seasons ago, Long, with out-of-state license plates on his car, parked in front of his grandmother's house at 7 Albion Place and someone ripped off his stereo. It made headlines in Boston papers and provided a lively topic for the interview sessions before the Raiders-Redskins Super Bowl.

"They wrote that I came from the slums, the ghetto, Gangland, U.S.A.," Long says. "It became a locker room joke. The people here didn't think it was very funny. They were offended. They're very proud people, working-class people, Irish mostly, and very close. They're suspicious of outsiders, and that's what I am now, an outsider. You'd think I'd be a favorite son in Charlestown. I'm not. I'm not a hero. I didn't play my football here. I left."

Heroes played for the Townies, the local semipro team in the Park League. The games were down by the Neck. Jack the barber coached them.

Playing football held no appeal for Long as a child. He could run fast and was big, too big. When he was nine he weighed 120 pounds. When he was 11 he was as big as the 13- and 14-year-olds. His uncle Billy, and then his cousin by marriage, Bob Murray, got him onto the Pop Warner teams they coached. He didn't stick around—for good reason.

"I was C-team age and A-team weight," Long said. "I didn't feel like going out there and taking a daily beating from kids two and three years older."

There was another thing, though, and it has been the dark shadow that has followed Long throughout his life. No confidence. Fear of failure, fear of being humiliated. On the street it was no problem. He could play street hockey, the No. 1 sport in Charlestown—"ball hockey," they called it—and he could play basketball and baseball in the playground, but football was different. It was organized, the real thing, uniforms, adults to yell at you, everybody watching. Pressure. The downside potential was too great.

Even as he climbed the football ladder, conquering each plateau as it came, the fear never left him. Two years after he finally committed himself to football he was a high school all-stater, seriously recruited by major schools. But to him big-time college football meant only the chance for big-time failure.

"I'd just finished reading *Meat on the Hoof*, by Gary Shaw, where he tells about what they did to guys at Texas when they wanted their scholarships back," Long says, "how they ran them off the team and put them through torture drills. I was terrified. What if I can't play?"

He signed a letter of intent at Boston College and immediately had second thoughts. "What happens if he gets hurt?" his uncle Billy asked a BC coach.

"The guy told me, 'Well, we only have so many scholarships a year,' " Bill Mullan says. " 'He'd lose it.' So Howie switched and went to Villanova, where they offered him a four-year."

By his senior year he was good enough to be chosen for the Blue-Gray all-star game in Montgomery, Ala.—as a late entry. Joe Restic, the Harvard coach and one of the assistant coaches for the Blue team, needed a spot on the roster filled.

He chose Howie, who had been a high school teammate of his son, Joe Restic Jr.

"I roomed with Colin McCarty, the middle guard from Temple who'd driven trucks with Joe Klecko," Long says. "No one talked to us. No one offered to take us out to dinner. It was the worst week of my life. They had a banquet the night before the game, and they introduced me to the guy I was going to play against, Zach Guthrie of Texas A&M. Texas? I'd never met anyone from Texas in my whole life. I'd seen him during the week. Great big guy, two-tone shoes, leather jacket, leather cap, toothpick in his mouth all the time. Never said a word. They announced his name at the banquet, then they announced me as the guy who'd be playing against him, and Frank Howard, the old Clemson coach who was emceeing the thing, pointed his finger at me and said, 'That's you, boy.' Scared? Hell, yes, I was scared."

And when the game started, when Long got his first taste of combat, the fear melted, and it was just football. He blocked a punt and pressured the quarterback all day. When it was over he was named defensive MVP. He said hello to his grandmother on national TV afterward and added, "Ma, it stinks here. I want to come home."

In his first training camp with the Raiders the fear came back. "I thought I stunk," he says. "I had no confidence—none. I couldn't understand why they'd drafted me in the second round."

He remembers lining up for his first live-contact drill and looking across the line at the glare of 300-pound Artie Shell. "I thought, Oh my God," Long says.

He sits in his grandmother's kitchen in Charlestown, his great frame crowding the room, his face alight and open as he tells these stories. It's the face of innocence, an Irish minstrel boy's face transported to the body of a massive grown man. This magnificent body, combined with those clean, chiseled good looks, already has the Hollywood talent scouts buzzing. Now where is there a part for a 275-pound choirboy? He is 25 years old with two years of All-Pro behind him, a wife who has completed two years of law school and a healthy baby son named Christopher Howard Long. It's all there ahead of him, a life of infinite promise, and yet almost every story he tells about himself, every anecdote, has an undercurrent of despair. It's not me, he seems to be telling you, this isn't really me that you see here in front of you.

Long achieved celebrity status in 1983, his first All-Pro year. Writers who met him for the first time during the Super Bowl week in Tampa in the tent put up for mass interviews were surprised by his soft-spoken, articulate manner and his wry, often hilarious way of expressing himself. One morning, with 30 or so writers crowding his little interview table, Long tipped his chair back, stared up at the top of the tent and proceeded to let loose a stream of consciousness that could become the definitive word on the surrealism of Super Bowl press days:

"Give me a day to die.... Are we in Kansas yet, Toto? I don't know where I am.... Oh God, I'm in a tent...."

Some kid, huh? Bright, great talent.

"Do you know what I was thinking the first day they had those press interviews?" he says. "I was thinking, Every player has his own table. What if nobody's at mine? How will I handle the embarrassment?"

Fear. Self-doubt. Curt Marsh, the Raider guard who roomed with Long at their first minicamp, remembers waking up in the middle of the night to see a frenzied Long wrestling the TV set off the wall and preparing to throw it out the window. "His eyes were wide open, and they had the glassy look of a maniac's," Marsh says. "I thought, Who am I living with? Then I realized he was asleep. I called, 'Howie! Howie!' There were nights when I saw him get up in his sleep and start fighting people. Once he almost went through a window...."

Long's wife, Diane, says, "He was always like a volcano about to erupt, always driven. Everywhere we went, he thought people were staring at him."

The story starts in Charlestown, one of the oldest towns in Massachusetts—it was settled in 1628. There are a few Colonial landmarks in Charlestown, but the pervading look is early industrial revolution, dark, soot-stained brick walls, abandoned factories, and the great gray shadow of the Projects. Long's first memories are street memories.

"There's the Bunker Hill Elementary School, the first

school I went to," he said as the car cruised the area last winter. "And this is Hood's, the dairy where my grandmother worked for 26 years. We used to play touch football on this little 10-foot-wide patch of grass between the dairy and the street. If you could catch a down-and-out pass on that field you were a serious player. And that's Eden Street Park across the street. See those three kids on the bench? That was me 12 years ago. Here's the place, Decatur Street, under the highway, where I got hit in the head with a bat. Me and this kid were hitting rocks, and as I bent down he cut loose with his home run swing and it caught me in the forehead. I didn't go down. I went to one knee. I had a lump this big. I walked home. Nobody was there; I went to bed."

"Howie was always bigger than everybody else," says his cousin Michael Mullan, a brewer for Anheuser-Busch, "but he wasn't tough. When you're that big and you ain't tough you've got a problem. Everyone wants a piece of a big guy. Kids would pick on him. I used to have to force him to fight. He'd be crying; he wouldn't do it. I gave him a choice—fight them or get smacked by me. After a while people left him alone."

Those memories haunt Howie Long to this day. The bitterness never leaves. "My cousin talks about throwing me into the street at seven or eight years old to defend myself," he says. "Can you imagine what that's like? What seven-year old kid wants to fight?"

At home there was no one to turn to. The Long family lived with his grandmother and Uncle Mike at 7 Albion Place, but his father, Howie Long Sr., was pulling long hours loading milk for Hood's Dairy, and his mother was bedridden most of the time, suffering from periodic attacks of epilepsy. Howie's four uncles, the Mullan brothers, had their own kids to worry about. There was only his grandmother, Ma, to feed him and clothe him. She knew what it was like to grow up alone. She was an orphan who finally had been rescued from a Catholic children's home in Yonkers. N.Y. by her aunt, Nellie O'Neil of Charlestown. She married Michael Mullan from Londonderry in 1925. He died of cancer in 1955. "He'd been a major in the IRA," Long says. "He lived next to the police station, and they tell stories about how he used to pass information along by a series of smoke signals from the chimney."

When Howie was nine, the Longs moved out of his grandmother's home to a house at 170 Bunker Hill St. "From that minute on, everything went downhill," Long says. "No one ever cooked in our house." He remembers sneaking over to 7 Albion Place, where his grandmother or his aunt Edie would feed him. Two years after the move his parents separated; a year after that they were divorced.

The memories remain, always dark, always haunting. He says that on the day the divorce went through, his mother "kind of went crazy" and went after his sister. He broke up the fight. After the separation he remembers his mother dragging him through the neighborhood at night, trying to find his father, hoping to catch him with another woman.

When the Raiders played in the Super Bowl in Tampa, the *Boston Herald* found Long's mother in Port Richey, Fla. She had remarried and retired. They took a picture of her with rosary beads in one hand and a picture of Howie in the other. "Mother's pride..." the caption read.

"A reporter from that paper called me up," Long says, "and asked me if I would get on a conference call with my mother. They wanted to do a *This Is Your Life* kind of thing. I told him, 'Don't you ever call me again.'"

After the divorce, the court had awarded custody of Howie, then 12, to his mother. "That was just their ruling, but nobody fought for custody. No one wanted the responsibility," he says. "Eventually I wound up back at my uncle Mike's house. I felt like the orphan everybody took in. Do you know what it's like to be 12 years old and not wanted?

"I would have liked to have lived with my dad, but when they got divorced he was working as a day laborer, sleeping in his car at night. Then he lived in a rooming house in City Square. He'd had a terrible life. He'd spent 13 years in an orphanage in Salem. Once we drove by it, an awful-looking place with barbed wire outside. As a kid I remember my father waking up at night in a cold sweat, ready to defend himself."

Howard Long Sr. had moved back into 7 Albion Place and lived with his ex-wife's mother and brother for nine years, until April 13 when he remarried and moved to East Boston.

He describes his relationship with Howie as "cordial, but we'll never be as close as we should be because of what has happened in the past. I'm not proud of what happened, but what could I do? I was struggling."

He is in his late 40s, youthful looking for a man with a 25-year-old son. Howie owes his height to his father, who stands 6' 8" and weighs 230, with black hair and sharply defined features. Sitting in the Mullans' kitchen, his hands gripping a cup of cold coffee, he speaks in subdued tones as he tells a story of Gothic horror about the Massachusetts of his boyhood.

"I lived with foster parents until I was four," he says, "and then I was sent to Plummer Farms School in Winter Island near Salem. It was a terrible, terrible place. You did 10 hours of farmwork a day and two hours of school. There was one teacher for the whole place. I was in the sixth grade at 17. There was no talking allowed inside the building. If you were caught talking, they made you hold your hands out, and you were beaten with a leather strap soaked in kerosene overnight. The kids who were too big for that were punched in the face. When I was 17, I was given a choice of staying in the home or going into the Army. I jumped at the chance. I'd never seen a dollar bill until I went into the service, never talked to a girl until I was 18. I met Peggy Mullan at a record hop in Charlestown as I was rotating out of the Army."

He studies the coffee cup and his hands tighten. "Seven of us went into the service," he says. "Six of them got dishonorable discharges. I was the only one who didn't. I've only met one guy who was in the home when I was there. He was a bum. I saw him on a bench in Boston Common."

He pauses again. "You know," he says, "there was a time when Howie and I almost didn't talk at all. I'm very happy for him now, for what he's done."

It's a life that could have gone in almost any direction, but underneath it all, underlying the bitterness and despair, runs a strong current of self-preservation.

"I never fooled around with drugs, and I was never an outlaw or a punk," Howie says. "Drugs scared me. I thought that if I did any kind of drugs I'd die. It was such an easy choice. It was as if someone said, 'Hey, kid, do you want a hot-fudge sundae, or do you want to hold your hand over a fire?'

"I was a street kid, but that meant hopping a ride on the back of the MTA down to Revere Beach—that's the beach that's made out of concrete—or sneaking into the Boston Garden to watch the Celtics or the Bruins. We had our whole plan of attack drawn up like a battle plan; we'd scratch it in the dirt. I'd cut school and go over to the Lori-Ann Donut Shop and eat doughnuts. I got a job at the pet store near Lechmere, unloading fish tanks. They gave me $10 for unloading a full long-bed truckload. I never broke a fish tank. When I asked for a raise, I got fired.

"My uncle John was a cop at the time, and he got me a job at this bar, the Rusty Scupper, sweeping up. I was 13, and I looked 16. I stood 6' 1", and I had this little broom and dustpan, and the place would be packed and I'd have to bend over and go around people's legs—'Excuse me, sir.'

"I loved it. They gave me a striped rugby shirt. It said Rusty Scupper on it, and I'd take it to bed with me. To me it was the Cadillac of sport shirts. My idol was a bouncer with a cast on his hand, a guy named Topper Rogers. He's a Boston cop. I wanted to be like him. Anyway Ma, my grandmother, came down and made me get out of the place."

By the time Howie was 14 and ready for his sophomore year in high school, a major problem had developed: He had become a truant. No classroom could hold him. He had missed 45 *consecutive* days of school. The busing riots were a convenient excuse, for many parents were hesitant about sending their kids to school. But Howie Long needed no excuses to stay away from class. There was too much going on outside ... fish tanks to unload, an occasional $20 to pick up longshoring on the docks when he could convince them he was 16. The Mullans had a conference. What should they do with this overgrown kid?

He could stay with Uncle George or Uncle Mike in Charlestown, but that didn't seem likely to work. It would just be more of the same. There was Uncle John, the cop, a solid officer who had once won the Medal of Valor for saving his partner's life. Uncle John had moved out of the area.

"I was the social climber," he says. "I moved to South Boston." But, no, his hours were too irregular. Then there was Uncle Billy, a supervisor with the Boston Housing Authority, a star for the Townies, who had played service football in France. He ran his house with the same military discipline he had learned in the Army. He lived in Milford, Mass., a suburban community 20 miles to the southwest, in a house that was crowded with two of his own children and two that he and his wife, Aida, had adopted. There were no luxuries, but Uncle Billy looked like he might be the answer for a truant teenager.

The family had already tried to enroll Howie in a vocational course to train him to be an electrician, but he had been turned down mainly because of those 45 missed days. Uncle Billy said he would take the kid, but he would have to obey the house rules. They packed a suitcase for Howie, and Uncle John took him downtown, bought him his first suit, and sent him to the suburbs.

Milford, Long says, was "high school, U.S.A. A beautiful place. They had cheerleaders, grass fields. I didn't know there was grass on the other side of the hill. I thought every place was like Charlestown. The first time I saw it, it was intimidating because it was so beautiful. The kids called me 'the Bostonian.' As an out-of-towner, I wasn't well received. I didn't have the kind of clothes the other kids had. I didn't have any parents in the booster club."

But Milford also had something else, a very dedicated coach named Dick Corbin. The first time he got a look at the 6' 2", 200-pound Long he suggested that he come out for football.

Corbin, who's the offensive line coach at Harvard now, says Long was a "survivor" as a sophomore but had become a "player" as a 6' 3", 235-pound junior tackle. In the winter between those seasons he played basketball and in the spring he threw the weights. The football team went undefeated his junior year and beat Pittsfield, 42–7, in the state championship. By his senior year, recruiters already had a pretty good handle on him.

"He broke his ankle on the first play of our second game," Corbin recalls. "The doctor said it was a four- to six-week injury. Howie said, 'Coach, my life is over.' In three days he had the cast off, and I saw him jogging around the field by himself, limping actually, and two weeks later he played."

In the classroom his dedication wasn't as evident. "When I first got there the teacher said, 'O.K., class, write a short story on your vacation.'" Long says. "Vacation? What vacation? I didn't even know how to start it."

He began cutting classes, and finally Corbin turned him over to his wife, Ruth Ann, an English and math teacher, for special tutoring.

"He was bright, you could see that right away," she says, "but he'd never had any discipline. In Charlestown he'd just been passed along. The interesting thing was that he always spoke with perfect grammar, even though he had no formal knowledge of it. That was probably his grandmother's influence.

"He let things slide, though. He'd show up an hour late for our appointment; he hadn't done the work. One day I told him, 'I can't work with you.' He was shocked. Everyone had always made allowances. After that he was O.K."

Life at home, according to Long, was a series of groundings. Those were Uncle Billy's traditional punishments, usually for missing the 9 p.m. curfew.

To this day, Long perceives his uncle Billy as a man of stern and unbending principle, but that doesn't give the whole picture. There's a fine strain of humor in the man, and underlying all is compassion, always great compassion. In the Mullan family Uncle Billy's house was the refuge for wayward relatives.

"That grounding was about Matthew's 40th life sentence," he says, calling Howie by his middle name, "the sentences to run concurrently. You know there were times when he wouldn't talk to me for two or three days. But the end of it is, look how he turned out."

Villanova received Long with these words from head coach Dick Bedesem: "He's unquestionably the finest recruit that our coaching staff has signed since we've been here."

Long was a big fish in a little pond. The Wildcats had losing seasons his first three years. "No film room," he says, "no reporters in the locker room; Ivy League level without Ivy League wealth."

Diane Addonizio, a classical-studies major from Red Bank, N.J., met Howie Long in her freshman year when he was a sophomore. She recalls him being moody and hard to know— "but attractive, boy was he attractive. I'd never met anyone that big who was that good-looking." The first real date they had was when Howie invited her to his room to watch an NFL game on TV.

"A little 12-inch, black-and-white TV that my grandmother gave me," he says. "A TV with lines on it and a coat hanger for an antenna. We watched a Dallas game. That's when they were still experimenting with Randy White at linebacker. On one play he got a running start and wham, he knocked the ballcarrier's helmet off. I started cheering. 'Wow, did you see that!' Diane must have thought I was nuts."

"Howie wasn't one of these guys who's too cool to have idols," says Diane, who married Long in June 1982. "He had pictures of Matt Millen and Bruce Clark from Penn State on his wall, and Mike Webster and Jack Lambert of the Steelers, and Joe Klecko from this area. Once he took me to a power-lifting competition at Villanova, and after we sat down he nudged me and said, 'Don't look around, but Joe Klecko just showed up.' He was absolutely in awe."

It took her some time to finally understand this strange, moody young giant she was so attached to. "He didn't send me a Valentine's Day card when we first started going together. That upset me, and I told him so," she says. "Then he explained how holidays never meant anything special to him. At Villanova when everyone went home for the holidays or the summer he was always the guy who stayed in the dorms. You know how a child's bed is special to him? Well, he never had his own. It was always a couch or something, while he was bouncing around from relative to relative. He was always living out of a suitcase, he always had his possessions on him. It took me awhile to understand that."

NFL scouts who came to test Long after his senior year saw another side of his character: He was always willing to work out, to run, to test—at any hour of the day or night.

"The Patriots worked me out in the snow," he says. "They

plowed the field. I ran 40s and 20s, did a vertical jump. I asked the guy for a pair of turf shoes. He gave me a Patriots key ring. I kept it. I thought it was the greatest thing in the world."

He was rated as a third- or fourth-round draft choice, but after the Blue-Gray game his stock rose. The Raiders sent their defensive line coach, Earl Leggett, to Villanova to work him out. "Earl had me set a couple of times and plant and come upfield 20 yards, and then he left," Long said. "I thought, Well, that's one team I can forget about, and I went up to my room and watched *Leave It to Beaver.*"

"I had seen his Blue-Gray films," Leggett recalls, "and we knew he'd run a 4.75 forty, but when you got around him you could feel the damn power and energy. You could just feel the brute strength."

Long finished his college career at 251 pounds. When he showed up at the Raiders' first minicamp he weighed 297, "just a biscuit away from 300," he says. "I thought everyone had to weigh 290 in the NFL. Earl looked at me and said, 'What happened to the guy I drafted?'"

When the regular camp opened, Long found himself across the line from Art Shell. "It was the first pit drill," he says. "I had checked out the line, and I saw that Matuszak was going against Lawrence, and Kinlaw against Dalby and Dave Browning against Shell, and I was going to get Lindsey Mason. I was getting ready for Mason when Shell came up and Earl said, 'Browning, step out of there, I want to see Long against him.' I thought, He's going to kill me. And he almost did. He hit me so hard he split the top of my right cheekbone and at the same time gave me the fists in the stomach. It was the most devastating pop I ever got in the NFL. My cheekbone still lumps up every year in training camp in the same spot."

In 1981 he was 21, the second-youngest rookie in the NFL, Houston cornerback Bill Kay edging him by four days. "Howie was the greenest of the green," Leggett says. "He didn't know nothing about playing the game." Leggett called him "My pro from Villanowhere." Each scrimmage, each game, became a death struggle. Eventually, all of Long's fears crystallized into one overwhelming urge to get the guy opposite him before he could deliver another dose of the Artie Shell treatment.

The rookies gave Long the nickname Caveman. The veterans were amused by him, by his intensity. What the hell, we're the Raiders. We've seen all types. "I didn't know what to make of them," Long says. "I remember going into a bar in Santa Rosa, where we trained—the Bamboo Room it was called—and Ted Hendricks was sitting on a stool and next to him was this life-size blowup doll. He said, 'Howie, meet Molly. Molly's my date tonight.'"

The Raiders would use Long in pass-rush situations as a tackle in the nickel defense. He remembers the Patriots' John Hannah and the Chargers' Ed White taking him to school. Mike Webster of the Steelers put him on his back the first play, and Doug Wilkerson of the Chargers "did tricks with me." But the intensity was always there. And in the fourth quarter, when things started to sag a little, Long would come on strong. He got his sacks and he wound up leading the team as a rookie.

He started the last five games of the strike year, 1982, and by 1983 he was a regular. He began following Leggett around like a puppy. The players called him Howie Leggett. Lyle Alzado arrived from Cleveland with plenty of giddap left in his aging legs and a willingness to share 11 NFL seasons' worth of knowledge with the young lineman. The club decided that Alzado should room with Long. "Lyle would bring a piece of chocolate cake and a glass of milk up to the room at 8:30, and at nine o'clock it was lights-out and the TV off," Long says. "I thought, Oh my God, I'm back with my uncle Billy again. I'd get a roll-away cot and sneak over to Calvin Peterson and Marcus Allen's room and watch TV.

"In the huddle Alzado was our leader, no question about it," Long says. "Still is. We say that Lyle will never retire. Eventually we'll prop him up on a horse and sew his eyelids open and he'll play forever. He'll be our El Cid...."

In his last two All-Pro years Long has become the Raiders' strongman on the defensive line, controlling the run and exerting pressure from the left end spot or as a tackle in the four-man pass rush. The night before a game he locks himself in his room with two cheeseburgers, a dozen iced teas and two reels of film. "If I don't look at films the night before, I feel naked the next day," he says.

He has mastered lots of subtle tricks of the trade—for example: "One thing I learned is never bend over in the defensive huddle. Stay up high and watch the other team's sideline, especially if the quarterback is over there talking to the coach. There's always that moment when he leaves him and starts back to the huddle and then forgets something and goes back. If you watch their lips, that's when you might pick something off."

Long's basic move off the line is devastating—it is the rip, an uppercut designed to break the opponent's grip and stop all forms of hand-to-hand combat. The hand fighters, he says, simply waste too much time. To counter Long's move, offenses use the tackle to set him up and then have the tight end crack down on his legs. That's where the trouble usually starts, setting off one of "the 80 or so fights I've had in the NFL," which have earned Long a reputation as a wild man.

"A lot of teams do it, but Kansas City is the worst," he says. "Willie Scott, their tight end, almost maimed me last year, and a big fight started. I told him, 'It might be legal, but do it again and I'll come down with my three-quarter-inch spikes and rip your ribs off.' That's the Catholic in me. Warn 'em first. Hey, look, I can't be responsible for what I do."

A few minilegends have already sprung up about Long. There was the time he went into the Seattle offensive huddle during a time-out and said to the trainer, "Give me that water. They don't need it. They're not doing anything."

"A few guys in the huddle laughed, guys that I know," Long says. "Ken Easley reminded me of it at the last Pro Bowl. He loved it."

There was the time Long screamed at Chicago guard Kurt Becker: "I'm going to get you in the parking lot after the game and beat you up in front of your family!"

"Yeah, I said it," Long says. "He'd spent the day flying over the pile and hitting defensive backs late. He was my target for the game, but I had missed him and sprained by back, so I was upset. Everyone has their favorite threat, and that's mine. Lyle's is 'I'll kill you and everything you love.'"

The Raiders' reputation as intimidators took some lumps

last year. Chicago outplayed them. Pittsburgh and Seattle ran the ball on them. Long sighs and admits, "Things were bad. Injuries, mistakes, some people just didn't play well."

Three weeks before the end of the season Long was wondering if he would have a shot at the Pro Bowl. His sacks were down, thanks to the double-team attention he was getting, but the statistics didn't show holding penalties by opponents, and the Raiders figure that Long and the Bucs' Lee Roy Selmon led the league in that category.

"I won't have the sacks of a Mark Gastineau," Long says, "and I won't get all those pursuit tackles. Our responsibilities are different. He's allowed to free-lance all over the field. I have back-side responsibility. I have to play the reverses and cutbacks. Let me know when Gastineau decides to play the run."

Al Davis, the Raiders' managing general partner, feels that Long is a player with "superstar qualities and room for improvement." Long says he'll dedicate the 1985 season to zeroing in more accurately on quarterbacks. "I came in too high a lot of times," he says. "They'd duck, and I'd miss."

The Raiders acknowledged Long's worth when they rewrote his contract after he staged a four-day holdout last July. They eventually gave him $3 million for four years, none of it deferred, a package that is the best in the NFL in terms of real money for a defensive lineman.

It's always a shock when people meet Long for the first time. Last winter his uncle John, the ex-cop who's now the driver and bodyguard for the agent Bob Woolf, took Long to meet Woolf. They talked for a while and finally Woolf said, "You know I don't know how to say this, but you're ... well, you're really not like I expected you to be ... you're...."

"Civilized," Long said.

"That's it," said Woolf.

"It happens all the time," Long said later. "I always spend the first five minutes convincing people I'm really Howie Long. They say, 'No, you're not. He's much meaner looking.' They figure I should be wearing a torn black jersey, going around raping and pillaging."

The Boys and Girls Club of Boston sees a very private side of him. He has come back and spoken to the group twice.

This fall he will treat 50 of the kids to tickets to the Raiders-Patriots game in Foxboro. "What I would have given if someone would have done that for me when I was a kid," he says. It's a simple matter. You've gotten something from life, you give something back.

Long's fears and his self-doubts are almost gone now. But sometimes at night they do come back, and he feels that maybe this has just been a dream, that he'll wake up and he'll be back in Charlestown again. Then he begins to wonder what might have happened—if.... What *if* his grandmother hadn't been around? What *if* his uncle Billy hadn't taken him in? What *if* Dick Corbin hadn't taken him in hand? What *if* he had been accepted for the electrician's course at vocational school instead of being rejected?

"Well, he'd be an electrician right now," says his aunt Aida. "A tall one. He wouldn't need a ladder."

"I never would have made it out of Charlestown if not for all those people," Long says. "I'd probably be working for the Boston Housing Authority, and I wouldn't be very happy. I wasn't a happy kid. But there was always someone there, always someone saving my ass—Ma, my uncle Billy, Dick Corbin and his wife and Earl Leggett."

"Call it luck, call it circumstance," Diane Long says, "but you have to wonder how many others there are like him out there, people who could have really done something if given a chance. They knew they were better than what they were, but they never knew what to do about it."

Long stares out the window of his Redondo Beach home, at the lights winking along the Pacific Coast Highway.

"God gave me good people around me, and He gave me size," he says. "It's kind of a miracle, really. Diane and I have talked about it. Where would I be now if God hadn't decided to rip me from stone?"

Got it Made, JoeMontana

BY   CURRY   KIRKPATRICK

JOE MONTANA WAS ALREADY A WILDLY SUCCESSFUL, HIGHLY PUBLICIZED QUARTERBACK IN 1985. BUT EVERYONE STILL YEARNED TO KNOW WHAT IT WAS LIKE TO BE THE VERY EMBODIMENT OF THE AMERICAN DREAM. CURRY KIRKPATRICK TRIED TO PIN DOWN ONE OF THE NATION'S MOST ELUSIVE HEROES.

What am I wanted for now, Sheriff?
To take me to the dance, JoeMontana.

Or better yet, to explain what the American Dream means to you, JoeMontana. A guy with a microphone asked JoeMontana that recently and JoeMontana, possibly confusing dream with democracy, repeated the routine shibboleths—"Life, liberty, freedom, is that how it goes?" he said—before adding a new one, "Oh yeah, and going out on Sundays to get beat up." Haw, haw. Elusive rascal, that JoeMontana. Just like on third-and-long. He doesn't want to be trapped. Or even touched. Doesn't want the people to know. Doesn't want anybody to figure out how absolutely delicious his life is. How wonderfully controlled, rich, secure and happy he finally has become. How JoeMontana, a skinny kid from the dreary Pennsylvania coal fields, could turn himself into a California beach layback. How could he outcelebrity his own name—a cute trick pulled off in recent times only by Madonna Louise Veronica Ciccone herself—and come off so ... so....

What am I wanted for now, Sheriff?

To explain why you're so lucky, JoeMontana.

Well forget it. Nobody can explain luck anyway. But so what if JoeMontana won the Super Bowl and married the spectacular Schick Sheriff back to back? (With a tiny rotor blade on the way.) Or that he makes a million point one a year and lives in a glorious hillside hacienda, where on a clear day he can see Catalina Island, Malibu, innumerable marinas and maybe the great but late Dan Marino as well? So what if JoeMontana, 29 years old, 6' 2", 200 pounds of Monongahela-by-the-Bay, Pennsylfornia, *is* the American Dream?

JoeMontana deserves all of this. First he had to juke that name—"Sounds like a gunfighter," says Terry Hanratty, the Notre Dame quarterback of the late '60s, hearing it for the first time. Now as a rule he's merely *JoeMontana*—ram right through that, one word. Really now, "Joe" is too, too plebeian, and how are you going to call a guy "Montana," which at last look was a state or something?

Remember also that JoeMontana had to spend the first 18 years of his life in the vicinity of Pittsburgh and the next five at Notre Dame—four regulation seasons and one injury-compelled redshirt year. That is enough dues-paying for several lifetimes. Moreover, he has had to scramble out of the pocket of two broken marriages and into the daylight from a reputation for a lackadaisical attitude and game-time inconsistency. Not to mention the silliest stigma of all: that an offensive football system "made" him rather than the other way around. Ultimately, however, JoeMontana hit pay dirt.

"JoeMontana's been searching," says his San Francisco 49er teammate Russ Francis. But no more that he has been searched after. Whose life is this, anyway? Was JoeMontana a flashy, womanizing show-off, as manifested by his ladies and his cars? He dated a Norwegian model between marriages; he tooled across *high school* in a Triumph Spitfire; his current favorite is a red Ferrari. Was JoeMontana a silent, bashful introvert? His wife, the former Schick law woman, Jennifer Wallace, says he is only now getting over being "afraid" of people. A veritable stranger, she had to pinch him in the butt (embarrassing him to a shade of cerise) before he would loosen up enough to complete their commercial.

Was JoeMontana a quaking-in-his-boots novice? In a game at Dallas in 1980, his second season in the pros, he actually tried to hide behind Bill Walsh so the 49er coach wouldn't send him into a terrifying blowout that the Cowboys would win 59–14. Was JoeMontana a macho commander? A little more that a year later he whistled a touchdown pass over the earlobe of Too Tall Jones and yapped "Respect that!" in San Francisco's 28–27 playoff upset of Dallas that created the 49ers' aura and lifted him to stardom.

Or did it? After San Francisco beat Cincinnati in the 1982 Super Bowl 26–21 the game story in this magazine listed Walsh's name 22 times, not necessarily all including the pre-scribed middle name "Genius." As for Montana, who had completed 14 of 22 passes for 157 yards and a touchdown and won the Most Valuable Player award, his name was mentioned a mere 10 times. Last January, prior to the 49ers' 38–16 Super Bowl victory over Miami, an SI cover featured both Montana and the Dolphins' Marino. In the eight pages inside the 49er was mentioned twice. Then he blasted the other guy off the map—his versatility, adaptability and ballet dancer's *feet* winning out over the cannon. And suddenly there was no other quarterback alive.

Backing up a bit, at the same time JoeMontana has been compiling the fairly outrageous statistics that now make him both the most accurate passer (in completion percentage) and the one with the lowest percentage of interceptions in pro football *history*, his overall quarterback "rating," according to an NFL formula you might get Edward Teller to explain sometime, is also the best of all the pros who ever took a snap. Still, the decade of the '80s has seemed at different times to be the signal-calling province of Joe Theismann or Dan Fouts or Doug Flutie or Bernie Kosar. Or of Marino. Or even of Warren Moon, whoever that may be. But wait a minute. What other quarterback ever won a national champi-onship in college and then won a Super Bowl in the pros?

Before JoeMontana, only Joe Namath. Before Namath, nobody. And in 1985 JoeMontana won another and a second MVP award as well.

Assuredly, JoeMontana is a nice fellow, quiet and restrained, polite and humble. But it's in the quarterback manual that the species is to be booed. All quarterbacks. Except that nobody can remember this quarterback ever receiving such treatment.

That is timing, and timing has always been JoeMontana's hole card—on and off the field. JoeMontana picked the NFL's strike-shortened 1982 season to have an "off" year—the 49ers were 3–6 but in truth the defense couldn't stop anybody, and JoeMontana's factored-out numbers would have been merely brilliant over a full slate. In August of '84 he discreetly negotiated a new contract estimated at $6.6 million for six years—he is the highest-paid player in the NFL—while teammates Ronnie Lott and Fred Dean took the brunt of public alarm by engaging in noisy holdouts.

Even during the acrimonious divorce in 1983 from his second wife, Cass, a stewardess four years his senior and, according to some 49er teammates, something of an overprotective woman, JoeMontana donned the white hat and rode the white horse. (The couple's two Arabian stallions were innocent parties in the litigation.) Reports in several papers said that Cass refused to relinquish her ex-husband's Super Bowl MVP trophy and assorted football paraphernalia. That the information was false did nothing to quell the Frisco uproar over JoeMontana, their JoeMontana, being done wrong. And what about this? Recently the 49er quarterback's replies to some fan mail were lost in transit, the result being that his answers were received months late. Unfriendly repercussions? One little girl wrote back thanking JoeMontana for being so kind to aim his reply so that it arrived on her very birthday. You gotta have timing.

Most amazing of all was how JoeMontana got away with moving from San Francisco to Los Angeles—a sin normally punishable by hanging. When he signed his contract, JoeMontana said he wanted to re-up for six years because he "loved" the Bay Area. Then he moved south with Jennifer. The fact that the newspapers revealed the new residence as being in

Palos Verdes Estates, 26 miles from L.A. proper, probably soothed some hurt feelings. Or else Jennifer may have smiled—an audible guaranteed to melt the harshest of critics—while the Montanas promised to find a second, in-season home in the South Bay. All the same, what San Francisco hero could have survived this horrendous faux pas but JoeMontana?

A few years ago when *San Francisco Chronicle* writer Ira Miller suggested JoeMontana be given a nickname, 10,000 monikers issued forth, including one proposal that what the man needed instead was a *real* name, specifically "David W. Gibson." Luckily, Sir Pass Goldflinger Big Sky Beaut Montana didn't change his name, and Montanamania continues unabated.

This summer at Macy's on Union Square, Montana made an appearance that in audience enthusiasm rivaled any of the past performances of Santa Claus—or even Calvin Klein at the perfume counter. Hundreds upon hundreds of people lined up for hours before JoeMontana's midmorning appearance. There were golden-agers, matrons, babes in arms—"the 49ers are undefeated in the kid's lifetime," one father boasted of his 7-month-old—who were joined by punkers with arrows, crosses and other terrific messages cut into their hairdos, creatures of indeterminate sex, shop personnel and streams of sighing young girls.

The subject did not have such a wonderful time. Even accompanied by the social and vivacious Jennifer, 27, a veteran trouper from her modeling days and her TV bit actress career (*Mork and Mindy*, *Dynasty*) JoeMontana looked painfully uncomfortable amid all the hullabaloo. Most public appearances are "a pain in the ass" to him, though he cooperates fully and understands their necessity. They are tolerable now only if his beloved Jen comes along.

Jennifer is a dazzling beach girl herself, right off the Redondo esplanade—beach "oriented," she emphasizes. She is credited with getting JoeMontana to settle down and open up in their 19 months together. Francis, the 49er tight end who knew Jennifer years ago in Hawaii, where she played beach volleyball and worked as a crew member on a large sailboat, says she is the "special partner" JoeMontana was looking for.

"He had been on edge for a couple of years," Francis says. "I think he's at peace now."

When the six-foot Jennifer met JoeMontana at that opening Schick shoot, his first impression was: "They finally got somebody they don't have to prop up on orange crates." They were married in February. The honeymoon was spent skiing in Utah and snorkeling off Virgin Gorda. She is expecting in November. "With Joe, this image of the athlete as public figure, star, hero—he's not into that," Jen says. "Everyone wants a piece of him, and he's never known who to trust. It got so that he didn't know what was real and what was unreal. I think he's eased up in that respect. He's accepted the responsibilities of celebrity. In the last year I've seen Joe just bloom."

On that summer day at Macy's, JoeMontana was cordial with everyone—fans, organizers, the Concord watch people from whom he receives terrific scratch for concealing his wrist with their product. But after an obligatory 90 minutes it was time to flee another pocket. The scene was precisely why the Montanas had moved from the city. The public had kept piling on. There was too much attention, acclaim. JoeMontana's face and name were splattered everywhere. There was no privacy. In Palos Verdes, JoeMontana could get lost behind the orange and lemon and guava trees by the pool and be protected inside the iron gates with the maximum-security system, the one with the sign in the front yard warning ARMED RESPONSE. Oh yeah, he also could go to the beach every few minutes or so.

San Francisco had become an environment in which JoeMontana had no control. There were no blockers. No options. Nobody was open. It was a trap, a loss. The only play was to get out of Dodge. At Macy's, JoeMontana told a reporter, "These public things are nice once in a while because the people get to see my wife and me up close."

Upstairs, JoeMontana tenderly kissed Jennifer goodby in the presence of a roomful of strangers—they were to be apart a full 10 seconds until meeting again out in the hall—and then both were whisked away by uniformed guards through the storage aisles down some more stairs, past a freight elevator and into a waiting limousine deep in Macy's basement, where nobody could make the tackle. When together—which is presumably till the 12th of Never—Joe and Jen don't hold hands, they *interlock* arms. Now JoeMontana was safely out of bounds again—or in another end zone. Also, it was abundantly clear, JoeMontana wasn't just in bloom, he was hopelessly in love.

Most of our greatest athletes are not naturals. Bjorn Borg and Larry Bird, to drop a couple of familiar names, had to sweat and toil and struggle until it all came true. JoeMontana is one of those few gifted from swaddling clothes with talent, all the right instincts and a flair for the dramatic as well. In Little League in Monongahela he pitched three perfect games, and at Ringgold High he high-jumped a 6'9" and saved his best performances for basketball, still a favorite sport. Even now he wins bets from his close friend, 49er wideout Dwight Clark, by dunking two hands backward. In San Francisco's first football game following the strike of '82, he threw 39 passes and completed 26 for 408 yards in a 31–20 rout of the St. Louis Cardinals. That's a natural.

"Sports was not something I had to work at," JoeMontana says. This got him in hot water at Notre Dame. But early on, his father drummed into him vast quantities of fundamentals. And later, his quick mind could, as 49er quarterback coach Paul Hackett says, "translate the X's and O's to eye level and then to reality." Work be damned—"I still hate practice," he says—JoeMontana has made it the easy way. On enormous physical ability and raw brainpower.

It was John Brodie, the former 49er quarterback, who suggested JoeMontana to Walsh. Phil Simms, who was considered one of the best of the college quarterback crop in the 1979 draft, would be long gone before the 49ers' pick, and Walsh was partial to Steve Dils, whom he had coached at Stanford. But when he watched JoeMontana work out with UCLA running back James Owens, Walsh was impressed with his "nimble" feet, quickness and balance on the drop. JoeMontana, who had never looked good in practice at South Bend, must have been playing charades. The 49ers drafted Owens on the second round and JoeMontana on the third, the 82nd pick of the draft. "I knew of his inconsistency,"

Walsh says. "I also knew about his competitiveness. If he could be great for one game, why not two, why not repetition? He was willing to learn. That was easy to tell. I knew he would improve. I was anxious to zero in on this guy."

Choosing up sides in the backyard, who always gets to be the quarterback? The best athlete, that's who. In fact as well as theory, the NFL doesn't quite work that way. The athletes go to the defensive secondary or to outside linebacker—or to basketball. Ah, but here was an athlete who almost offhandedly happened to be a quarterback. Recall the Catch that culminated the Drive that beat Dallas and got the 49ers into Super Bowl XVI. Yes, Clark made that phenomenal leaping grab in the back of the end zone with 51 seconds left to win the game. But here's what JoeMontana did just to get the ball loose and up there: He avoided a frightening defensive rush, dashed to the sideline searching desperately for someone to break clear, baffled both Cowboys, Jones and Larry Bethea, who were about to sandwich him, pumped once off-balance to get the two Dallas defenders in the air, then leaned in another direction as they were coming down and threw off the wrong foot.

You don't, as they say, coach that. Moreover, you don't scout it or prepare for it, either. JoeMontana does not have the rifle of a Marino or a Steve Bartkowski or a Neil Lomax or even a Matt Cavanaugh, the 49ers' second stringer. But scavenger feet, an intuitive head and a thirst for spectacular improvisation will slice up coaching expertise and standard fortifications any day—just like in the backyard. Who can forget the Miami defenders in last January's Super Bowl running around frantically looking for San Francisco receivers? And then here came JoeMontana—racing down the field behind their backs chasing *them*: "I got half my catches from Joe at Notre Dame just avoiding confused defenders," former Irish tight end Ken MacAfee once said.

"Street ball" is 49er running back Wendell Tyler's description of JoeMontana's style. "Just like back home on the block. I move when he moves. In two years of this here, I've got the feeling. You pick up on his groove to get into your own."

Walsh surely cringes at the notion that his complex offensive designs—JoeMontana remembers rehearsing 127 different plays for a game with Buffalo, then it rained—might be considered in the realm of improv. His initial philosophy was that the short pass is as effective a tool at controlling the ball as a bull moose running game if you have an intelligent point man who can read defenses, delineate situations and throw with accuracy. This offense was developed for a mechanical fellow named Virgil Carter when Walsh was an assistant at Cincinnati in the 1970s and the Bengals had to throw to make first downs. In 1981 JoeMontana took this strategy and turned it into an art form as the 49ers rolled to their first championship. It is said that along the sidelines in that watershed playoff victory over Dallas, Brodie and O.J. Simpson, Frisco kids from birth, were so caught up in the emotion that Brodie broke out in tears.

Last season, with Tyler and Roger Craig adding a running attack to the 49er monster, the entire NFL could be seen sobbing. Now opposing defenses had to cover every inch of the field in fear of runners and receivers and of JoeMontana everywhere. The quarterback's days of being overly patient—that is, in waiting too long looking for the perfect option and then hurling wild—were over. Now there was hardly ever such a thing as a 49er broken play for long because JoeMontana would quickly fix it.

When JoeMontana keeps the football, the fun begins. "It's a burden on us, sure," says Francis, "but a challenge, too. Our scramble drills cover all the possibilities. It's a relief to run down the field and see nothing but trouble, everything getting very hairy, and as you turn your head you see JoeMontana scrambling. He has seen the problem before you get there and now he's going to finish the play anyway. And you know he *will* finish it."

After six NFL seasons, JoeMontana already tiptoes with legends. Unitas and Starr: But they wouldn't be caught dead in the open field, or else they might be dead. Tarkenton and Staubach: JoeMontana has a better arm than the former, is more accurate than the latter. Though not necessarily as hard to catch, he is probably faster than both. "I don't know if anybody can run him down," says 49er guard Randy Cross. "The only reason Gastineau caught him in [this year's] Pro

Bowl was because Joe stopped running to throw." Namath: the same elegant drop and setup. The same upbringing in Western Peeay. But after his Super Bowl, Namath basically faded into interceptions and summer stock. JoeMontana still has two good knees and can move sideways. "He's Fred Astaire," says Namath.

It has never been the arm with JoeMontana. "Weight room! Weight room!" the 49ers scream when one of his long practice heaves flutters short. Nor is his angular body particularly known for its hunkability quotient. "Who is this, the *punter*?" Clark said seriously upon their first meeting.

When JoeMontana has instead is the dramatic ability to get his body *in position* to throw—from all imaginable angles, through any multiples of crunching hits. "Escapability," Hackett likes to call it. "JoeMontana knows how important his feet are. Over a period of six weeks going over game films last season, we might have mentioned his feet three times. Last year on only five passes did his feet cost him an interception. That's just unbelievable."

JoeMontana still knows how much he doesn't know. He knows the lifeblood of a quarterback, the edge, especially his edge, is in a command of the Walsh system. Simply, he *has* to be a human memory bank for the 49er plays, progressions, personnel and various formations. Furthermore, JoeMontana not only knows the 49er offense, he also understands it—which is altogether a different kettle of, uh, Dolphin. This summer Hackett marveled at how JoeMontana could repeat whole game plans four months after the fact. Hackett's forte is innovation; he is renowned for challenging Walsh mentally. In weekly quizzes on the game plan Hackett will have the set of plays in front of him, but, he says, "I'll miss more that Joe does." Is it any wonder JoeMontana was the right quarterback for this job?

JoeMontana has subtly acquired a share of team leadership, though not off the field, of course. "If you didn't know Joe, you wouldn't know he was JoeMontana," says Tyler. But out there on the grid....

"There's not a lot of lemmings on this team," says Cross of the champs. "So JoeMontana's your perfect field general for a bunch of individualistic maniacs. No rah-rah. His leadership has come slowly, by example. He's always thinking a step ahead. A lineman's input isn't life and death to him, and he'll be polite. But you get the impression you might be a nuisance. He'll go 'oh sure' and give you that one-thousand-miles-away stare. I call it playing football in the third person. He's there and he's not there."

Well, folks, he's just taking what they give him.

Wrong. In the 49ers' possession plan JoeMontana takes what they don't want to give him. Walsh has called JoeMontana a "sensuous" athlete and compared him to "a great writer or musician" in the way he can manipulate the point of emphasis of a football game. "JoeMontana stretches our limits," Walsh has said. "He redefines what is sensible." This is marvelously heady stuff. And, by the way, it's all true.

The two men have had their differences as well, Walsh complaining at times that JoeMontana has depended too much on bosom buddy Clark for a target; that he has been overly reckless breaking away from blockers; that he spent valuable time on extracurriculars (TV shows, endorsements, appearances) in the season following Super Bowl XVI. But criticism cuts both ways. "The TV stuff was on Mondays, a nonstudy day, and I didn't miss any practice sessions that year," says JoeMontana. "On my choice of receivers, whose neck is it? I'll go with a guy having the hot year every time. They say I force the ball sometimes, but I don't call any of those third-and-eight plays. I don't call *any* plays."

This may stick in the craw. Last season with time running out and Detroit and the 49ers tied, JoeMontana entered the huddle and was asked somewhat facetiously what plays Walsh had told him to run. "He didn't give me any − − plays," JoeMontana snapped. "He told me to get the − − ball in the − − end zone." It took 11 plays to set up the decisive field goal, and the 49ers won 30–27.

"I can kid Bill—but not about philosophy or egos, stuff like that," says JoeMontana. "I like to think the system was built around the quarterback and that I add something special. As much as Bill puts in, we're the ones who have to execute. But maybe that's just for my own mindset, to keep me motivated. One frustration is that throwing deep is not part of the plan. It's so hard to sit and watch other teams do it and know, damn, we can do that. But throwing down the field is not something a team can perfect in practice, and whenever we miss in a game he [Walsh] gets scared and I get nervous. Then we back off. I think I'm at a point in my career where I could play anywhere in any system, but I don't want to have to find out."

Greater love hath no man for another that he refuses to throw him to the hyenas in his rookie season (San Francisco was 2–14; JoeMontana threw just 23 passes all year). Walsh also protected him in JoeMontana's second year, when the 49ers were 6–10. At the beginning, Walsh played him behind Steve DeBerg, using him only in propitious situations—not against headhunters, rarely inside his own 50, always to spur confidence. If not looked after this way, who knows, JoeMontana could have ended up Archie Manning.

Once against the Jets, DeBerg took the team to the New York five-yard line, but JoeMontana came in and scored on a rollout. Then he completed four of six passes for 60 yards. Then, exit. In his second season JoeMontana started a few games, then handled the headphones and clipboard for three weeks, then started a few more. "I was setting the stage," says Walsh. But in the 14th game of 1980, after the 49ers fell behind New Orleans by 35–7 ("Attack, don't absorb," Walsh said at the half), JoeMontana marched the team on four touchdown drives totaling 331 yards and engineered another drive in overtime that led to a field goal and a 38–35 victory. This was the greatest comeback in the history of the NFL. JoeMontana never looked back. Of course he had been there before. He has always been Comeback Joe.

It was in JoeMontana's junior year at Ringgold High that it first happened, a 35–35 tie with heavily favored Monessen from across the river. It was the kid's first starting assignment on the varsity, but Joe Sr. had prepared him long and well. Running pass patterns. Swaying the tire through which his son aimed his deliveries. Lying about the kid's age to get him in peewee ball. Both Montanas insist the proper word is "encourage," not "push," for what Joe Sr. did for Joe Jr. in sports. But others who were there know different. "He never had a choice," says Theresa Montana, wife and mother.

Joe Sr., 52, silver-haired and part Sioux Indian, was born a year to the day after the future mentor, Walsh. When little Joe was three, his father quit his job as a telephone equipment installer for Western Electric, which kept him on the road, and took an office job at the Civic Finance Company in Mon City, as Monongahela is called in the local vernacular, so he would always be there, a benevolent sage for an only child's pursuit of excellence in athletics. And there he remains—although now JoeMontana has mounted a strong lobbying effort to get his parents to move to California.

The father always has been the son's best friend. And the father's father wasn't far behind. "Hooks" Montana, a semi-pro player for the New Eagle (Pa.) Indians, once drove all the way from Texas to Cleveland hoping to see JoeMontana play in the Notre Dame–Navy game, even though his grandson was a redshirt that season. At halftime a stroke came on. Within seconds Hooks was gone. JoeMontana says Hooks knew he was about to die and wanted to pick the place. If that is so, no Notre Dame fan ever passed from this earth a happier fellow. Notre Dame 27, Navy 21.

JoeMontana himself turned down a basketball scholarship to North Carolina State in favor of football under the Golden Dome, but he was terribly homesick from the start. Not only that, among the three quarterbacks on the freshman roster he ranked last. In his second semester he married a hometown honey, Kim Moses, which was not so unusual in that time and place. At Notre Dame, Nick DeCicco, JoeMontana's roommate, and Nick's father, Mike, the university's academic adviser, tried to talk him out of wedlock—no more panty raids at St. Mary's, Joe, no more transplanting goats from the South Bend Zoo to the athletic dorm. But in Mon City lots of people married young. Hardly anybody ever left to go off to college.

So the teenagers went through with it. Kim took a job in the Notre Dame Sports Information Office, and JoeMontana soon gave her plenty to type up. Because coach Dan Devine favored others—the kid didn't exactly practice hard, remember—JoeMontana spent much of his sophomore year coming off the bench and didn't start till the fourth game of his junior year. In between, 1976, he sat out the season with a separated shoulder, although to this day he vows he could have played the second half if Devine hadn't held him out. (MacAfee insists that if JoeMontana had played he would have won the starting job, had a leg up on the Heisman Trophy and would have won it in 1977.)

In his modest fashion JoeMontana does not dwell on his truly amazing storybook career at Notre Dame: among other heroics, six games in which he played a total of a little less than 40 minutes and brought the Irish back from 88 points behind.

North Carolina, his sophomore year: JoeMontana plays 1:02 and guides the Irish from a 14–6 deficit to a 21–14 victory. Purdue, junior year: JoeMontana, the *fourth* Notre Dame quarterback sub, plays six minutes and passes for 154 yards and 17 points to bring the Irish from 24–14 behind to a 31–24 win. Stuff like that. By now Devine had figured everything out, and he left JoeMontana in charge for the balance of 1977, at the end of which the Irish smashed Texas in the Cotton Bowl and won the national championship.

But this was a bittersweet time. JoeMontana and Kim were having problems in the same period the Notre Dame quarterback was all over the wire services kissing the Cotton Queens upon landing in Dallas. The publicity did not sit well with some people in Mon City, where Kim was the girl next door, and if there is anywhere on the planet cynicism still lingers about JoeMontana, it is in his own hometown.

"It's very hard to go back, anywhere, it really is," JoeMontana says softly. "But Mon City is not the kind of place people who leave go back to. Not in spirit, not all the way." Last spring he took Jennifer back to Mon City, but he has not maintained close ties there other than with his parents, and the visit was somewhat awkward. "I know what the people probably think," he says.

What they think is that JoeMontana went Hollywood long before he even saw California, and in a way he did. While still a senior at Notre Dame he kept orchestrating cinematic finishes right out of a Tinseltown dream. As in the '79 Cotton Bowl: It was 17° with 30-mph winds for JoeMontana's last college game. He was cut and bleeding from the raw rock salt on the field. He showed a temperature of 96°

before being covered with blankets in the locker room and force-fed with chicken soup. By the time a doctor got his breathing back to normal it was late in the third quarter and the Irish had fallen behind Houston, 34–12. *JoeMontana redefines what is sensible.* Before enough rosaries could be said to cover the situation, Montana had whipped Notre Dame to within 34–28, and with four seconds left he nailed Kris Haines with a perfect quick-out pass for what would have been the winning touchdown. But Haines slipped. In his very last huddle JoeMontana told Haines, "Don't worry, you can do it." And he called the same play. And he threw the same pass. And this time, with the clock having run out, Haines caught it. Notre Dame: 35–34.

Soon after, JoeMontana left for the Southern California beaches to await the pro draft and his future. "I love the ocean," he says. "It's scary. Lots of things are happening out there." Again, just like third-and-long.

All during Super Hype XIX, while the media fiddled with Marino, JoeMontana, with his great heart and competitive desire, must have burned. One Florida writer, comparing the two, even referred to JoeMontana in print as a "wimp." But the 49er quarterback eschewed woofing and kept his poise. There isn't a mean bone in JoeMontana's body, but even a laid-back ocean lover has pride. After the game, the first thing JoeMontana said was, "Where's the guy who called me a wimp? I hope he saw this." And he pointed to the scoreboard.

What should most concern the rest of pro football, however, is something else JoeMontana said, this time while warming up before that game. Here it was just moments before the SuperDestinyArmageddonMarinoMachoaManoMontanarama Bowl, and the San Francisco quarterback was taking snaps in the end zone and talking to himself. Hackett heard him. "I feel like I'm floating back here," Joe mumbled. "I'm drifting, dammit. Next year in training camp I've got to get this setup right."

Uh oh. The beach boy has finally acquired some work habits. He's happy in love, besides. Now how far does this stretch the 49er *limits*?

TEAMS

◆ ◆ ◆

'You're a Part of All This'

BY ROY BLOUNT JR.

IT'S NOT EASY TO CONFUSE WRITER ROY BLOUNT JR. WITH
MEL BLOUNT, THE PITTSBURGH STEELERS' FEROCIOUS SAFETY,
YET THAT AND OTHER MAGICAL THINGS HAPPENED DURING
THE SEASON BLOUNT—THE WRITER—TRAVELED WITH MEAN JOE,
ARROWHEAD, ELMER FOOD AND THE REST OF THE STEELERS.

I backed off, took a little run and butted Mean Joe Greene
right in the numbers. Really. I had sneaked down onto the
Steelers' sideline during the last two minutes of their Super
Bowl victory, which I felt a part of. On a SPORTS ILLUSTRATED
assignment I had spent the whole 1973 season hanging around
with the Steelers, on the sidelines and in a lot of other places,
to write a book called *About Three Bricks Shy of a Load... The
Year the Pittsburgh Steelers Were Super but Missed the Bowl*. Now,
with the clock ticking down, the Steelers were about to con-
sign my title to ancient history. I had more or less taken the
position in my book that being humane, or something, was
better than winning. Now that my friends had the Bowl all
but sewed up, I could see that ultimate victory did have a certain charm, and I was doing my best to join aptly in the exul-
tation. But I was burdened by a little red-and-blue bag I had

been given in the auxiliary press box. Inside the bag were wadded-up mimeographed play-by-plays and the remains of my press lunch: strange sandwiches called "muffelettes" and some other things, chicken fingers, I think. It is complicated to tote muffelette scraps and embrace Ernie (Arrowhead) Holmes at the same time.

Holmes is the only person I know who is 6' 3", weighs 260, has a big gold tooth and wears his hair shaved off except for what forms the head of an arrow pointed at you. Later that night at the Steeler party I was reminded of how unsettling Holmes looks when I said to two different people, "That's Ernie Holmes over there, you want to meet him?" and each of them said, "Oh my God." Two years before the Super Bowl, in a serious emotional crisis, he had shot at a policeman in a helicopter. During the Super Bowl he was largely responsible for reducing the Vikings' offensive line to quivering jelly. Two weeks before the Super Bowl he had been telling me to "get away" in an ominous tone. Now, I just shut the muffelettes, and to some extent the jelly, out of my mind and grabbed Holmes and bounced around with him. And beat on L.C. Greenwood, who off the field wears a gold medallion given him by a lady, which has "TFTEISYF" on it, which stands for "The First Time Ever I Saw Your Face." And did the grip with Mel Blount—under whose picture in the local paper my name had appeared once that week—and tried to outglow Dwight White and yelled, "Moon! Moon! Moon!" at Moon Mullins and slapped the shoulder pads of Andy Russell, who slapped my shoulders (another problem: no pads) and cried, "You're a part of all this!" I guess I would have felt better if I had been celebrating the signing of an eternal amity pact among all the nations of the world, but I don't know.

Greene and Terry Bradshaw hugged each other. During these last minutes Bradshaw and his quarterback rival Terry Hanratty and Joe Gilliam and their hard coach Chuck Noll and six cameras all had their noses or lenses within inches of each other, figuring the next play or recording the figuring, and they were all grinning, even the cameras. Greene and Holmes bent way over from the waist and bumped their heads together triumphantly.

The Steelers had the game wrapped up, and I wasn't feeling

objective at all. The final gun went off and we all roiled around like an invading army that had just started to whoop after taking a castle, and Greene and Franco Harris picked Noll up on their shoulders and—behold, the winning smile on Noll's face. I had never seen Noll's mouth so wide open. It was as though the Dragon Lady had gone all soft around the eyes and said, "Oh, baby." Glorying, I headed off the field with the players and got nearly crushed between Greene and the Vikings' Carl Eller, who were being crowded by yelping, snatching fans, but who said to each other, emotionally, respectfully, something profound, which in retrospect I believe was "Good game." I looked for Ray Mansfield, the Steelers' newly famous center, so I could pound on him, but I didn't see him until afterward in the press interview tent, which looked alarmingly like a sideshow—Steelers in blood-spotted white-and-gold suits, standing on platforms above milling, curious reporters. "How does it feel?" "What do you weigh?" Right after the gun, Mansfield told me later, he had been busy retrieving the ball, which was lying on the field unnoticed. "Players were running right past it. Even fans," he said. "All of us had been fighting for it so long, and now it was just lying there. It looked kind of sad." He gave it to Russell, who presented it to Art Rooney, who had been wanting it for 42 years.

Up in the stands Julie Marks, 12, a friend of mine who had never seen a football game before but had been yelling "Deee-fense!" at the top of her lungs, also noticed the ball lying free and then Mansfield carrying it away. "Do you think," she asked her mother, "they would give it to me?"

Everybody wants to get into the act. I was into it because of my book, copies of which had reached the players at about the time—early this past December—when the team, which had been on-again, off-again, suddenly became a juggernaut. I feel that some, if not most, of the credit for this transformation should go to the players and the coaches, and perhaps to Radio Rich, who has 34 radios in his room at the Pittsburgh Y and has been hanging around the Steelers longer than I have; but on the afternoon before the Super Bowl, Greene did offer an unsolicited testimonial. I had brought Reggie Jackson of the Oakland A's into a small room-shaking festivity involving

Greene, Holmes and Dwight (Mad Dog) White, who had a viral infection. "This guy's book had something to do with us being here," Greene told Jackson. "He raised some bleep that he dug."

I don't know what specific bleep I could pinpoint as helpful, but the great thing was that I had been acknowledged as ... a factor. Me, a factor. Like the wind and the turf and the cartilage in the running backs' knees. Like all the other press during the week leading up to Super Bowl IX, I had often felt the urge to mutter "IX, SCHMIX," or when some player or coach said, "It's only another game," to rise up and shout, "It certainly is!" But when you see yourself as a factor, your attitude changes.

PROFESSOR STUDIES SUPER BOWL, SAYS HAS MYTH QUALITY read the headline in the New Orleans *Times-Picayune* on Thursday morning before the game. Andy Russell was reading the story aloud at breakfast. "Sociologically speaking," said the lead, "the Super Bowl is a 'propaganda vehicle' which strengthens the American social structure."

"I can't stand that stuff!" Greene shouted.

"More than a game, it is a spectacle of mythical proportions which becomes a 'ritualized mass activity,' says Michael R. Real, assistant professor of communications at the University of California at...."

"——" Greene cried. He seized the paper and tore it to shreds. "I'd like to run into that guy," he said of Michael R. Real.

The Steelers have a number of stars and leaders of various kinds, but Greene is their sun. The main strength of the team is the defense, of the defense the front four, of the front four, Greene. There may well never have been a lineman at once so smart, strong, fiery and, especially, quick as Greene when he is inspired. People who watched the films of the Steelers' playoff victory over Oakland said that on one play Greene began his rush a millisecond after the snap and hit the quarterback half a millisecond after the ball did (he was penalized for being offside and thought himself that he must have been, but the films showed that he wasn't). And that he once went straight *through* Oakland Center Jim Otto, like a 275-pound chill through a man with no coat. They kept slowing down and stopping the film to see exactly how he went through Otto—between the two T's maybe, or headfirst through one of the O's. They could never figure it out. One moment Greene and Otto were head to head, and then they formed a blur together, and then Otto was more or less where he had been, only lying down (and perhaps spelled "Toot"), and Greene was entangled with the Oakland backfield in a pile. The only lineman to compare Greene with, says Steeler Defensive Line Coach George Perles, is the great end, retired, of the Colts, Gino Marchetti. "Alan Page," said Perles, when the distinguished Viking tackle was mentioned. "Joe could whip Alan Page and stand on him."

Throughout their closing surge this season, as they blew New England, Cincinnati, Buffalo, Oakland and Minnesota off the field, the Steelers relied more and more heavily upon a unique Stunt 4-3 defense, designed by Perles around Greene. Greene and the intimidating Holmes would smash a hole in the middle of the line; the nimble White and Greenwood would pinch in from the sides; All-Pro Linebackers Russell and Jack Ham would stick to the short-passing targets (Minnesota's Fran Tarkenton said they did it "maybe as well as anybody in history"); and everybody in the secondary meanwhile was 1) liable to break a receiver's back and 2) drooling for interceptions. That was basically the defense last year, too, when the Steelers failed, but toward the end of this season it eschewed fancy variations and revolved around Greene, and nobody did anything against it, except Oakland's estimable Ken Stabler with his long passes that were not enough. The Steeler defense was a guerrilla operation, featuring vicious, opportunistic hitting, hell-for-leather pursuit and the repeated generation of loose balls—balls bounding free, popping up, squirting out and rolling around. The game ball Mansfield picked up was probably not much more baffled, lying there, than it had been all afternoon. My favorite turnover of the day was when Minnesota's Chuck Foreman ran into the middle of the line at the Steelers' five. He fumbled in the midst of a huge seething pileup, and Greene, standing beside the tangle, appeared to reach into it and slap the ball up into his arms like a bear scooping a fish out of a stream. What actually happened, said Holmes, was "I hit Foreman...."

"What did you hit him with?" I asked.

"Stuck my head in there," he said sort of modestly. "And the ball got loose and squirted back through Ticklehoff's legs"—Holmes called Viking Center Mick Tingelhoff "Ticklehoff," not meaning any offense, I think—"and Joe picked it up." It was almost as though the Vikings had snapped it to Greene, which seemed appropriate.

There were other factors in the Steelers' improvement this year. Competition among the three quarterbacks produced a much steadier Bradshaw. "He got rattled a couple of times in the huddle," said Rocky Bleier after the Oakland game, "but now we're not getting uptight about it. We settle him down and he comes through." Last year Bradshaw threw key interceptions that deflated the team. This year, after winning the job back, he kept coming up with spirit-lifting third-down completions. That is the difference, or difference enough, between a dumb quarterback and a smart one. I had quoted a Steeler saying last year, "You want your quarterback to be tricky, wily, like Bugs Bunny, or Daffy Duck. Bradshaw's too much like Elmer Fudd." When that came out, Bradshaw called his attorney and asked, "Who is Elmer Food?" But knowing how to pronounce Fudd is not essential. Johnny Unitas last year said, "All I know about sentiment is it comes between '——' and 'syphilis' in the dictionary," which wasn't true, and when I asked Fran Tarkenton before the Super Bowl about peripheral vision, he said, "Periphial vision is bull." Which is also, Tarkenton's pronunciation aside, untrue. Hanratty is the Bugs Bunniest of the Steelers' three quarterbacks; and Gilliam is the most exciting, the one you'd go for if you were building your team around the quarterback. (And he is the one some other team is likely to go for soon—he is too restless to be your ideal No. 2 man, and he has told teammates that he asked Vice-President Dan Rooney for "one point five over five," which is to say a five-year, $1.5 million contract, and got his feelings hurt when Dan seemed amused.) But the Steelers believe in Bradshaw now, hence Greene's hug.

Also this year Harris ran hard again, suppressing his leg pains and ceasing to "dance." Wounded vet Bleier became the solid, good-blocking halfback needed to complement Franco. The offensive line improved. Tackle Gordy Gravelle "arrived." Jim

Clack switched from center to guard, and he and Mullins pulled vigorously ahead of the 230-pound Harris. The new offensive line coach, Dan (Bad Rad) Radakovich, was regarded with no warmth by his charges, who were fond of his predecessor, Bob Fry, whom Noll fired. Radakovich told Mansfield after the Oakland game, "Good work, Ranger, but remember, I've got the young guy [rookie Mike Webster] waiting in the wings." But Radakovich drilled them exhaustingly in new techniques that opened big holes for Harris and allowed the quarterbacks to be sacked only 21 times in 17 games. Rookie Receivers Lynn Swann and John Stallworth added dash to the offense, and Jack Lambert, another rookie, mastered middle linebacking in one year. Bleier talked Russell into lifting weights, and Russell for the first time in his career went uninjured. Russell talked Bleier *out* of lifting weights late in the season, and Bleier was less tired toward the end.

Usually it is only after you see how the season ends up that you can figure out what the factors were, or which ones were good. For instance, it now appears that having your reserve quarterback's wife shot at in the off-season could be a good omen. That happened to Rosemary Hanratty (by accident, since it was someone else the man was angry with). But a more reliable indicator of the Steelers' fortunes is Joe Greene's behavior each year during and after the second Houston game.

In '72, when half the team was hurt or sick for that game, Greene rose up and beat the Oilers almost singlehandedly, sacking the quarterback five times. The Steelers went on to win their first division championship. In '73 Greene was so disgusted with the Steelers' lack of spark against Houston that he took himself out of the game, an action many of his teammates resented. The Steelers fizzled badly in the playoffs. In '74 the Steelers lost the second Oiler game, 13–10, on Dec. 1, which looked bad. "After that we just about packed it in," says Art Rooney Jr. "We were getting ready for next season. People were saying, 'That Paul Brown, he's a genius. Doesn't have half the talent Noll does and he still wins.'" But Greene was saying something different, and Noll was on top of things.

Greene has been heard to complain that Noll is not emotional enough. A good deal of the time Noll is what you would have to call grim. Early this season, not long after the players' strike was settled, Safety Mike Wagner was walking through the Steeler offices with a check for something like $4.17 that he had been issued because earlier he had been slightly under-paid during the exhibition season. "Look here, Coach," he said lightly to Noll. "This is all they paid me."

"If you're just in the game for money," Noll said stiffly, "you'd better get out of it." Once, during the Steelers' dark losing days, Cornerback Lee Calland came into the dressing room at halftime weeping. He rose tearfully, dramatically, and began making a heart-rending appeal for a better second-half effort. "Shut up, Lee," said Noll, and Calland sat down and Noll fell to diagramming plays on the blackboard.

So Noll didn't feel called upon to whip up his troops after the Houston game this season. Greene did. He went to certain members of the offense and told them bluntly that they had better shape up. He said if the Steelers didn't make the Super Bowl he was going to quit them.

"If you do," Russell told him semi-jocularly later, "you better not come back and play against us, because we'll kick your tail." But Greene had established his own intensity, at least, for the rest of the year. He is a proud, emotional player, who demands that his context be worthy of and responsive to his fiercest and most acrobatic efforts.

A week or so after that came copies of my book, which raised the stuff Greene approved of, and as the Steelers were picking up steam and moving toward the playoff game with Oakland, Noll tossed in a little provocation of his own. He came into a team meeting with his lips compressed even more tightly that they usually are when his back is up. Before Oak-land's first-round game with Miami, Raider Coach John Mad-den had said of the Raiders and the Dolphins, "When the two best teams in football get together, anything can happen."

"I'll tell you what *anything* is," Noll told the Steelers. "*Any-thing* is that Oakland isn't getting into the Super Bowl." The room was charged. Greene jumped up and began waving his fists and yelling. The fat was in the fire.

The Steelers soundly whipped Oakland. They felt better about that than they did about beating Minnesota in the big one. The year before, in the first playoff round, Oakland had made them look bad. "I never thought I'd see a team of yours embarrassed like that," Art Rooney Jr. told Noll in the Steelers' first draft meeting after that game. Although Noll's instinct for talent and Artie's scouting operation have, by means of the draft, built the Steelers' material up from almost nothing to a young abundance—three Rookies of the Year in six seasons—the partnership has been abrasive, and those words must have galled Noll. He had been tense then, goading people the week before that '73 loss. He was loose this time, before the '74 win, the win that got them into the Super Bowl. He even cracked jokes about the locker room horseplay in which Kicker Roy Gerela gashed Lambert's ear with a tossed Coke can. The Steelers went into the game happy and came out happier. When I went into the cramped visitors' dressing room at the Oakland Coliseum after the 24–13 win—into the room where the Steelers' season had ended in defeat the year before—Stallworth yelled, "No more bricks!" and we slapped hands, and White said, "Now you got to write: *A Full Load*." "*A Load and a Half*," said Gilliam.

I sat down next to Holmes expecting a friendly talk, and he said, in a suppressed furious growl, "What'd you put that stuff in your book for?"

Now if there is one person on the Steelers you don't want to have furious at you, it is Holmes. His given first and middle names are Earnest Lee, and that is the way he likes people and the way he beats on people. He does things earnestly enough to seem vulnerable as well as formidable, and I hated for him to think I had sold him short. Things had been very vague while I was with the Steelers the year before, as to what they were saying for publication and what they weren't. In general, it was up to me to decide. While I was with them they had tended to forget I was a writer because I was always drinking with them and eating chowder and playing liar's poker instead of taking notes. Several of them told me they assumed I would never actually write anything for that reason. I knew that what I had written had hurt the feelings of three or four players I liked, and that made me feel bad. But I hadn't expected Holmes to be one of those players. "*What* stuff?" I asked him.

"Said I had the mind of a 6-year-old child," he replied in a low tone that caused a tremor in the stool I was sitting on.

"Oh," I thought, "my God." What I had in fact done was quote Holmes as saying, one afternoon when we were drinking martinis and eating chowder, "I'm trying to get my mind right. I haven't wanted to talk to reporters much since the incident." He was referring to that time after the '72 season when he broke down under the pressure of personal problems and started shooting from his car at trucks and wound up in the woods firing, accurately, at a police helicopter flying overhead. "There isn't a moment," I had quoted him as adding, "from the time I go into the dressing room until the game is over that I'm not praying. People think I'm talking to myself; but I'm praying. With the mind of a child and the brains of a 60-year-old warrior."

That had struck me as such a poetic statement I felt he would be proud to have it repeated. Nobody with a small mind could have expressed such a thing. Now I felt as though I had quoted Wordsworth as saying, "*I wandered lonely as a cloud*," and he had chewed me out for accusing him of not having any friends.

"But *you* said that," I said. "And it was about your state of mind when you were praying. And it was a *great....*"

"Get away," he said, and that's more or less what he said on the plane back to Pittsburgh whenever I tried again to explain. "Stay away from him," people said, but I didn't want to leave it at that.

Otherwise, it was a pleasant trip. "Last year on the plane back from Oakland," said Mansfield, "Ham kept asking me, 'When did you know you had it lost?' This time, it's like he's in a daze. I know he's in a daze because he says he doesn't want to play gin."

Ham was not too bedazzled to advise me that my title should have been *One Year Shy of a Book*. Tony Parisi the equipment man said, "I'm giving you an exclusive. I knew they were going to win this one. You know why? Because before we left for Oakland nobody asked me for a box."

"A box?"

"To ship their stuff home in. Last year before Oakland, a lot of guys asked for boxes."

White said on the P.A. phone, "Mr. Rooney has something to say in the jubilance of what we've done," and Art Rooney, the Chief, the Steelers' founder and owner forever, said something that nobody remembered.

"The first time my father brought Johnny Blood home," Art Jr. said later, "us kids expected him to jump on the table and take off his clothes or something. But he was very polite, we had dinner, he talked about, you know, pertinent things of the day, and at 9:30 he and my father left. I can't tell you how disappointed I was. Here was this legendary guy, and that's all he did. And that's the way it's been with my father. He hasn't said anything much. Mainly, he's worried about making sure he gets a Super Bowl ticket for every policeman and fireman in Pittsburgh."

The Chief, however, doesn't have to say anything dramatic in order to be a powerful presence on a victory-over-the Raiders flight home (though personally I would rather make a remember-the-terrible-old-days drive to the racetrack with him), and when we got into the airport there were 10,000 Pittsburghers waiting, at 1:15 a.m. Later, several of the Steelers said they were glad when they got out of that crowd. "I got more beat up by them than I did in the game," said Greenwood. "When I got in the car finally, I just sat there for a minute. People were banging on my windows: 'Open up, we're your fans! I said, 'Yeah....' "

But I loved it. I was congratulated by Frenchy Fuqua, who had been back in Pittsburgh with two broken wrists; and kissed by Ham's fiancée, Joanne Fell, who looks better than anybody else in the world; and for a distance of what must have been a mile, all the way from the gate down the long corridor and through the baggage area and way on out into the parking lot, I proceeded like a loaded blood cell along a narrow artery through hungry tissues of people, who were jammed into every inch of space on both sides of us, and they were all cheering. They were reaching out hands to shake. I shook them all. Girls sitting on friends' shoulders were bending down to kiss my head. People were yelling, "Great game!" at me, or "Great cigar!" (since I was smoking an Art Rooney stogie of great size). It was like heaven, everybody happy, everybody loving you. Holmes bared his chest and raised his arms in triumph, and the crowd thundered, "ARROWHEAD!" It went on and on, through the warm, bright airport out into the cold, dark lot, as though it were going to go on forever, through day and night and all the seasons, and one person toward the end even recognized me for what I was and (rather than snorting "You're no player") cried out, "Great book!"

I went away from Pittsburgh for a few days then, after the Oakland win, and dreamed two Ernie Holmes-related dreams. Once he was reaching to shake my hand, I guess, but then maybe not, and I was in some kind of craft—a team plane—a helicopter? The other time my head was shaved completely, no arrowhead even, and I looked silly, exposed.

I rejoined the team in Pittsburgh, then flew with them to New Orleans. During the 10 days leading up to the Final Reckoning I headed toward Holmes a couple of times but ran into someone else on the way. Then, on the day before the Bowl, I entered the room where Holmes, Greene, White and a bunch of marveling friends were drinking bourbon and Coke and beer and Mateus and dancing and rejoicing over the coming victory, and the first person I walked head-on into was Arrowhead, who said, "Hello, Arch Enemy."

The Steelers were loose all during Super Week. They enjoyed the attention of the press. "Centers are totally overlooked people in this world," Mansfield told an interviewer grandly, "and things like the Super Bowl are good to bring the personalities of people like me out." After the first two nights, which were no-curfew nights—from which I retain an image of Mansfield standing for some reason on top of Russell's rental car—they faithfully returned to their rooms at the Fontainebleau by 11 p.m. But within the fold there was considerable shouting and running around in the halls and drinking and entertaining of guests. One of the diminutive "security men" posted in the players' hall was scandalized. "If the Vikings' coaches impose more discipline on them," he told a Steeler in a tone of deep concern, "you guys are going to be in trouble." Noll, unlike Minnesota's Bud Grant, permitted the Steelers' wives to stay with them on Friday and Saturday nights, although he had never allowed cohabitation on the night before a game even at home during the regular season.

"Yes, there will be a bed check," said Russell. "He wants to see our wives in their nighties." Kidding. Kidding.

And Holmes was loose when he called me Arch Enemy. "I'm not your enemy," I said, "I'm a good man. And so are you." I suppose that sounds kind of silly. You had to be there. We shook hands, and then he took my picture. A good many of the Steelers have recently gotten enthusiastically into photography. In this party in a small room of the Fontainebleau, Holmes, White, Greene and several of the friends present all had cameras, and they were all taking pictures of each other. A wrestling match between an Oriental and a Latin was proceeding unattended on the TV set. Flashbulbs were popping. Rosé was flowing. Music was playing. "Of all the writers here, writing all those words all week," said Greene, whose shirttail was out, "nobody has said what it means. We're *happy* to be here. We're feeling *good*." Holmes was dancing the Bump with a tiny self-possessed girl whom people called "Texas." "Get *down*, Texas," people yelled, and Holmes started bumping her hip with his head. Greene hurriedly focused his camera. "Shows what kind of a photographer I am," he said. "I missed it." Holmes started to bump with his head some more, for the picture, but Texas made some slight indication that she'd rather dance the Bump in a serious normal way, thank you. "I'm sorry," Holmes said politely.

White was there, with his viral infection. I had visited him in the hospital a couple of days before. He'd been lying there losing 18 pounds because he hurt too much to be hungry. In the rooms around him were old ladies with complicated wire-and-tape apparatus in their noses and mouths, lying there silent as Dwight. An old lady turned over in her bed and said, "Oh!" vexedly to no one. An old man was helped off the toilet and into a wheelchair by a nurse—"Now sit," she said. Dwight was morose; at least 75% certain, the doctors said, not to play. Now, in the motel on Super Eve, he was still sick, but out bouncing around anyway. The room seemed about to burst. White was saying, "Doc Huber sat down on the bed and put his arm around me and said, 'I know how you feel.' I was crying like a little punk. I said, 'Know how I *feel*? You don't know how I *feel*! I'm gonna be in there. I may fall out, but I'm

gonna fall out *in* the Super Bowl.' They rolled aside the rock,"
he proclaimed with arms flung wide, "and I came walking out,
standing up!"

"You're ready! You're ready! I can tell you're ready," Greene
told me as Reggie Jackson and I left the party. Jackson is a
good-sized person himself and usually at least as expansive as
anybody in the room. "I have never seen people so *physical*,"
he said.

And as the world knows, they were physical on the field the
next day. Before the game Glen (Knotty Pine) Edwards, the
rough-as-a-good-bark-covered-stick free safety, sat in the dressing room and noticed that his teammates were unaccountably
sitting around like zombies. That was the first time they had
been subdued all week. "Where the hell am I, anyway?" he
said, and everybody broke up. Pine, whom the Steelers elected
as their most valuable player this season but who attracted
widespread notice only when he hurled himself egregiously at
the head of Cincinnati Quarterback Ken Anderson as Anderson went out of bounds on TV, was in the press interview
room one day during Super Week and nobody was interview-
ing him. "Nobody wants to talk to a dude like me," Pine said.
But in the Bowl itself he came up with one of the biggest
plays, nailing Viking Receiver John Gilliam so viciously that an
all-but-completed pass deep in Steeler territory bounced high
out of Gilliam's arms and into Blount's. Edwards wasn't invited into the interview tent after the game either. In the dressing
room he said he'd probably spend his championship money on
a new house. He bought one last year, but he thought he'd get
a different one. And he'd take a vacation. He didn't know
where. He went to the Bahamas last year and didn't like them.
Edwards once told somebody that when he went places in
Dallas with Greene and White people made a big fuss over
them, all of them, including him. When he went back home
to Florida, however, people said, "Hey, Pine. Hey, Pine. You
still up there?" "Hey, Pine. They cut you yet?"

In the victorious dressing room the Chief entertained a
bunch of reporters by telling them that he never showed emotion at ball games. "Even in my betting days at the track,
when I was betting a fortune, a guy standing beside me would
never know it." Once during training camp last summer a

teamster official at a party tried to introduce James Michener, the novelist, to the Chief. "Oh, he's with me," the Chief said. Michener was in town gathering material for a sports book. The Chief hadn't heard of him as a writer, but since Michener had once run for Congress in Bucks County, Pa., he knew of him as a politician, and they had come to the party together.

The teamster official was impressed. "Whoever you're with," he told the Chief, "it's always a top guy. If it's a politician, or a hood, or a union man, or a gambler, it's always a top one." Now the Chief was with the top football team, but he didn't look any more distinguished or any less rumpled than usual. I told him it had been an honor to be associated with him. I felt almost tearful in the back of my eyes. He looked embarrassed.

Everything seemed sort of washed out in the dressing room and in the interview tent, where Greene was saying mildly that his thoughts turned to the Vikings, in sympathy. There was something disconcerting about the Steelers becoming winners. The Rooney regime's charm always had something to do with rising above defeat. Now that the Steelers are kings of the mountain, would they stiffen up? When Tex Schramm of the Cowboys phoned the Chief a few days later and expressed hope that the two teams could do some friendly trading, the Chief reminded him of the kind of trades Schramm used to try to foist upon the old irregular Steelers. "One time they sent us a player with a broken arm," the Chief recalled fondly after hanging up. "I called up Schramm and said, 'We've got just two days till the season starts, and you send us a man with a broken arm!' 'Well,' Schramm said, 'he has an Irish name, doesn't he?'"

The Chief seemed happier over that story than he did over winning the Super Bowl. I wonder whether such stories will collect around the new Steelers. Kathy Kiely, college-sophomore daughter of the Steelers' public relations director, said on the plane back to Pittsburgh after the Super win, "This is the first and last hurrah."

The welcome-home parade in Pittsburgh the day after the Super Bowl wasn't as good as I expected either, not as good as the one after Oakland. The Super reception was nice along the highway in from the airport, where people had been standing in the cold for four hours waiting—a nicely dressed middle-aged lady standing alone waving her sweater, two kids banging potlids together, a new fan club holding a sign identifying itself as "Bradshaw's Brains." But when we got into downtown Pittsburgh, people beat so hard on the top of the convertible I was in that their blows reached my head, and they leered unhingedly in through the car windows. It was unnerving. I hope nobody ever looks at me that way again.

So I guess the climax of the Super Bowl for me was back there on the sidelines, jumping around like a fool, or maybe in the bus after the game when Holmes said, "I don't know. This thing has got me off into something I don't hardly know how to express. It's just ... too much. After the game I wanted to start slapping reporters."

I said maybe I'd better get on another bus, but he said no. He looked at his ring finger's middle knuckle, which was as big as a golf ball. He was trying to decide where to wear his Super Bowl ring. "I think I'll put it behind the knob," he said.

Holmes' eyes looked glazed, he was so fulfilled. "Them guards was in there *quivering*," he said of the Vikings. "It was like they were little kids. Joe was down there saying, 'You bleeping faggots!' I think they were terrified."

Greene got on the bus. "How'm I look-in' *now*!" he cried.

White was regretting that his illness, despite which he had played almost the whole game, was going to keep him from partying that night. "That's half the Super Bowl," he said.

"No," said Greene. "No. This is it. This is all of it. Right here." I looked around the bus. I *felt* like I knew what he meant, but I'm not sure. Greene has a certain mystery about him. Tarkenton told Russell that a man from Greene's hometown told him Greene was 30 three years ago. He is listed as 28 now. At that little party the day before the game Greene said something about being 28, and White said, "On the books, anyway," and Greene grinned. Can Joe Greene have hidden five years away somewhere? I don't know. I didn't ask. I didn't care. I wasn't feeling like a reporter. I had been sucked into the Super Bowl and I felt good. We were all factors on that bus. Eat your heart out, Michael R. Real.

A Team for All Time

BY RON FIMRITE

SIX MEMBERS OF THE MIGHTY GREEN BAY PACKER TEAM OF
THE 1960S HAVE BEEN ELECTED TO THE PRO FOOTBALL HALL
OF FAME. SO HAS VINCE LOMBARDI, THEIR LEGENDARY COACH.
AS RON FIMRITE DISCOVERED IN 1986, LOMBARDI'S TEACHINGS
CONTINUED TO INFLUENCE HIS FORMER PLAYERS' LIVES.

Could there ever have been such a team? Was the coach, that
saintly tyrant, really of flesh and blood or simply the invention of fabulists? Were there actually such persons as Golden
Boy, Fuzzy Thurston and Ray Nitschke, the last a player of
such renowned toughness he scarcely flinched when a coaches' tower collapsed and fell on his head?

Well, yes, there was such a team as the Green Bay Packers
of Vince Lombardi, and pro football should be eternally grate-
ful that the Packers, the stuff of myth and legend, should have
become the first Super Bowl champions. It was this team that
stamped the event with legitimacy and respectability.

Even the most scholarly fan might have trouble recalling
who won, say, Super Bowl V, Super Bowl X or even XV,
but everybody knows who won I. The Packers themselves
will never let you forget it. Several of the players have

written books on how wonderful they all were, and one of them, guard Jerry Kramer, is now up to four books on the subject, the last, *Distant Replay*, published only a few months ago. But they *were* wonderful, surely one of the best teams in history, possibly the best. The Super Bowl I victory gave them their fourth championship in six years. Super Bowl II would add a fifth. Six of their players—Bart Starr, Nitschke, Jim Taylor, Forrest Gregg, Willie Davis and Herb Adderley—have been elected to the Pro Football Hall of Fame, as has their famous coach. The Hall really isn't big enough to contain the Lombardi legend.

If he had never done anything else, Lombardi would have achieved lasting recognition for the maxim attributed to him, "Winning isn't everything. It's the only thing," which ranks right up there with "Nice guys finish last" as an immortal utterance. Actually, he said a lot more that made better sense, such as, "You don't do things right once in a while. You do them right all the time." Or, "The harder you work, the harder it is to surrender." Or, "Fatigue makes cowards of us all." Or, "All men are not created equal. The difference between success and failure is in energy." Lombardi-isms, his players call them. Quotes about Lombardi may prove equally durable, particularly two by Henry Jordan, the team's defensive right tackle who died of a heart attack at 42 in 1977. "He treats us the same," Jordan once said. "Like dogs." On another occasion he said of the dictatorial coach, "When he says sit down, I don't look for a chair." But it was the power of Lombardi's remarkable personality that held such a disparate group of athletes together for so long. "We were all Lombardi's sons, all his children," Kramer wrote in his latest book.

It may well be true that Lombardi's methods, his preachiness, his fanatical devotion to the work ethic would not win him this sort of unflagging loyalty from today's far wealthier and certainly more independent athletes. But the Packers of Super Bowl I were scarcely robots. The Golden Boy, Paul Hornung, and Max McGee, the wide receiver, were legends in their time not so much for what they accomplished on the field, which was considerable, as for what they accomplished off it as intrepid bachelors in the barrooms and boudoirs.

Starr and tackle Bob Skoronski were, on the other hand, the straightest of arrows. Nitschke was an avowed tough guy, and so, in a far less obtrusive way, was safety Willie Wood. Willie Davis and Ron Kostelnik, the defensive left end and tackle, were dutiful and hardworking, and both have made fortunes outside of football, as businessmen. So, for that matter, has the carefree McGee. Jim Taylor, the hard-driving fullback, was tough and tightfisted. And Kramer, by his own admission, was of a restless and adventurous nature. Some of the Packers came from broken homes. One, receiver Red Mack, spent part of his childhood in an orphanage. Many were dirt poor as youngsters, and few of them earned anything remotely approximating the comparatively lavish salaries their successors are taking home today.

Their common bond was Lombardi, actually the love of Lombardi. Some years after Lombardi's death in 1970, Kramer asked Adderley if he thought often of his old coach. "Every day," Adderley replied. "And I love my father, who is also deceased, but I don't think about my father every day."

Lombardi was himself a man of profound loyalties—to his church, his family, his players, the game and the National Football League. He approached that first Super Bowl game with a missionary zeal. The 1966 season was the last for the American Football League as a completely independent entity. Spurred on by the the AFL's relentless raiding of its rosters, the NFL finally agreed to a merger of the two leagues in June of that year. In '67, interleague play in the exhibition season would begin. A realignment of the merged leagues would follow. Super Bowl I, then, would match the AFL's last true champion, the Kansas City Chiefs, against the lordly Packers on Jan. 15, 1967 in the Los Angeles Coliseum. Lombardi was not about to suffer the humiliation of losing such an epochal encounter. "We got a pregame speech every day," Kostelnik recalls.

Lombardi, the onetime law student, was building a strong case against the upstarts from the new league. Chiefs defensive back Fred Williamson particularly outraged his sense of fair play. A favorite Williamson tactic then was to deliver a devastating (Williamson thought) forearm shiver to an opposing receiver just after the ball was caught or sometimes just after the whistle had blown. Williamson, who nicknamed himself the Hammer, noisily proclaimed before the game that Packer receivers could expect no mercy from him. Lombardi made it clear to his players that the Hammer should likewise expect no mercy from them. He wanted his braggadocio and his cheap shots taken care of cleanly but forthrightly.

One Packer receiver, McGee, was not the least bit concerned about the Hammer or any other Kansas City player. At 34, McGee was winding down a long and certainly colorful career. He had caught only four passes all season playing behind Boyd Dowler, the large (6' 5", 225 pounds) and speedy receiver from Colorado. He had, however, caught a decisive touchdown pass in the fourth quarter of the team's 34–27 win over Dallas in the league championship game, playing only because Dowler had injured a shoulder late in the game. Dowler was apparently hale and hearty now, and McGee was counting on a restful afternoon in the Southern California sunshine. With this in mind, he determined to do Los Angeles the night before the game with a pretty blonde from Chicago, whom he had met on a nocturnal adventure. Lombardi had warned his players earlier that curfew violators would be fined the huge sum of $5,000, so McGee was dutifully in his room when assistant coach Dave (Hawg) Hanner took the customary bed check. But he was out of it in a flash after Hanner advised him, foolishly, that it would be his only check of the night. McGee returned to the hotel, he estimates, at 7:30 the morning of the game.

Later in the day, McGee found himself next to Hornung on the sidelines. Hornung was suffering from the pinched nerve in his neck that would prematurely end his career, and, like McGee, didn't figure on playing much. Hornung was correct in that assumption. He didn't play at all. Whimsically, he turned to his friend and inquired, "What would you do if you had to play?" "I'd be surprised," McGee replied.

Shortly after the kickoff, Dowler reinjured his shoulder and Lombardi called "McGee!" McGee seemed stunned, but he thought his coach had somehow just learned of his curfew violation and was going to levy the $5,000 fine then and there. No, it was worse than that: Lombardi wanted him to play.

With a storybook team, life should imitate art, and, indeed, the sorrowful McGee had the game of his career. The first ball McGee caught went for a 37-yard touchdown in the first quarter, the first score in Super Bowl history. He caught six more passes that day for a total gain of 138 yards and another score as the Packers won easily, 35–10. He had a field day against the Chiefs' relatively inexperienced cornerbacks, Williamson and Willie Mitchell. The Hammer did little pounding that afternoon, and in the fourth quarter he was knocked unconscious tackling Donny Anderson.

Lombardi's great team would also win Super Bowl II, beating the Oakland Raiders 33–14. And then, sadly, it would be all over. In 1969 Lombardi would leave Green Bay for the Washington Redskins, and a year later he would be dead. Hornung's injury would force his retirement. McGee would retire after the '68 Super Bowl, and the Packers would never play in another one. Jordan died, Thurston would fight a bout with cancer, and defensive end Lionel Aldridge suffered severe emotional problems. All of their lives went in different directions, some down, most up, but they never lost that sense of community that made them so strong in their playing days. Their time as athletes has passed, but what a time it was.

Lord of
the Rings

BY RICHARD HOFFER

AL DAVIS SPENT A LIFETIME BUILDING THE RAIDERS INTO A PRO
FOOTBALL DYNASTY. BUT BY THE LATE 1980S HIS ONCE-PROUD
TEAM HAD BECOME JUST ANOTHER NFL CLUB. IN 1989 RICHARD
HOFFER EXAMINED BOTH DAVIS AND THE INTIMATIONS OF
MORTALITY THE RAIDER OWNER SAW IN HIS TEAM'S DECLINE.

Al Davis is suffering an unlikely crisis of mystique. The
sight of him striding a sideline, rigged out in his white bell-
bottoms and shiny black shoes, no longer stirs a sense of
dread. Davis's team, which has made four Super Bowl
appearances over three decades, now loses as often as not.
When his Raiders do win, it is with the same gentlemanly
flair exhibited by every other team in the NFL. His players
do not dominate, they do not inspire terror, they do not
engage in the cartoonish, roughhouse tactics their logo
promises. "Weak sisters," sniffs Lester Hayes, a rogue cornerback who got out before Silver and Blackdom, as he has
forever named the franchise, turned into Mr. Rogers'
Neighborhood. For all we know, that pirate is winking
behind his eye patch.
  Strange times in Silver and Blackdom, huh? In recent

years Davis, 60, watched a life's work, a testament to his will, crash down about him. Never mind the distracting years in court. The Raiders, who are 7–6 and fighting for a wild-card playoff berth in '89, missed the playoffs in each of the past three seasons, the longest the team has ever been out of the money.

Davis presides uneasily over this dormant dynasty. Never much of a loser, he now resorts to desperate measures. Hiring Mike Shanahan from the Denver Broncos in February 1988 to coach his Raiders was a wild departure from form. Davis admitted his mistake no later than Game 1 of the Shanahan era. Shanahan might be a good coach, Davis said, but he wasn't a Raider coach. Four games into the 1989 season Davis made that literally true, replacing Shanahan with Art Shell, the offensive line coach, who brought Raider heritage to the job. Davis had never fired a head coach in his life.

Strange times? Davis is considering hauling the franchise back to Oakland, having fought the NFL and the city for years so he could leave it. The attraction might be not so much that he would reap a relocation windfall but that the Raiders used to win in Oakland. It was in 1963 that rookie coach Davis turned a 1–13 team into a 10–4 contender, and the club enjoyed a mighty success for seasons to come. In Oakland. If Davis can work miracles only in one ZIP code, so be it.

These are, in fact, stranger times than you might know. The head buccaneer, who has always said he would rather be feared than respected, has allowed himself to be drawn into the gentleman's club of NFL owners, a sporting barony that previously represented nothing more to him than an opportunity for big-money litigation. Rival NFL owners paid Davis $18 million to settle the antitrust suit he brought against the league over its efforts to block him from moving the team to Los Angeles, but some of them now actually hail him as a force for reconciliation in league matters. He is practically Establishment.

You look at Davis's return to tradition, to respectability, perhaps even to Oakland, and you wonder. You hesitate to say his enormous self-confidence is slipping. But you do notice that Davis is suddenly hounded by defeat and mortality. He is not as defiant. Is it from turning 60? Is it from regular trips to Hall of Fame inductions at which the greatness of the Raiders is seen more as past than prologue? And all these people dying around him, friends and former players. Davis has taken a strange pride in his ability to breathe life into more than just franchises. He has nursed enough people back from the brink to hint at supernatural powers. "It's tough to dominate death," he said years ago, after helping to bring a Raider employee, Del Courtney, out of total paralysis. "But we got it done with Del." Just another Raider success story. But now they just ... die.

This summer Davis lingered on the practice field and surprised a small group of writers by ticking off a number of recent deaths. There was Don McMahon, a high school buddy who died while pitching batting practice at Dodger Stadium. There was Don Clark, the USC coach who gave Davis his first big-time assistant's job. Former player John Matuszak, who embodied all things Raider, died, as did promising safety Stacey Toran.

"The football I'll get straight," Davis told the writers. "My biggest thing now is this death business. I've always been able to control the elements of my life, dominate my environment without hurting others. But this death business.... I can't beat it. I can't win." Strange talk in Silver and Blackdom. Had anybody ever heard this monumental force of personality express a doubt?

Al Davis does not suffer inspection needlessly. Most cross-examination, and he has had his share, is forbidden unless required by law. Pity the fool who presumes otherwise. Television reporters awaiting Davis after a recent meeting with the Los Angeles Coliseum Commission were advised they could neither film nor quote him. But they could continue to exist. Davis reacts to interview requests with a look of alarm: he actually pulls his pompadoured head back as if to put even more distance between himself and the public. "Oh, ah don't do those things," he says in that much-imitated Southern accent, eccentric in a Brooklyn boy.

He maintains a small circle of pals in journalism, trusted

friends from his AFL days. That he speaks to them is testament to his loyalty and friendship, of course, yet it would
not be cynical to note that these pals are strategically placed.
At one point Davis had a confidant at each of the three network football shows. It is characteristic of his notion of
public relations that Davis has always tried to maintain some
control over the journalism that attends his every move. In
the old days he rewarded reporters with Christmas gifts as
well as bons mots. Those he felt did not properly reflect the
Raider spirit would suffer freeze-outs or worse. Even today
it is nothing for Davis to tell a beat reporter that he will
speak to his editor, or publisher if necessary.

Who can blame him? One of the few times he made himself available to anyone beyond this small circle, he was
wildly disappointed. A close friend arranged an extensive
magazine interview for Davis, and it went so badly for
him—the worst part was that certain blasphemies were laid
out for Davis's mother to read, but there was also a refer-
ence to Hitler that could be construed as favorable—that
Davis reportedly didn't speak to that friend for a year.

In the past Davis's secrecy, and the suspicion it generated,
was a powerful weapon for creating confusion among his
foes. Nobody in the league knew what he was up to. Alone
among the owners, he disdained the NFL scouting combine, preferring to keep all intelligence to himself. This attitude fueled a comic paranoia; one rival coach shook his fist
at "bugged" light fixtures in a locker room, and whenever a
helicopter passed over a practice field, some naturally
assumed that Davis was in it.

You do not need a genius, which is how many people have
described Al Davis, to explain the Raiders' comeuppance.
The NFL draft was designed to enforce parity, punishing
winners and rewarding losers. Like any team denied high
picks over a long period of time, the Raiders have suffered.
The offensive line got old, the defense just got bad, and a
quarterback never developed.

Still, Davis never relied solely on the NFL draft. He was
so far out of the mainstream that for years he could have
been said to be holding his own draft, one that neither

interfered with nor resembled the league's version. Davis depended on an astounding network of unofficial scouts, all loyal to the Raiders and nobody else. Former Raider great Gene Upshaw says it was hard to meet anybody who did not represent himself as a Davis operative. "I'd run into some high-school coach," he says, "and he'd tell me he was a Raider scout. Everybody was a Raider scout."

Davis also depended on his own instincts. He drafted Mark van Eeghen out of Colgate after watching him run through a rainy-day drill in a gym. Davis prospered with all sorts of strange picks like that. Howie Long, the All-Pro defensive end on today's Raiders, was plucked out of Villanova in the second round of the draft. Defensive tackle Bill Pickel came from Rutgers, also in the second round.

That's Davis's history. None of the Raiders of yore fit a computer printout, either. "He never had normal players," says Tom Keating, a defensive tackle from the glory years. "Fred Biletnikoff was certainly not the fastest or strongest receiver, just a guy who had unbelievable hands. Al had a lefthanded quarterback and a 47-year-old placekicker who thought he should be playing instead of that quarterback. We had a team full of people like that. We had an owner like that."

Davis took other teams' mistakes and turned them into Raider All-Pros. Castoffs like Matuszak, Lyle Alzado and Jim Plunkett all prospered under Davis. He played every angle. He obtained playing rights to Willie Wood, who had retired to a coaching job with the San Diego Chargers, just in case the Chargers, a division rival, thought about activating him against the Raiders. Davis once hung around a celebrity golf tournament in Las Vegas just to see if any football players were unhappy or otherwise available.

But his touch has deserted him in recent years. No reclamation project has buoyed the Raider defense, and no running back has come out of the tail end of the draft to lead the team in rushing, as Marv Hubbard, an 11th-round pick in 1968, did from 1971 to '74. In picking a coach, Davis stumbled even worse. Regardless of his prospects in the NFL, Shanahan could never have made it as a Raider coach. Davis might have thought he wanted some fresh air in an organization that had been hermetically sealed, but he quickly realized that Shanahan was all wrong. He made it clear that Shanahan was fired less for his silly disciplines (players could not sit on their helmets) or even his 8–13 record than for his refusal to throw long to Willie Gault. Davis mumbled something about shotgun formations, too.

Indeed, it was Davis's early-season return to the Raider way that corrected a disastrous beginning. Shell is no mere memento from the glory years but a forceful man determined to put the old philosophy back into effect. Against the Bengals last month, the Raiders' fourth win in five games under Shell, L.A. opened with a 63-yard pass to Gault. Bo Jackson suddenly was sweeping outside for big yardage—92 on one play—instead of banging into the left side of the line. And the defense brought back memories of Hayes's "kick maximus gluteus" unit; Bengal quarterback Boomer Esiason went down spitting up blood. This was all heartening but still inconclusive. The Raider way, after all, means Super Bowl rings on the players' fingers.

As the Davis mystique has faded, so has the Raiders' old image. The team does not dominate, a word that is ordinarily well represented in Davis's public statements (so are "attack," "commitment to excellence," "pride and poise" and "getting it done"). The Raiders are no longer the misfits who prospered in Oakland, inspiring talk of a "criminal element" in football. "They are on a par with the Atlanta Falcons," says Hayes. "There is no more fear of the Raiders. The fear factor is now null and void."

The owner, too, is softening his relations with traditional enemies. When the owner of the Cleveland Browns, Art Modell—whom Davis often characterized as former commissioner Pete Rozelle's running dog—offered to solve a fractious dispute among owners by resigning his position on the NFL's television committee, Davis was the first to insist that he stay. When Rozelle, long Davis's enemy, announced his retirement, Davis was the first to shake his hand. Strange times? Perhaps, as Hayes says, "the man is but a mere mortal."

If it is arrogant to put yourself beyond the working laws of the NFL, what do you call someone who places himself outside the rules of life and death? A mere mortal? Davis might be surprised to hear that. Might have been at one time, anyway. Concerning mortality, Davis intends to seek an exemption, both for himself and for friends.

"Death is the only thing I'm afraid of," he told Pete Axthelm in an ESPN interview this spring. "It's the one thing you can't control."

His friends have been hearing this for years. In an interview seven years ago Davis admitted, "I'm just nutty about death." He said, "I lost my dad in a strange way, and it does bother me.... So all this other stuff is kid stuff, because I believe I can overcome all other things and dominate."

As it turns out, he was being modest. He thought—and with some reason—he could dominate death, too.

1n 1979 his wife, Carolee, whom he has described variously as a "big-time New York girl" and a "wild woman," went into cardiac arrest and sank into a coma. Davis has said that the doctors told him she would be a vegetable if she ever woke from the coma, an unlikely event in itself. Davis responded with a stubborn fury that is all his own, and within a week he'd set up shop in her hospital room, taking this matter into his own hands. Getting it done. He stayed by her bed around the clock, talking into the nights. Over and over he would say, "Wake up, Carolee, the plane is waiting for us, we've got to get to the game." After another week and a half Carolee came out of the coma, willed back to life by her husband.

"I don't think there was any virtue in that," Davis told Axthelm. "She was my friend. I would do it for any friend." Davis gave everyone on the hospital staff who had attended to Carolee—an interim family that included doctors and nurses and orderlies—a new television set. Carolee sits beside him in the owner's box at all the home games.

With others, though, Davis wasn't able to get it done. He tried to intervene in the fatal illnesses of two sportswriters, Jack Murphy and Wells Twombly. For the latter, a San Francisco columnist, he even arranged a liver transplant.

So many deaths. "It's busted him up," says Jimmy (the Greek) Snyder, a member of the Davis inner circle. "That's one thing he can't put up a game plan against." Certainly it mocks all his assumptions. Upshaw, now executive director of the Players Association but still in touch with his old boss, says, "He always told me, 'If I could just conquer that, if I could just conquer life and death.' It's always been a mystery to him. It's a mystery to all of us, but he thinks about it a lot more than most."

Little artifacts of defiance—as when he said after a pet dog died of cancer a few years ago, "There are places I know now [that might have prolonged the animal's life]"—are being replaced by hints of resignation. People and pets do die, contrary to his best intentions. As for himself, he continues to lift weights, which he hauls along to training camps and NFL meetings, not to gain strength but to preserve his health and maintain his "lines." He drinks ice water with meals, though he has been seen with a Diet Pepsi. He has no known vices outside of fashion, in which he makes an interesting statement—that the development of style was halted abruptly in 1963. Everything about him seems concerned with the preservation of the past, which is strange in a man given to forward thinking.

Is it possible that nothing works anymore? What else is being mocked these days? How about loyalty? How did that get to be such a joke?

Raider players continue to be the best paid in the league. Lyle Alzado once got a $100,000 raise he didn't ask for. But Davis's devotion to his players is best measured in other ways. Upshaw recalls that Davis chartered the biggest jets for his team, giving each player his own row of seats. Pregame meals were catered according to individual players' tastes. The assumption was that nothing was too good for a Raider. Like Super Bowl rings. The NFL pays for the rings, but Davis designed such outrageous diamond-studded fixtures that in 1981, after Super Bowl XV, the league set a maximum base value for each ring.

For an owner, Davis has always been strangely considerate of labor. He flew former Raiders to Super Bowl games, back when the team was in them, and he continues to fly former players to home games throughout the season. Whenever a Raider is inducted into the Hall of Fame—there have been six, and they have all asked for Davis to present them—he arranges for former teammates to be on hand. One former Raider, long since traded away, got into trouble with drugs, and Davis secretly financed his rehabilitation. And, says Upshaw, "If a player passes away, like Dan Birdwell did in 1978, he flies us all in for the funeral."

Now, Davis is not a modest man. Somebody who keeps weights in a room off his mirrored black-and-silver executive suite to keep up his looks is obviously a man of some vanity. Front-office workers recall with delight the time he emerged from his suite in new sunglasses and asked a secretary what she thought of them. Not much, she said. The sunglasses were never seen again. Another favorite story: Presentation of the trophy at Super Bowl XV was delayed while an assistant searched for a comb to smooth the Davis ducktail.

Still, he defers as much acclaim as possible to the players. He rarely goes to awards banquets for fear of denying the players their proper due. The gesture occasionally backfires. He got some heat in 1983 when he stiffed the Los Angeles Press Club; friends say he was just being careful not to steal attention away from the team.

When Upshaw and Davis visited Irwindale, Calif., to see one of several proposed sites for a new Raider stadium, Upshaw asked if it would be named Al Davis Stadium. Davis was surprised at the suggestion. "Not in a million years," he said, adding that the hall of fame he intends to build with the stadium will be devoted entirely to the players.

So why then did Marcus Allen hold out this summer? Gil Brandt, former personnel director of the Dallas Cowboys, says Davis was shocked by the holdout. "He had a hard time understanding that," Brandt says. "Al had a hard time believing, as well as he treats his players, that Allen would hold out. That never happened before. Maybe players have changed."

Oh, what doesn't change? The NFL has changed. Twelve years after Rozelle removed Davis from the competition committee, he reappointed him to the inner circle, embraced him once more as "a football man," the kind of guy who could bridge the widening chasms among owners. Al Davis? Wasn't it just yesterday that the league paid a fortune for interfering with his move to L.A.? And here's Modell, as representative of the old guard as any, saying, "I'd rather have Al inside the league than outside."

Ever since Davis was chosen commissioner of the old AFL, with the apparent order to force a merger (other NFL owners still believe Davis was disappointed he couldn't destroy their league first), he had been a stick in the NFL's eye. Even as a colleague he was a nettlesome presence. Davis was the "1" in too many 27–1 votes to have been anyone's favorite, but until he began hauling owners into court they had conceded that he had a certain charm. Former Browns coach Sam Rutigliano intended a kind of compliment when he said, "Al can steal your eyeballs and convince you that you look better without them."

His mischief in the AFL days marked him forever as a scoundrel—signing players under goalposts, more or less kidnapping them in planes and offering contracts with the inflight meals. There is a story that Davis once saw Brandt in a hotel men's room and quickly called the front desk to say Brandt would be taking all his calls in Davis's room. Davis then fielded all the scouting reports while Brandt studied his wallpaper. "I don't see how that could happen in a hotel, and I find it hard to believe," Brandt says. "But let me say this: I wouldn't put it past him." Lore like that was hard to live down.

It was hard to hold against Davis, too. Even a straight arrow like Tex Schramm, former president of the Cowboys, confesses to a certain affection for the miscreant. "I don't put him in the category of being dishonest, but he will tread as close to the line as he can," Schramm says. All the same, he adds, he enjoys the heck out of Davis.

But Davis steadily depleted that reservoir of good will as he engaged owners in lawsuits. Davis is held responsible for having dragged the late Steeler owner Art Rooney, most beloved of NFL men, through court in 1977. But of course Davis was going to stand by his player, George Atkinson, who had been branded part of a "criminal element" by

Steeler coach Chuck Noll. That marked the beginning of Davis's exile; Rozelle removed him from the competition committee.

As bitter as it got when Davis sued the NFL after the other owners tried to prevent him from moving his franchise, the final straw seems to have been his testimony on behalf of the USFL in the 1986 trial of that league's antitrust suit against the NFL. "Unforgivable," sniffs Tampa Bay Buccaneers owner Hugh Culverhouse.

But the NFL is now polarized, with new owners—guys who made their millions in oil, electric shavers and shopping centers—expecting sophisticated marketing ideas to go with their franchises. The old guard underestimated the division and found that they couldn't name a commissioner. Suddenly both sides found something to like about Al Davis.

Steeler president Dan Rooney, a "football man," notes Davis's protection of tradition. "I don't go for the genius stuff," he says, "but he's a bright guy, knows football and can grasp the issues. He's not the devil he has made himself out to be."

Rooney was reminded of this when, after his father's funeral last year, Davis sat down with some of Dan Rooney's sons and nephews and talked about football and Art Rooney for two hours. "I thought it was wonderful," Dan says.

And the new owners like Davis's free thinking. Now, teams move at will—the Colts and Cardinals changed cities under the NFL's modified rules. Davis's idea that a city might owe a franchise for its benefit to the community—an idea that has led to an auction, with Irwindale, Sacramento, Oakland and even Los Angeles bidding for a team—has also attracted attention. "I like that," says Jerry Jones, the new man in Dallas.

Cities, mindful of an owner's short attention span, are now scrambling to please teams. After the Oilers threatened to move to Jacksonville, Houston found $40 million for stadium improvements all on its own. Team owners are not unmindful that the Cardinals struck gold when they moved to Phoenix. And now Oakland, which has had trouble funding its school system, is putting up about $50 million for football's potential benefit to the community. In other words, the ultimate beneficiaries of Davis's efforts to change the NFL's rules have been the owners themselves. Davis, meanwhile, still doesn't have the type of stadium for which he moved to L.A. in the first place.

Time passes doesn't it? Schramm says of Davis, "I don't think he's had a happy 10 years. He's always talking about the one thing he can't control, death, and he probably has the feeling life is so short. Maybe he wishes he could have changed the last 10 years.... Maybe he's tired, he'd like to do football instead of all that other stuff."

Davis bought into the Raiders for $18,500 and has seen that stake grow considerably. He now owns close to 30% of the team, which was valued at $80 million two years ago, before the bidding for franchises got intense. Davis once asked Jimmy the Greek what passes for rich these days. "I told him a guy had to have better than $20 million, and he said, 'Just 20?' He's got a great sense of humor."

If Davis is rich, he doesn't assume the life-style. His extravagances are limited to the ridiculous largess he bestows upon loyalists. John Madden's son Mike, now on the Raiders' staff, remembers looking for his dad after a game. He was 12, and Davis spotted him pacing around. "What do you want for Christmas?" Davis asked. Mike said any kid would appreciate a motorcycle. "O.K.," Davis said. Mike added that, all the same, he probably wouldn't be allowed to have one. Too dangerous. "What about a car, then?" offered Davis. Too young, said Mike. "How old do you have to be?" asked Davis. Too old. "Let's think big here," Davis persisted. "How about a store, then? Could you run a store, hire and fire people?"

"I'm 12 years old, looking around for my dad, and all of a sudden I'm running a store," Mike says today.

Davis, for all his apparent power and fame, does not exploit his celebrity in a town that would surely enjoy it. Three or four nights a week he drops in at Carmine's, a small Italian restaurant in West Los Angeles. He dines alone, a telephone at one side, a pile of reading material at the other. For nightlife he returns to his home near the Raiders' training facility and watches game tapes.

For Davis the only important wealth is the legacy of the Raiders. But the Raiders are often losers now, and he blames himself. He frets that he robbed his team of its home-field advantage by moving it into the vast Los Angeles Coliseum. He agonizes over each defeat, each injury. After a loss, he moves through the dressing room like a wraith, approaching each player as if they'd both lost a loved one.

"He doesn't have anything else, you know," says John Madden. "His life is entirely the Raiders." Hard times in Silver and Blackdom, then, when the franchise fails to excite fear and suspicion, does not dominate. Of course, nobody thinks that Davis, even at 60 and with signs of mortality all about him, lacks the conviction that, one more time, he can get it done.

The history is, Al Davis has always gotten it done, achieved his will with an arrogance that is at times appealing. Del Courtney, a former big-band leader, became Davis's right-hand man in the Raiders' early years. One night in 1971, before the team was to leave for a game in Kansas City, Courtney got up from a restaurant table and keeled over. Stricken with Guillain-Barré syndrome, he was completely paralyzed. For nearly three months he lingered in intensive care. Because he was unable to move even an eyelid, nobody knew if he could so much as hear. Doctors didn't think he would live. "Did Del make it through the night?" asked a doctor on rounds, unaware that Courtney could, in fact, hear. "Well, no way he'll make it through another."

Late each evening, after practice and meetings, Davis would appear at Courtney's bedside. Courtney says, "He would stand there and say, 'Del, I don't know if you can hear me, but things are going good at the office, made a couple of good trades.' Other times, he'd say, 'You're probably lying there worried about your security. Well, nobody's been in your office, nobody's gonna take your place, and not a penny is being deducted from your salary. And if you're worrying about your horrendous hospital bill, we're picking up every cent.' "

On and on he went, each night. *The Tribune* in Oakland

had prepared an obituary for Courtney. At one point doctors announced Courtney had one hour to live and phoned relatives, saying, "If you've got anything to say to Del...." And still Davis kept showing up. "He said, 'You're not gonna die, Del, you're gonna fight.' He kept saying that. I guess it got to me," recalls Courtney, who has retired from the Raiders and is once again leading a band. "He said, 'Del, you're a Raider. Raiders don't die.'"

Of course that was 1971 and Al Davis was just 42 and greatness was in the Raiders' future. It was possible to believe anything.

COACHES

◆ ◆ ◆

A New Life

B Y   G A R Y   S M I T H

DRIVEN, INTENSE, SINGLE-MINDED—THESE ARE JUST A FEW OF
THE ADJECTIVES THAT HAD BEEN USED TO DESCRIBE DICK
VERMEIL. BUT IN 1983, AFTER 23 YEARS IN THE GAME, VERMEIL
KNEW IT WAS TIME TO GET OUT. GARY SMITH SPENT SOME
TIME WITH THE MAN WHO OVERCAME AN OBSESSION.

Every glass of wine ages on its table. Every chair and every
Kawasaki dealer in the ballroom is turned toward the podi-
um. At a front table, a small, gray-haired Japanese man, the
emperor of Kawasaki, listens with his upper body tilted forward and his eyes narrowed. He has never heard of the
speaker before, but in his country they once asked men
like this to pilot Zeros down the smokestacks of enemy
battleships.

"You got players who won't perform up to their level, don't
keep them on your roster!" Dick Vermeil cries. "Get them
selling! Give them time to think your way, and at the end of
the year, if they don't, then cut 'em or waive 'em!"

His jaw is thrust out challengingly. Everything about him
seems to have just burst out of a three-point stance, except his
hair, which many years ago agreed to lie perfectly in place for

the rest of his life. Now the jaw swivels from one side of the ballroom to the other.

"There's not a man in this room who works as hard as his dad," Vermeil declares. "Limits are self-imposed—there's no limit to human energy!"

He pauses. This speech was written and memorized back when coaching football was still his life, back when certainty was still his comrade. The jaw loses some of its jut.

"I found my limit," he admits.

He plunges back into the speech, and the fire catches inside him again. "My kids say to me, 'I'd never work as hard as you.' I'll tell you, one day there's going to be a wide-eyed awakening in this country when the young people see the results. There are seven days in a week and 24 hours in a day. If you're working a 40-hour week, you've got a helluva lot of hours at your Kawasaki dealership that you're wasting. I never gave a damn if it took 20 hours a day. I had a sign in our locker room that said, THE BEST WAY TO KILL TIME IS TO WORK IT TO DEATH."

He pauses. He's too honest for this. "Instead of 17 to 19 to 20 hours, I should have moderated it. I should have kept it to 14. I worked time to death ... and it killed me."

He returns to the script, and the fanaticism returns to his voice. "People in management have *got* to learn to handle the negatives," he preaches. "People that interpret temporary setbacks as failure allow frustration to blind them."

Pause. "I've been guilty of this. You're looking at a failure. I licked 90 percent of the problems. The only problem I couldn't lick was myself."

The speech ends a few minutes later, and an ovation erupts. The motorcycle dealers stand in line to meet him. Some will go home talking about the football coach, some will go home talking about the human being.

Vermeil puts on his overcoat and steps into winter, still uncertain which he would rather be.

Every morning of his life as a football coach, Dick Vermeil would pull a yellow legal notepad from his office desk and make lists. With a first-grade teacher's neatness, he would write a number, circle it and then print the task to be performed.

Exclamation points, as if by a zest all their own, would spring from his pencil at the end of his sentences.

One of his lists would be for his wife, Carol; he would call her in mid-morning and read it. One would be for his administrative assistant, one for his personnel director. The longest would be for himself. In recent years, before starting his lists, he would listen to the small tape recorder he kept beside his bed to transcribe the ideas that awoke him during the night.

It seemed all his life would be like this. List it. Do it. Check it off. He was one of a generation of sprinters, of young American males shot down a straightaway out of the starting blocks of the Depression, neither their feet nor their eyes ever leaving their lanes. Vermeil's sprint would simply be faster and straighter and more dramatic than the others'.

The sprint began on the Calistoga (Calif..) High cinder track, upon which he walked, alongside his football coach, on a spring day during his senior year. The school counselor had glanced at Vermeil's grades and recommended a future in his father's garage. Vermeil saw himself coaching football. "If I'm going to do it," he vowed to Coach Bill Wood that day, "I'm going to do it right."

It was as if, upon parting with his coach that afternoon, he had sat down and written a list.

1. EARN COLLEGE DIPLOMA AND MASTER'S DEGREE! BECOME HIGH SCHOOL HEAD COACH!
   1.1 BECOME HIGH SCHOOL COACH OF THE YEAR!
   1.2 WIN LEAGUE TITLE!

He wanted Carol to stay at home with the children, and so when he was finished with his hours of coaching at Hillsdale High in San Mateo, he would change clothes and work some more. At various times he had a job at a food warehouse, dug swimming pools, drove an ice-cream truck, pumped gas, fixed cars under a single hanging light bulb in a silent garage at midnight. "That man's going places," people would say. They had no idea how fast.

2. BECOME JUNIOR COLLEGE HEAD COACH

    2.1 BECOME JUNIOR COLLEGE COACH OF THE YEAR!

He was 27 and personable and handsome, and the coeds at Napa College, a J.C. in Northern California, wished he would stand still long enough for them to flirt. He couldn't. He was busy bullying a wreck of a football program to a 7–2 season in his first and only year there (1964). His reputation began to spread.

3. BECOME MAJOR COLLEGE ASSISTANT COACH!

4. BECOME NFL ASSISTANT COACH!

5. BECOME MAJOR COLLEGE HEAD COACH!

    5.1 WIN ROSE BOWL!

    5.2 BECOME PAC-10 COACH OF THE YEAR!

The new head coach of UCLA was 37. Not a wrinkle crossed his clothes or face; even his charisma was crisp. "Men", he told his staff as the first day of practice approached in 1974, "I want to get off to a good start. We'll meet at 6 a.m."

His assistants blinked and nodded. They should have known their lives would change when Vermeil interviewed them between midnight and 3 a.m., after his day as a Ram assistant coach was done. That first work day, they adjourned at 1 a.m.

No one could sprint with Vermeil. He led his assistants onto UCLA's 5½ mile cross-country course and strung them out for miles, crying at the finish, "That was great, let's do it again!" Three assistants moved into the local Holiday Inn three nights a week.

The whip came down and left the same quick welt it had everywhere else. The Bruins finished 6-3-2 in Vermeil's first year. On two separate occasions Assistant Coach Lynn Stiles's family awoke to discover him asleep in his car in the driveway. A friend drove Vermeil home each night so he would not be found on the side of the road, dead asleep or just dead.

One day in his second season at UCLA, Vermeil had his staff peering at a film of the previous year's game against Oregon State. Suddenly he punched a button, froze the picture on the screen and blurted, "My God!" The assistants leaned forward, but all they could see was a sideline shot of Vermeil's second-oldest son, David. "God," he said, "has David ever grown a lot in a year!"

"He said it as if the only time he ever saw his kid was on the sideline," recalls former Assistant Coach Carl Peterson, now president and general manager of the USFL's Philadelphia Stars. "Not *during* the game, when he was there with him, but on film a year later."

Vermeil's oldest son, Rick, who was in high school at the time, was growing his hair to his shoulders, skipping classes and stretching out on the beach. "It's tough to walk a middle road with a dad like him," says Rick, now 25 and an athletic-equipment salesman in the Philadelphia area. "I rebelled. I resented him because he could work so hard and was so driven and so successful—the whole ethic and image he portrayed. He'd say be home at 10; I'd come home at 3. He never pushed me into sports; he just wanted me to be the best I could at whatever I did."

UCLA went 9–2 that second year. Vermeil shocked Woody Hayes and Ohio State 23–10 in the Rose Bowl.

6. BECOME AN NFL HEAD COACH!

The phone rang in Vermeil's UCLA office: Mr. Leonard Tose, owner of the Philadelphia Eagles.

"Tell him I'm not interested," Vermeil called to Peterson. Now the sprint was accelerating even faster than Vermeil had charted it; he had planned to win a national championship before moving on to No. 6 on his list.

Peterson remembers the moment. "Dick said to us, 'I can't go now. I want to be an NFL head coach someday, but if I go now, I won't be able to take all of you. I'd need veteran pro coaches up there.' He's absolutely the most loyal man I've ever met. We said, 'My God, Dick, this is financial security. You've *got* to talk to him.' "

Finally Vermeil agreed to meet Tose on a Friday morning, assuring his assistants beforehand, "I'm not going to take it." He went home that Thursday night and asked his family to vote on whether or not they should move. Carol: No. Rick: No. Dave: No. Nancy: No.

At noon Friday he called Peterson. "Well, I took the job," he said.

Before he could draw in a deep breath, he was standing in front of the Philadelphia media. He told them his emotional approach would not change. "I think people basically are the same from 18 years old to 32," he said. "I think football players play because they like the game, not because they make money."

On July 4, 1976, Vermeil already had his assistants gathered at his first pro training camp. Darkness enveloped Widener College in Chester, Pa., and all was quiet in the dorm room except for the whir of a projector.

Suddenly there was a staccato burst of loud pops and then an explosion. Vermeil bolted to a window and looked out into the night. "What the hell's going on?" he shouted.

Peterson blanched and said, "I forgot to tell you, Coach. There's a fireworks display at Widener's stadium."

"What the hell for?"

"It's July 4, 1976, Coach, the 200th birthday of our country."

"I don't care whose birthday it is! Go tell 'em to turn if off!"

The team that reported to Widener a week later was fragmented by losing, drug rumors and the '74 NFL players' strike. First- and second-round draft choices for the next three years had been traded away. "It was the most forlorn franchise in football," says San Francisco 49er Coach Bill Walsh, who was then an assistant with the San Diego Chargers.

Vermeil dug in. He wallpapered the locker room with slogans. He ordered the Eagles to keep their helmets on and chin straps buckled during the agony of two-a-day practices. Then he ordered wind sprints. Then he ordered the players to lie down on benches and pump pig iron in puddles of their own sweat.

Doubters were dismissed with shocking abruptness. When starting fullback Mike Hogan was arrested on drug charges, Vermeil cut him without waiting for advice from a judge or jury. A free agent named Mike Siegel was sent packing in mid-practice for missing three blocks; he stripped and dropped his uniform on the ground piece by piece before disappearing from the field wearing only his shorts.

But believers felt an honest arm coil around their backs as they trudged away from a three-hour practice. They shared beef and beer in his house, and tears in his locker room. Vermeil cried when he had to cut them, and sometimes, even when logic demanded it, he refused to. They hated him for his toughness and loved him for his compassion and sincerity, and somehow, in the midst of this emotional jackknifing, their Sundays became holy war and they gave up everything for him.

"As athletes," says former Eagle Linebacker Bill Bergey, "we all want to achieve something for ourselves. But with Dick, you go way beyond that. You play for The Cause."

"I always thought he'd have made a great priest," says Monsignor George Sharkey, the team chaplain.

For Vermeil, The Cause began each Monday at 8 a.m. and lasted until one o'clock the next morning, until between 4 and 6 the next, and 2 the next. He would sleep on his office pull-out sofa bed during what remained of those three nights and finally leave his little world at 7:30 p.m. Thursday to go to WCAU-TV to tape his weekly show. "Thank God for the TV show," his assistants would sigh.

Common suffering and Vermeil's loyalty kept the staff from rebelling. But after the 1981 season, Offensive Coordinator Ed Hughes left, telling friends he feared a heart attack.

By Vermeil's second year, the outmanned Eagles were coming within a touchdown of far superior teams. But already Carol Vermeil could see the sprint dehydrating her husband. At last she and Eagle General Manager Jim Murray persuaded him to visit the team psychiatrist. He entered the house a few hours later, his jaw set.

"Well?" said Carol.

"It would take me a week," said Dick, "to straighten the guy out."

7. BECOME HEAD COACH OF A SUPER BOWL TEAM!

By the third year, Vermeil was UPI's NFC Coach of the Year and the Eagles made the playoffs as a wild card team. He buried his head on Tose's shoulder in the locker room and sobbed after the game that sewed up the playoff berth. He hijacked Cornerback Herman Edwards' Super Fly hat at the team party, put it on and danced.

He opened Christmas presents a week late at home so there would be no disturbing his preparation for his first playoff game. His team lost. "If I described what it felt like inside me to lose," he says, "you would write me off as a lunatic. They'd call me one-dimensional, but when I lost, it was the only dimension that people evaluated."

But the Eagles were winners now, and winning only made the tension worse. He set curfews for himself and broke them. He canceled vacations. He gulped coffee for breakfast, ate a Carnation Breakfast Bar for lunch and sometimes had a hoagie, while sitting on the toilet, for dinner. He'd try sleeping pills or hot chocolate or a glass of wine to get to sleep, and still he'd awaken wondering what Shula and Landry and Noll were doing. When he went home, his mind did not, and once dinner ended he'd plug himself into stereo headphones and a Neil Diamond tape and collapse on the couch. He lectured his players that their families were their No. 1 priority.

His sense of responsibility was overwhelming him. He personally redid an entire section of the playbook after an assistant coach drew the circles and squares representing offensive and defensive players freehand, instead of tracing them with a stencil. He accommodated virtually every media and charity request, speaking at up to 50 functions a year. He became frightened—but only for a moment—when long spasms shot through him as he gaped at films. On occasion he seemed to be asking for release from something he could not control. "Sometimes I wish Leonard Tose would fire me," he said.

Al Davis, the Raiders' owner, would phone him at 3 a.m. EST, perhaps to escalate his fear of not working hard enough. Some coaches and executives squirmed at the work standard Vermeil was setting for the league and some of them resented it. "Vermeil got under my skin by making a big deal of sleeping at the stadium and saying that he worked 16 hours a day," groused Dallas Cowboy General Manager Tex Schramm. "I know what other coaches do, and they just don't talk about it."

Because Vermeil heaped so much blame on himself for everything that went wrong, criticism was more than he could bear. Once he had to be tackled to prevent him from climbing into the stands after a heckler at the Vet in Philadelphia. On another occasion he said he felt like decking his wife for second-guessing a play call. "He put on this air as this tough little French sonofagun," says Peterson, by that time his personnel director, "but underneath it he was more sensitive than anybody knew. He'd say he never read the papers. Bullcrap. If he didn't read them, he'd say 'What'd they say, Carl?' For all his success, his confidence level wasn't always strong enough to pull him through."

By his fifth NFL season, 1980, Vermeil was a Super Bowl coach. "That was the best coaching job in the NFL in the last seven years," says Walsh. "There are other great coaches, but they had great organizations around them. Vermeil beat them with his own guts and a few people who followed him. Players of his he'd brag to me about, I wasn't that impressed with. He convinced himself and them they were great. He lived their lives."

The Raiders ran off the Eagles in the '81 Super Bowl 27–10. Instead of receiving praise, Vermeil was criticized for burning out his team with long practices and meetings.

Vermeil returned to Philadelphia, to a quandary. He had dragged 45 overachievers to Super Bowl status in an emotional sports city ravenous for more. More? Vermeil added an hour to his daily work schedule.

8. BECOME...?

I'd love to spend more time with the kids, the husband says. God, they're adults now.

There are so many things we should have talked about all those years, the wife says.

I'd love to go deer hunting in Colorado or Montana. I could sit in a goose pit or a duck blind for hours and freeze and enjoy it.

Sure. And maybe take some time to read, Dick. Maybe play some cards.

I'd love for the two of us to get in a car sometime and drive cross-country. I'd love to go to Italy and see where my great-grandfather came from.

I'd like that. I'd like to have some nice conversations.

I'd like to see our friends. Hell, I don't know half our friends. I'd love to try broadcasting and get the whole family involved so we could work together.

Why can't we, Dick? Why can't we...?

January 1982. A car plowed into Carol Vermeil's Ford on the driver's side, fracturing her right elbow and her pelvic bone and sending 50 stitches' worth of glass into her head, just missing her left eye. "They said she could have easily been killed," Stiles says. "You could see the effect on Dick. For the first time, it really hit him: How important is anything compared to life?"

Vermeil went to San Diego to coach in the Olympia Gold Bowl and had his team of college all-stars hitting so hard during his first day of practice that there was nearly a mutiny. "I'd promised the players a light week, a vacation," says former Kansas City Chief Running Back Mike Garrett, who was player coordinator for the game. "His first day he has them killing each other and they're pulling me aside, saying, 'This guy's crazy. You've got to cut this out or we're leaving.' My teammates called me Mr. Intense at USC, and this guy was two octaves higher than me or anyone I've ever seen. He was personable, but I'd have been terribly afraid to play for him. You couldn't even drink a glass of water slow around him."

April 1982. They thought it was seasickness. The Vermeils were on a sailboat in the Caribbean, taking the vacation they had fantasized about but postponed for years. They felt terrible. They came home to a diagnosis of hepatitis.

For 45 years Vermeil had made unreasonable requests of his body. A remarkably accommodating machine with a pulse rate of 48, it had occasionally protested but in the end had always submitted. Now a doctor was telling a man who had missed just a half-day of work in his life—for Nancy's birth—to live on his back for three weeks. Before a week had gone by, the Eagles' film man was seen staggering out of the office under a huge box of paper work and film, heading for Vermeil's house.

A few weeks later Carol's blood count had improved, and she received permission to break quarantine. Dick's hadn't; he was told to go back to bed. "He called me," recalls Peterson, "and he was angry. He said, 'Goddamn, she beat me getting well.' He was even competing with his wife to get better!"

Draft day came, and Vermeil could lie still no longer. Against his doctor's advice he left his house for the Vet. When he walked into the draft room, every Eagle coach and scout was wearing a surgical mask.

By now Vermeil's sense of humor had shriveled. "You sons of bitches," he growled. "I don't think that's real funny."

Training camp began, and Vermeil did not ambush the mistake-makers the way he once had. Part of it was a conscious effort to pace his team, save more of its frenzy for the end, and part stemmed from the hepatitis hangover he could not shake.

July 1982. Charlie Johnson, 30, perhaps the quintessential creation of Vermeil's labor pains, asked to be traded. Too soft in the body, two years behind his football-playing contemporaries because of a stint in Vietnam, he was not chosen until the seventh round of the 1977 draft. He agreed to do it the Vermeil way. He became a locker-room leader and weightlifting fool. He became a Pro Bowl starting noseguard three straight years. And "He became tired of waking up with a headache from head-butting every day," says Philadelphia Quarterback Ron Jaworski. "He didn't mind the headaches on Mondays, after a game, but he decided his career wasn't going to last very long having full contact in practice the way we did."

Vermeil took it like a slap from his firstborn son. He realized Johnson was not alone. Veterans who had accepted the relentless repetitions and long practices in the program's formative years found them self-defeating now that the Eagles were a playoff team. In seven years under Vermeil, one player insisted, he had fresh legs in just one game.

Once, after three straight losses, the Eagles' staff had polled the players for theories. Frank LeMaster, a friend of Vermeil's as well as one of his linebackers, responded that the players were mentally and physically burned out. At the end of the season, LeMaster got a two-page letter from Vermeil, saying the reason he was tired was because he *thought* he was tired. LeMaster, who had placed No. 1 on the squad in camp-opening conditioning tests, swallowed hard.

"We didn't always agree with Dick's methods," says Jaworski, "but when we were celebrating victories on Sunday nights, we didn't complain. I never remember seeing a defense I wasn't completely prepared for. But everybody dreaded Mondays, even after we won."

At the end of July, Vermeil shipped Johnson to Minnesota for a second-round pick. After that he ached every time he walked past the picture in his house of Johnson carrying him off the field after a victory over the Vikings.

September 1982. Gene Upshaw declared that the NFL players' strike was on, and Vermeil finally had to accept the possibility that a football player's primary pursuit might be money. He continued to go through the mechanics of addiction even during the strike, popping game films for placebos. Tose ordered him to go home on Thursdays, but he came back every Monday.

His players? Surely the Eagles would work longer and harder on their own than any NFL team, wouldn't they? Instead, they decided that full-scale workouts would be a signal to the owners that they were chafing to return, and with the headmaster's whip removed, they scattered like schoolchildren at recess. A fearful thought struck Vermeil: His commandments hadn't been internalized.

The weekends came, and in the stillness Vermeil heard himself think another disquieting thought. There was no pressure, no Sunday judgment on the floor of the 70,000-seat cement bowls ... and he *enjoyed* it. Carol and he would drive three and a half hours to a cabin he had recently bought in the mountains of Pennsylvania. She was shocked when he began pulling off to the side every few miles, stepping from behind the wheel and calling, "Look how *red* the leaves are. Look how *yellow*."

"I'm saying, 'Right, Dick, this is the East Coast, and they get red and yellow every year,'" Carol remembers, "He'd take five steps and stop and point again. You can't believe how many rolls of film he used up on trees."

At the cabin they would start dinner and a fire, and pour each other wine. And when the sun broke the next day, he'd hike with his Labrador retriever, or if his boys had come along, they'd hop on motorcycles and hit the trails, the boys grinning and gunning ahead to spray rooster tails of dirt back into his face.

In the middle of November the strike ended. Vermeil felt bad that that didn't make him feel good.

He tried to hurl himself back into the same work schedule without the same illusions. It didn't work. He watched film at 2 a.m. and saw nothing. He began to cry during routine locker-room speeches. His neck was so tense that when driving he could not turn it to see in the left lane. At home, he was farther away than ever. "I'd say, 'Dick, I cut off my arm today, but I don't think it's too bad,'" says Carol, "and he wouldn't even blink."

The first Sunday after the strike, the Bengals manhandled an Eagle team whose players were still grumbling about the new union contract. The second week Vermeil hit bottom. At Wednesday's practice, while his team walked through the plays installed for that Sunday's game at Washington, he sat red-eyed in the parking lot. The most powerful motivator in the NFL could not motivate himself to get out of a car.

On Saturday, while his daughter, Nancy, was graduating from Penn State, her father faced a team bus ride to Washington. As the bus filled up in the Vet parking lot, he sat in his car, once again immobilized.

He dined that night with Monsignor Sharkey. The priest had given Vermeil a book entitled *Burn Out* two years earlier, and Vermeil had dismissed it. Now he had read the sections of it underlined by his wife and finally admitted it was happening to him.

After dinner he gathered his team for his ritual night-before oratory. Crying, he told them that if he could not find a way to inspire them, he would "waive Dick Vermeil." At 9:30 p.m. he sat down for a snack. He looked over to a table where his veterans sat, expecting to find them quietly preparing for the game. His crusaders were hunched over copies of the new contract. The next day the Eagles lost again.

"Some guys had started turning Dick off," Jaworski says. "He'd get emotional, and it was 'Here we go again.' The bang effect was gone. And we were so much more programmed than other teams, we couldn't just come back after eight weeks and start winning."

When the Eagles lost their third straight game the next Sunday, Tose was waiting for them in the locker room. "You might as well go back on strike!" he raged at the players.

Vermeil was—and is—a friend of Tose's, but he knew he must act. He took Tose by the wrist. "You men know what I think of Mr. Tose," he rasped. "That wasn't Leonard Tose saying that."

The season was torpedoed; the Eagles sank into last place. "I was afraid we'd get a phone call in the night," says Vermeil's brother Al, until recently an assistant with the 49ers, "saying he'd gone to sleep and hadn't woken up. Cardiac."

In other NFL cities, men were living in hells similar to Vermeil's. Last year seven other head coaches—Marv Levy of the Chiefs, Leeman Bennett of the Falcons, Walt Michaels of the Jets, Chuck Knox of the Bills, Jack Patera of the Seahawks, Ray Malavasi of the Rams and Ray Perkins of the Giants—were either fired from or quit what has become professional sport's most distorted job. In a mobile society in which the fabric of community and neighborhood is unraveling, sports more and more are becoming the synthetic replacement, football more and more the favored thread—and head coaches more and more the paranoid victims.

A ninth coach, Bill Walsh nearly fled, too, just a year after winning the Super Bowl. The last month of the season Vermeil and Walsh volleyed phone calls back and forth, trying to motivate each other. The reasons the job has become so preposterous over the last decade, Walsh says, are these:

•Communications. "The media bring every little detail to the public's attention now, which puts more stress on the ownership to win and builds the fans' expectations higher each year."

•Increasing salaries. "In a lot of cases, as the salaries grow the returns we're getting from players are diminishing."

•Rule changes. "The way they've changed the passing rules, a good team can't dominate the line of scrimmage anymore. The more passing there is, the more variables there are—and the more chance the lesser team will win."

•Parity. "The way the talent is spread in the draft and the way the scheduling is set up, you can go from first to last [as the 49ers did in '82] just like that."

•Drugs. "They have a dramatic impact on the performance of your athletes. They stop sleeping and eating right. In three weeks a great athlete becomes a shell of himself. The coaches who brag the most about their lack of drug problems usually have the biggest problems."

•The USFL. "It's just going to add one more thing for the coach to worry about, and spread the talent even more.

"You have to take the Noll and Landry and Shula approach," Walsh concludes. "Delegate authority to your assistants, relax and breathe deeply. Then we'll probably have assistants burning out. What it all comes down to is that there are now more factors than ever that an NFL coach cannot control."

Says Landry, the Cowboys' coach for all the team's 23 years, who once warned Vermeil during pregame player drills to slow down: "A long time ago I tried to judge what I could and could not control and stopped worrying about what I couldn't. This was a bad year for coaches because the strike meant there was more we couldn't control than ever. The trouble is, NFL coaching is not musical chairs, like it is for baseball managers who get fired. You don't often get another job if you don't succeed; they're going to kick you out with no pension or medical benefits, and you'll have to struggle all on your own. It's free enterprise at its extreme, and that can mean devastating pressure."

From the NFL's inception, its head coaches have survived an average of 3.2 years with a team. That sort of job and a man like Vermeil was one very cruel piece of matchmaking.

On Jan. 2, at the Eagles' final game, Vermeil cried through the national anthem. He spent the next week summoning a courage most men never find or, at 46, have long since lost— the courage to acknowledge that one's values are warped. He knew now what he must do, but after a 23-year torrent of dogma, he found it almost a physical impossibility to work the strange words up his throat.

The following Sunday the Vermeils finished dinner and sat facing each other in their paneled basement.

"I don't know if I can make this decision," he admitted.

"I've already made it," Carol said.

"What do you mean?" he asked. In 23 years she'd never entered into a career decision.

"We're getting out."

"Do you really think so?"

"Yep. Let's do it."

Just then Murray, the Eagles' general manager, telephoned. Now Vermeil was fighting something deeper and stronger and older than the football coach in him, something that made him feel almost as if he was choking as he spoke the words.

"I'm getting out."

Louie Vermeil peers out of the Owl Garage. On his right, just a foot away from this 100-year-old barn he converted into a car-repair shop, stands the Church of Our Lady of Perpetual Help, from where priests used to hurl the name of God against Louie's hammerings and grindings on the Day of Rest. On his left stands his white house, a landmark in California's Napa Valley for having sheltered a dreamer named Robert Louis Stevenson and a doer named Richard Allen Vermeil. In front of Louie is a yard full of junked cars and trucks, grave-robbed for their organs and corroded by rust. For five decades, rust and Louie have worked the same hours here.

"You'll laugh," he says, "but as a young man I was fascinated by the thought of working 24 hours straight. I did it, too."

His hat is tilted back on his head and his glasses are tilted down on the front of his nose. His jaw comes out after you even more than his son's. His hands are arthritis-cramped into two tool grips. Grease, an old and eager friend, has left a lick on his forehead.

He slams the hood on a Pinto tune-up and at 72 permits himself the heresy of a 4:30 quitting time. He swivels toward the house. In 1972 he suffered a damaged left hip when he was hit by a race car while officiating at Calistoga Speedway, of which he's president. He used a broomstick shoved under his armpit while working the next day. Three years later he consented to see a doctor and lay still for an artificial hip socket.

"You should have seen how many cars we had backed up here during World War II because nobody could get parts anywhere and I had to make them," he says. "I had a Model A pickup that sat out here a whole year before I could get to it."

He worked seven days and nights a week during the war, built a reputation as Northern California's finest machinist and then *he* burned out. In 1946, along with an old high school football teammate, he rebuilt the engine of a 1935 Ford convertible, painted it black with red stripes, bid his family good-by and drove East. He planned to close the Owl Garage when he returned and find work that was less draining. He saw the Indianapolis 500 and he saw Buffalo, which reminded him of San Francisco, and then all this foolishness got to him. "I felt guilty," he says. "I thought, 'What the hell am I doing out here, goofing off?'" He returned to the Owl and never vacationed again.

Now the man whom locals call The Bear pushes open the back door of his house, brushing past the painting that says WELCOME TO VERMEIL'S NEST. It has been 50 years that Louie and his wife, Alice, have been chirping and scolding each other here like a pair of bluejays.

Alice, a woman with a round, friendly face, white-rimmed glasses and blond hair arranged in a small bun, is searching her kitchen for a lost item. "What'd you lose, Mom?" grunts Louie. "Your mind?" Then, in an aside, "Don't ever compliment 'em. They'll stay in a rut."

Alice laughs and calls him a knot-headed Frenchman. It is a kind of thing their son Dick never dared say. "I'd come home and tell him I threw three touchdown passes," Dick remembers, "and he'd say, 'Good, go change a flat.' I started working with him the first day after I graduated from grammar school. His automatic response was always to jump your ass. I never saw him sit and relax. I do remember seeing him once, in swimming trunks, at a picnic on the Russian River. Hell, I didn't know if he'd float."

As the eldest of three sons, Dick faced the same hard choice his own eldest son would encounter later: Match the old man's work capacity for the reward of a small nod—or rebel. He craved the nod too much.

Louie and Alice sit at the kitchen table and laugh, recalling the time that Dick quarterbacked Calistoga High to a 14–7 loss in the championship game with St. Helena's. In punt formation, he had chased down a bad snap in a driving rain, had run with the ball and failed to make the first down. "Shoulda punted—you had the time," growled Louie afterward, and Dick burst into tears. While the rest of the team and half the town held a season-ending party in his house, Dick stayed in his room and cried. He didn't know until years later that the man who would not hug or praise him listened on the radio to all of his games as a quarterback at San Jose State, sitting in his car in a rainstorm on the nearest hill when reception was poor.

"I was a critic," Louie says. "I didn't want him to think life was easy. I'd praise him behind his back to everybody. I never realized how much he wanted me to praise him. Hell, my dad worked until he was 86 years old, and whenever I worked for him I'd bust a gut.

"Dick's a little too softhearted. I'd a chewed those players' asses out in Philadelphia. There are three tough nuts in that league—Shula, Grant and Landry. I don't think Dick could hold a candle to 'em."

"But he'll be back," interjects Alice. "Don't you go getting too excited about all this. I've got a bet with his father: Dick will be back coaching within a year. I *know* I'm right."

"I just bet to be ornery," grumps Louie. "Hell, I can't *agree* with her. He'll be back. It'd be like me leaving the garage. Yeah, he'll be back."

There is a driving rain in Culiacán. Vermeil wades through lagoon mud up to his knees and then turns his face to the rain to watch and wait for the flutter across the western Mexico sky. There it is. He jerks with the kick of his Browning automatic, again and again, and birds drop like thick precipitation. The other hunters in his party finally stop, sore and tired, but when Vermeil is happy with the hurt in his right shoulder, he switches the shotgun to his left and goes on and on. "This is the first time I've ever gone hunting and thought only about hunting," he says.

He is relaxed and talkative, and all the natural charm has returned. Yet every sunrise still calls forth a new referendum on life without football. He *hopes* he can live without it. He *hopes* he becomes so good a commentator for CBS on Sunday that he can bear, perhaps even enjoy, all the relaxation in between. His demon has been staggered, not slain. "If he does not achieve as a broadcaster," says his brother Al, "oh my God."

And so the battle to become comfortable with who he is, instead of what he does, still swings back and forth. "It's 50-50 I'll be coaching," he says. "Hell, I already feel so good I could start tomorrow. If I'd taken another few weeks to decide, I might have stayed. I'm still not sure burnout applies to me...."

Then: "I'll probably spend some time with a psychiatrist. I have to learn to handle my own drives, to stop trying to control so many variables...."

Then: "I don't need a therapist to tell me that. Cripes. I've got more common sense in one hand than most of them have in their body. I'd rather have had the upbringing I had than the reverse approach to work—even rather than moderation. Look what it's done for me. How many people have experienced the highs and lows that I have through football? I might come back as an assistant to a Shula or a Landry, to see how they do it. But hell, if I'd approached it as just a game, I might still be coaching at Hillsdale High. I don't have any regrets...."

Then: "It's time I put my family over my occupation. I'm not an example of what a guy ought to be...."

Darkness covers Culiacán, and at a table in a restaurant Vermeil and his companions, including UCLA alumnus Rob Hixson who had been vainly asking Vermeil to come hunting here for years, fill themselves with shrimp, octopus, whitefish sauteed in onions, marinated scallops and melted Mexican cheese with sausage. They douse it all with wine.

Dinner ends: the margaritas and mariachi band begin. "You know," says Vermeil, "there *are* other things in life."

Suddenly he jumps up from the table, strides into the middle of the music and commandeers the trumpet. He throws back his head and pours out two songs that he has not attempted since he was a boy, and brown-skinned men who have never seen a football game smile and cheer.

Dick Vermeil laughs so hard he has to remove the horn from his lips.

"Hell," he cries, "I didn't know I could do that!"

Wiseguy

BY   FRANZ   LIDZ

HOUSTON OILER COACH JERRY GLANVILLE POSSESSED A SHARP TONGUE AND A REPUTATION AS A TOUGH GUY. HE ALSO LEFT TICKETS FOR THE LIKES OF ELVIS, JAMES DEAN AND THE PHANTOM OF THE OPERA. SO FAR AS WE KNOW NONE OF THEM EVER VISITED HIM. FRANZ LIDZ DID.

The quips come in sudden spasms. "When I was born," says Jerry Glanville, the coach of the Houston Oilers, "the doctor looked at me and spanked my mom." On a 300-pound player he cut during training camp: "This guy was so fat it looked like someone sat in his lap and didn't leave." On why he would never own a horse: "I don't want to keep anything that eats while I'm sleeping, including a wife."

Nowhere is Glanville's patter more spirited than on his Monday evening radio show. Amid balloons and streamers and clinking glasses in the High Chapparal Room of the Marriott Astrodome, Glanville trades genial insults and talks football with telephone callers and patrons of the hotel. Normally, the ambience of the *Jerry Glanville Show* is cocktail-party cheery. But on a recent Monday most of the audience seemed glum and slightly embarrassed, like guests at a bash where the host has committed some indiscretion nobody wants to acknowledge. A few fans were angry. The Oilers had just committed a 23–13 loss to the patsy New England Patriots to fall to 2–3, which was a little unsettling for a team many had picked to win the AFC Central Division.

The critiques being thrown Glanville's way bordered on unnecessary roughness. The irate fans lambasted his strategy, his leadership, his manhood. Glanville told them he was thinking of putting out a novelty item called Glanville-in-a Box. "It'll have detachable limbs." he said. "You can hurl them at your TV during Oilers telecasts."

Finally, an old-timer in the crowd stood up. He wore satin gym shorts and a morning-after stubble. No shirt. "The fans all think you deserve to be fired," he said. "The media say your days are numbered. Well, if a student gets an F, you don't fire the teacher. And Mr. Glanville, you're the teacher." Glanville set his mouth in a small smile, adjusted his microphone and said, "I want to say personally that I appreciate my son coming to the show."

Lately the mood at the Marriott has perked up considerably. Two weeks ago, the Oilers upset the Bears 33–28 in Chicago, and on Sunday they beat the Pittsburgh Steelers 27–0 at the Dome to move into a first-place tie with the Cincinnati Bengals. Yet Glanville remains as unfazed by the recent good fortune as he was by the bad. He knows those clamoring for his dismissal have simply turned down the volume for a while. "I'm always a game away from a hanging," he says.

Glanville had been an NFL assistant for 12 years when the Oilers promoted him to head coach late in the 1985 season. In the four years before he took over, Houston had gone 1–8, 2–14, 3–13, 5–11. "When I got here in '84, we had the nicest guys in the NFL," he says. "Their mamas loved 'em. Their daddies loved 'em. But they wouldn't hit if you handed 'em sticks."

He recalls a 1984 game against Pittsburgh in which half a dozen Steelers jumped offside and flattened Houston quarterback Warren Moon, whose teammates stood around gaping. "It made me nauseous," says Glanville, who was then the Oilers' defensive coordinator. "I knew then we'd never be any good if we didn't protect each other like family."

Glanville re-created the Oilers in his own brash image. He installed a buckshot four-wideout offense called the Red Gun and instilled a smash-mouth spirit in the defense that some think crosses the chalk line of football propriety. The Oilers became known as the Bad Boys, the Astrodome as the House of Pain. Houston went 9–6 in 1987 and made the playoffs for the first time since '80. Last year the Oilers were 10–6 in the regular season before losing to the Buffalo Bills in the second round of the playoffs.

"Now we're so cocky we'd play Russian roulette with a guillotine," says Glanville. Laughter erupts in a sly cackle from the side of this mouth. Like a prizefighter's laugh. Or a bully's. "Jerry's a very tough guy," says Todd Menig, an old friend. "But he's also a gentle, soft human being. A lot of it has to do with growing up without a father."

Glanville, the son of a Ford salesman, grew up in a Detroit housing project. His parents divorced when he was in the 10th grade, and after that he lived with his mother in Perrysburg, Ohio. Her father and brother were both part-time coaches, and she told Jerry, "Do whatever you want in life, just don't ever coach."

So before graduating from Northern Michigan in 1964, he worked on an assembly line at a Chevy plant and toted 100-pound bags of flour for General Mills. "People tell me I have a hard job," he says of coaching in the NFL. "I don't even consider this going to work." He played linebacker for Montana State and Northern Michigan, where his distaste for history class was mitigated by a love for psychology.

"I'm still mad at my history teacher," says Glanville. "He was such a drone that he cheated me out of 10 years of enjoying the subject. The only reason I majored in psychology was that my first psych professor was full of energy and enthusiasm. I know now you can't accomplish anything without those things."

Those things sum up Glanville in all his parts: shameless grandstander, tireless volunteer who visits the terminally ill, swaggering stoic who strutted into the House of Pain on Sunday after having been bitten on the foot by a water moccasin the day before, irrepressible wise guy who tells trainers, "Never X-ray injuries: X-rays show bad things." This is a fellow who once stopped his car on an interstate after a loss to tell his future wife, Brenda, to take a hike. Brenda's crime was saying, "But Jerry, it's only a game."

Glanville never debunks a story. "My life is partly truth, partly fiction," he says. "I guess you could say it's a contradiction." Glanville didn't come up with that line. Kris Kristofferson did. Glanville thinks Kristofferson is one of the three greatest poets of the 20th century. The other two are the late folk singer Harry Chapin and country balladeer Jerry Jeff Walker.

"Jerry Jeff is one of my top assistants," Glanville says. In defeat, Walker consoles Glanville on his car CD player. "The man with the big hat is buying," Glanville sings along in a strong but not necessarily musical voice, "so drink up while the drinking is free."

A compact 5'9", 175 pounds, Glanville turned 48 on Oct. 14, but he looks 10 years younger—well, maybe five. He's somewhat disappointingly garbed in jeans, a denim jacket and a quite ordinary striped shirt. But on his feet are what appear to be footballs. In fact, they're boots cobbled out of football leather. "If a player fumbles a lot," he says, "I make him carry them."

Glanville is renowned for appearing on the sidelines in black. He screams around downtown Houston in a black-on-black Corvette and a 1950 Mercury, which he calls "my James Dean special." A replica of a Tennessee license plate on the front of the 'vette reads 1-ELVIS. Glanville insists that Elvis "is alive and living in Grand Rapids, Michigan." He knows this because he read it in a supermarket tabloid. Glanville believes everything he reads that isn't about him.

Last year Glanville visited Graceland. He toured every room except the kitchen, which was locked. "I was sure Elvis was in there," Glanville says. "I heard him. I *smelled* him. He was fixing a peanut butter sandwich." Before a 1988 preseason game in Memphis, Glanville left a pass for Elvis at the Liberty Bowl's will-call window. The King never picked it up, but Glanville enjoyed the attention the gesture attracted. Later in the season he left passes to Oiler games for Buddy Holly in Dallas, James Dean in Indianapolis, Loni Anderson in Cincinnati and the Phantom of the Opera at the

Meadowlands. "People think I'm crazy," Glanville says, "but I don't have to be. If I can convince them I may be, then I've accomplished all I want."

Criticism, he tells you, glances off him like a deflected pass. Yet he has been feuding with the Houston press since the Oilers lost eight straight games in 1986. Ed Fowler of *The Houston Chronicle* branded him a "bobo in black," accused him of having a siege mentality and claimed some of his plays were concocted in an LSD laboratory. When Fowler and another *Chronicle* columnist called for Glanville's firing during the '87 season, he retaliated. Glanville told callers to his show he wouldn't answer questions until they promised to cancel their *Chronicle* subscriptions. "I only hold a grudge till I die," Glanville says.

He has been accused of encouraging dirty tactics among his players since 1979, when he was the defensive coordinator of the Atlanta Falcons. He cooked up a furious pass rush called the Gritz Blitz and ordered the secondary to dive bomb helmet-first on every play. Falcon defensive back Bob Glazebrook once plunged into a pile so ferociously that he broke the arm of teammate Jeff Merrow. Glanville almost teared up when he heard Glazebrook had asked for the X-ray and cast as mementos. "God," he said, "I love pro football."

Glanville knows how to fire up players. In fact, he whips them into a frothing frenzy. "Jerry teaches us to expect everything, but fear nothing," says linebacker Robert Lyles. "We don't go out to hurt anybody. We go out to tackle them hard on every play. If the sucker's moving, our goal is to get 11 guys on him. Put the flag up. Surrender. He's dead. It's over. He's a landmark. It's hit, crunch and burn."

"Just seeing him wear black gets me juiced," says second-year cornerback Cris Dishman. "Black oozes a bad-boy attitude." Dishman may be too bad for his own good. He glowered over injured Minnesota Viking tight end Carl Hinton in this year's season opener, screaming and taunting him. The next week, in San Diego, he received a personal foul penalty that turned a third-and-22 for the Chargers into a first down. Moon took Dishman aside and asked him to tone down his act. So did Houston general manager Mike Holovak. Glanville talked to him, too, but Dishman says, "There's no toning down with Jerry. When you tone down, you're loose, and when you're loose, you're out of a job."

Steeler coach Chuck Noll believes Glanville goes too far. After Houston beat Pittsburgh 24–16 two years ago, Noll stretched the obligatory postgame handshake into a midfield finger-wagging lecture about cheap shots. Glanville had to jerk himself free. "I think Chuck was infatuated with my hand," he says.

On the practice field, Glanville is a sputter of comic agitation, razzing his players into fits of helpless laughter. "Jerry's just a crazy old white man people listen to," says running back Mike Rozier, whom Glanville calls Lassie when Rozier dogs it. Once, when a pricey defensive lineman showed up late for training camp after a contract dispute, Glanville snatched the player's nameplate off his locker and hung it over the door to the lavatory. "Jerry keeps us all sort of humble," says running back Allen Pinkett. "It's impossible to have a big ego here. Jerry says we're family."

At Saturday workouts Glanville holds Kids Day and Pets Day. Sons, daughters and gerbils run routes with their proud papas. "We had to separate Wives Day and Girlfriends Day," says Glanville. "A couple of guys brought both."

For all his loudmouthing, Glanville doesn't talk much about his speeches to church groups, his fight to reopen an inner-city boys' club or his work with runaways, drug addicts and the homeless. He visits the children's wards of Houston hospitals every Wednesday morning, sometimes dragging along players. He practices his bedside manner on cancer patients and quadriplegics, not just kids in for tonsillectomies. "Jerry would come in the middle of the night if I asked him," says Jim Alcorn, chaplain of St. Luke's Episcopal Hospital. "He has incredible compassion toward these kids. He finds a way to touch them."

It's not always a happy experience. "I've seen him stand in the halls in tears," Alcorn says. "I've seen kids die in his arms. Many athletes can't take it—they come and leave. But Jerry isn't smart enough to leave."

At the moment it doesn't appear that he'll be leaving the Oilers anytime soon, either. But he knows that can change. The local press has speculated that Glanville could be replaced by owner Bud Adams if Houston doesn't advance further in the playoffs than it did last year. Glanville doesn't seem dismayed. "You know what NFL really stands for?" he says. "Not For Long."

He utters this while sitting behind his office desk, surrounded by memorabilia of his dead heroes: a liqueur bottle shaped like a bust of Elvis and a traffic ticket "issued" posthumously to James Dean. He reaches back and grabs a recent group photo of NFL coaches. "Six of us get fired every year," he says. "I'm in an elite fighter-pilot group. I know one day I'm not coming back, but I go out anyway. And one day I'll say, My god, they got me, too."

Glanville leans forward, elbows on knees, his mouth resting in one upturned palm. "Till then," he says, "I'll drink up while the drinking is free."

Deep into His Job

BY ED HINTON

AS THE '90S GET INTO FULL SWING, THE DALLAS COWBOYS ARE THE FRANCHISE THAT SEEMS POISED TO DOMINATE THE DECADE. ONE MAN RESPONSIBLE FOR THIS IS OWNER JERRY JONES. THE OTHER IS AN OLD TEAMMATE OF JONES'S NAMED JIMMY JOHNSON. IN 1992 ED HINTON VISITED WITH THE DALLAS COACH.

Down near the docks in Port Arthur, Texas, a once rowdy seaport and refinery town that has seen its day, sits the public library. It's a source of local pride not only for its staunch, clean appearance amid abandoned buildings on deserted streets, but also because it serves as the town's museum. Near the rows of books are tributes to the region's best-known citizens, mostly musicians and athletes, with their sheet music and high school yearbooks and game jerseys on display. From Tex Ritter to the Big Bopper, from Bum Phillips to Tim McKyer, a wonderful menagerie of free spirits who dreamed bigger dreams than Port Arthur, even in its heyday, could handle are celebrated there. Two of the more prominent exhibits are busts of Janis Joplin and Jimmy Johnson, former schoolmates at Thomas Jefferson High, class of 1960 and '61, respectively. A smart girl and a smart boy, equally driven but in different directions—each was somewhat disgusted by the other's burgeoning talents and antithetical personality. Janis, a painter of some merit and a folk singer in those days, had the look of a beatnik and was called Beat Weeds. Jimmy could solve algebra problems at a glance and write term papers worthy of A's the night before they were due. He was a football lineman with the scars of childhood street ball showing through his burr haircut and was called Scar Head.

By a quirk in scheduling, Janis and Jimmy once had to put up with each other in a history class for an entire school year, she seated behind him. He would tease the weirdo, "give her a hard time, irritate her," he remembers; she would scoff at the jock and ignore him as best she could.

Worlds apart sat adjacent that way in Port Arthur. At one end of Procter Street, the main drag, stood the whorehouses, the gambling joints and the brawling saloons—all flouting Texas law for merchant sailors' cash. At the other end of Procter was a populace conservative in thought and speech, living on quiet, tree-lined streets and faithfully attending church. Port Arthur was a Texas boomtown, sprouting refinery pipelines and freighter masts, and as it was just 50 miles from the Louisiana line, it was also a Cajun town, with signs for boudin and the strains of twin fiddles. Port Arthur was segregated, but there was a middle ground where working-class whites and blacks lived so closely that their children could come home from "separate but equal" schools and learn to know each other well.

"Jimmy never thought there was any difference between him and the blacks," C.W. Johnson, Jimmy's daddy, said recently while driving through the old middle ground, where the Johnson family lived until 1962. "And he didn't like it when anybody said anything about it, either."

In their disregard for racial barriers, Beat Weeds and Scar Head were alike. They came to understand how life worked on the other side of the middle ground, and they took that insight with them as they continued on their divergent paths. Janis took it into a blues-singing frenzy, only to drop dead of a drug overdose at 27. Jimmy took it into football, where his savvy for massaging the human spirit in all its ethnic patterns would become an invaluable coaching tool.

After a vice cleanup in the mid-1960s and then the oil bust of the '80s, Port Arthur turned into a sleepy town with few signs of youth or ambition. But the unscarred library and its treasures inside stand as testimony to a brighter day. The bust of Janis is five-headed, the sculptor's interpretation of her multidimensional personality. The bust of Jimmy is conventional and features his trademark coiffed hair and hint of a smile. His face is portrayed as calm and unflinching, as it was when he arrived at the University of Miami in '84 to a cool welcome—he succeeded the beloved Howard Schnellenberger—and then set his players' spirits free, won a national championship and narrowly missed two more. It is the same smile he wore when he went to Dallas in '89 and was greeted by flat-out loathing—he displaced the legendary Tom Landry—and went about the task of tearing down a rotting facade and rebuilding the Cowboys. But like Janis, Jimmy has a personality that is multifaceted.

"It'll be quite a story, when all is said and done," says Cowboy running backs coach Joe Brodsky, 58, a Johnson skeptic in 1984 who became such a Johnson convert that he up and left the Miami area after 55 years to follow Johnson to Dallas. "How could a guy come in and take shotgun blasts in the face in two different programs and win a national championship with one and the Super Bowl with the other? Now won't that be a pisser?"

A Pretty Good Wizard   For Johnson the hay is pretty much in the barn, as they say in Texas. At 49 he's got things just about the way he wants them—at last. "I'm doing what the hell I want to do," he says, meaning coaching football, drinking beer, eating ribs and living alone in a big house with four aquariums teeming with saltwater fish. There are no loose pets, no wife and no kids around. His sons Brent, 28, and Chad, 26, are more like friends of his now; the three of them are closer than they've ever been. Jimmy's former wife of 26 years, Linda Kay, has gone to Venezuela to find a new life, waived, you might say, when Jimmy reorganized his own life three years ago to best suit the way he wanted to go about coaching the Cowboys.

All that remains for him to do now is to plug in another

blue-chip player here and another real find there, win a Super
Bowl or a few—"And we *will* win," he says—and then go off
and lie on a beach, to be left alone for the rest of his days.

It was happy hour on a recent afternoon in a popular
restaurant in Valley Ranch, the Dallas suburb that has the
Cowboys' ultramodern practice facility and offices as its hub.
Johnson was having a beer with Rhonda Rookmaaker, his
girlfriend, but even more, "my buddy," he says. She's clever,
and their relationship is largely a merry duel of wits and one-
liners. They live three blocks apart, in a posh development
about a Troy Aikman–to–Michael Irvin bomb from the Cowboys' training complex.

Yeah, Jimmy Johnson's got it like probably a lot of middle-
aged American guys would love to have it. Some guys go
through the mid-life crisis. Jimmy is in mid-life bliss. "At least
I'm not criticized for being phony," he says. "I'm just self-
ish." He pours another beer over ice and, acknowledging the
black-hat raps, especially from his days at Miami, where he
was perceived as the leader of a band of renegade players,
says, "I'm not a bad man."

That, it is pointed out to Johnson, makes him sound like
the Wizard of Oz. When Dorothy pulled back the curtain,
found a mere man there and said, "You're a bad, bad man,"
he replied, "I'm a very good man. I'm just not a very good
wizard."

Johnson is amused by the analogy. "I won't even go so far
as to tell you I'm a good man," he says. "But I *am* a pretty
good wizard."

Earlier that afternoon, at the first day of minicamp, Johnson
had spotted his Tin Man. ("Poor son of a bitch," Johnson
says of the movie character, "didn't even know he had a heart
till somebody told him. That's my job.") Rookie cornerback
Clayton Holmes, a third-round draft choice out of little Car-
son-Newman College, was walking meekly off the Cowboy
practice field, obviously awed by his surroundings. "Hey,
Clayton, I saw you doing some really good things out there,"
said Johnson, out of the blue, from his seat on a bench near
the locker-room entrance. Holmes looked up, surprised that
Johnson even knew his name.

"Got a lot to learn, Coach," said Holmes.

"We think you can play here. We like you."

Well, you should have seen Holmes's face.

"Now," Johnson asks at happy hour, "how was he going to know he really can make this team unless somebody told him?"

Push enough buttons, and a pretty good wizard can go from 1–15 in his rookie season in the NFL to 7–9 and Coach of Year the next season. Push a few more buttons, and the following year he goes 11–5, delivering on a preseason promise to Cowboy fans that Dallas would make the playoffs in 1991. Now Johnson is the toast of Texas, and "the people who were so ugly before, now they're licking his shoes, and you just want to go *uh!*" says Rhonda, pretending to smack someone across the face.

Tony Wise, the Cowboy offensive line coach, and Johnson go way back; they hooked up as assistants at Pitt in 1977 and have worked together almost every year since. Still, every few weeks, Wise comes up feeling like the Scarecrow did at the end of *The Wizard of Oz*. "Jimmy doesn't get in drills, and so many people have viewed that as a real chink in his armor—that he lets his people work," says Wise. "But he's fantastic at coming by, dropping hints, getting me thinking. Two weeks later I'll say, 'Jeez, Jimmy, I think we ought to do such-and-such.' And he'll say, 'That's a hell of an idea, Tony.'"

"Jimmy is a very shrewd man," says Irvin, who has played for Johnson in both Miami and Dallas and is the Lion of sorts in this scenario. "He'll make you do some things you don't want to do, and you *know* you don't want to do them, but for some reason you'll do them and enjoy it."

Irvin, who had an All-Pro season in 1991 with an NFC-high 93 receptions, was perceived at Miami as the quintessential Hurricane hot dog, who, among other things, ran right up into the Orange Bowl bleachers after a touchdown catch. Johnson was regarded as the guy who turned those hot dogs and other assorted hell-raisers loose on the rest of the country. The Miami players really stirred things up before the 1986 national championship game, in the Fiesta Bowl against clean-cut Penn State. Some Hurricane players wore camouflage fatigues as they deplaned in Tempe, Ariz.; all of them walked out of a steak fry honoring both teams; and during pregame warmups some Miami players swore at Penn State players and coaches. When Penn State coach Joe Paterno's "good kids" won the game 14–10, Middle America cheered.

Johnson cuts to the bottom line when he talks of the resentment that built up against his Miami teams. "We had a lot of black players out front," he says. "I think a lot of the resentment came that way. The black players knew that, and the black players knew how I felt. I don't know that there was racism involved in the resentment, but there was some ignorance involved—people who have had few dealings with other ethnic groups. I mean real relationships, not getting somebody to clean you house."

Does Johnson genuinely have such a great rapport with his players? "With the blacks? Yes!" says Irvin. "He'll sit there and listen—I mean, really listen. You know he's in your corner, no matter how the media caves in on you. It takes the load off. Then when you go on the field and the man says, 'I want you to run down there, catch that ball and run into that wall,' who are you to say no? You say, 'O.K., Coach, you were there for me, and now I'm going to give it up for you.' And you run into the wall."

At Miami, Johnson was "such a father," says Irvin. "We'd have these Thursday-night meetings where he would go around the room to each individual, and you had to tell him what you planned on doing in 10 years. He wouldn't let you say football. And you had to tell him what you were doing toward that goal.

"Now it's just football," Irvin says of the relationship between coach and player in the NFL. "I know he loves football, but I think he misses being that fatherly figure to so many kids."

"I don't want to lose the feeling I have for players," says Johnson, "but the pro system almost causes you to be cold and insensitive, when you have to release players yearly."

But the tough personnel moves that have to be made in the NFL also offer Johnson an opportunity to work his wizardry. And never has he been more of a wiz than when he instigated the famous Herschel Walker deal in October 1989. While jogging with his assistants during a lunch break, "Jimmy was talking about what we could do to get this thing turned quicker," says defensive coordinator Dave Wannstedt, who also hooked up with Johnson for the first time at Pitt. "What did we have of value on the club?"

The answer was easy: Walker, who rushed for 1,514 yards and caught 53 passes for 505 yards the year before, was the only Pro Bowl player Dallas had left. But Johnson doesn't believe in building an offense around one player. Besides, he sensed something in Walker. "Jimmy's into all that psychology baloney," says Wise, forgetting how well it works on Wise himself. "Jimmy said, 'I'm concerned about whether Herschel's heart is in it for the long run.'" And so to the shock of his assistants running beside him, Johnson decided he would try to deal Walker for a package of players and draft picks.

To their everlasting regret, the Minnesota Vikings made the trade Johnson dreamed up on that run. In return for Walker, Dallas got five players and seven high draft choices, two of which were first-round picks the Cowboys used to trade up so they could draft Emmitt Smith, the NFL's top rusher in 1991, and Russell Maryland, who became a starter at defensive tackle last season.

In all Johnson has made 44 trades since coming to the Cowboys, mostly wheeling and dealing draft picks to accelerate his rebuilding program. In the 1991 draft the Cowboys had seven picks of their own plus 10 picks acquired in trades with 10 other teams, for a total of 17 players drafted in 12 rounds. Johnson makes those picks pay off by joining his staff in probing college campuses for prospects. Johnson believes he and his coaches, as well as scouts, have to size up a prospect themselves, and when Johnson drafts the player, he turns him over to the assistants so they can do their jobs. "He truly gives responsibility," says Wannstedt, "but he expects results." That goes for practice as well as for games. Wannstedt runs the defense, Norv Turner the offense. Johnson takes in the big picture and the tiniest nuances.

"He was probably one of the most underrated coaches in the country when he was at Miami, but he wasn't there long enough for people to realize how good he was," says Florida State coach Bobby Bowden, whose team lost four times in five games against Miami while Johnson was the Hurricanes' coach. "I called him a defensive genius after they beat us 31–0 [in 1988]. I guess I always had a lot of secret respect for him."

SCAR HEAD   By the vacant lot where the Johnson house once stood runs DeQueen Boulevard, in Port Arthur's old middle ground. The boulevard has a grass median, 10 yards wide. "We'd play tackle football there—no helmets, no pads, with some local kids, the black kids," says Johnson. "I mean, we'd have some knock-down-drag-outs. I've got scars on my head because when you got knocked out-of-bounds you'd go into the street. They were guys I hung around with. Baby Joe and I.E."

C.W. and Allene Johnson and their first son, Wayne, moved from Clarksville, Ark., to Port Arthur in 1942, the year before Jimmy was born. The Johnsons moved into the house on DeQueen Boulevard in 1949, when C.W. left his job as an oil-refinery mechanic to become a supervisor at a local dairy. "It was a company house," says C.W., who could walk right out the back door to the dairy.

At the elementary school for white children, Jimmy's best friend was Jimmy (Max) Maxfield, who dubbed him Scar Head. In junior high Scar Head and Max became partners in a successful "tour" business. Smooth operators, they had gained entrée to several of the better bordellos, whose keepers wouldn't let them partake of the hired help or allow them to drink but thought they were cute and let them look around. "So Jimmy and I would charge other kids 25 cents to take them in for a look at these evil places," says Maxfield, now a pharmacist in Houston. "The whores walked around in little nighties, and they'd come sit on your lap and the kids would go nuts. They were happy to pay the 25 cents for our little tour."

The quarters came rolling in for a few weeks, until one night Scar Head and Max were bringing in a tour group and never made it to the front door. Across the street, on the hood of a car sat C.W., who had suspected what they were up to and followed them. C.W. wasn't the kind of daddy to use the belt. Just the sight of him and a word would do. "I just said, 'Let's see how fast you boys can get out of here and get home," C.W. says.

Still, C.W. wasn't always so wise to his youngest son's shenanigans. Once when Wayne was nine and Jimmy was six, C.W. caught them smoking in a movie theater. He took them home, gave each one a big cigar "and made us light 'em up," says Wayne. "Now Jimmy knew how to smoke just as much as I did. But when Jimmy lit his cigar, he started blowing the smoke out of the end, rather than drawing on it. Daddy said, 'Aw, Jimmy, you don't even know how to smoke. Wayne put you up to it.' Daddy made me smoke both of 'em, and I got sick. And Jimmy was lying in bed laughing. He knew what he'd done."

Jimmy had his parents fooled into thinking he wasn't a drinker in high school, until the night he forearmed one too many cars. At the time the forearm was the most feared weapon in high school football in the South, and Jimmy would practice his technique on parked cars. "Jimmy would forearm a car once every couple of weeks, just to keep his hand in," says Maxfield. "I once saw him forearm a '56 Chevy—the model that had the big 'V' under 'Chevrolet' on the trunk—and he forearmed it so hard the 'V' flew off, all the way across the street in the air."

But one night, "for some reason this girl kind of infuriated me," Jimmy recalls. "I'd had too much to drink. I went *foom!* and bashed in her door. She was so upset."

Jimmy went home to bed, but then the girl's father phoned. "When Jimmy came to the phone, he said, 'Hello,' and then 'aaagghh,' like he was going to throw up," says Allene. "That was when I knew he'd been drinking. I just sat down and cried."

Wayne, who hadn't even seen Jimmy earlier that evening, walked in on the commotion. "I said, 'I know the girl. I'll take care of it,'" says Wayne. "And Daddy turned and said, 'Oh, *you're* the one.'"

"Jimmy had convinced us that Wayne had made him drunk," says C.W.

"I never blamed Wayne," says Jimmy. "I don't lie. They *assumed* it was Wayne's fault, because there were very few times I was ever bad."

"Jimmy was a con artist. Probably still is," says Wayne, without malice. Now a refinery maintenance foreman in Baytown, Texas, Wayne speaks of his little brother with pride.

C.W. doesn't recall exactly what Jimmy's IQ test score was but says that "160 rings a bell." Jimmy made good grades and played his heart out as a guard and linebacker for Buckshot Underwood, an old buddy of Bear Bryant's, at Jefferson High. Once, in a game, "Jimmy was running downfield and pointed to his mouth and hollered that he'd got a tooth knocked out," says C.W. "Buckshot hollered back, 'Keep goin'! We'll get you a new one!'"

Maxfield thought Scar Head's speed and strength came naturally, but C.W. says that "all one summer, while he was working for me at the dairy, he wore lead weights around his ankles." Most of the Southwest Conference schools plus Alabama joined the chase for the squat-bodied kid with the shocking quickness and the ferocious forearm. But his parents were Arkansas folks still, and Jimmy went where he knew their hearts were.

JIMMY JUMPUP On the practice field at Arkansas, a few teammates called Johnson, a 5' 11", 195-pound noseguard, Jimmy Jumpup because "when he'd get knocked down, he'd be up so fast," says Jerry Jones, a Razorback guard who would not forget that trait in Johnson. Jones would go on to become an oil and gas wildcatter, which is as pure a high-stakes gambler as you'll find in business. Nobody plays hunches harder than a wildcatter looking for a lock, a hole card, a secret advantage in searching out oil deposits. Nobody is better at keeping his edge to himself until the right moment. It turned out that Jones was pretty good at it, and he became a multimillionaire by the mid-1970s.

When Jones bought the Cowboys in 1989, he promptly fired Landry and played his hole card by hiring Johnson away from Miami. And he caught hell from the Texas media for buying a plaything for his old Arkansas roommate to coach. Says Jones, "To think that I would spend $140-something million—everything I'd ever worked for—and make a decision based on a friendship, is unfair to Jimmy, and it demeans me." What he had done was to keep track of Jimmy Jumpup through the years, the way a big investor tracks a promising little company.

In truth Johnson and Jones were paired in a hotel room on Friday nights before Arkansas road games, but that was about the extent of their rooming together. Both married as undergraduates and lived off campus. And they weren't nearly as chummy as they have been made out to have been. "We haven't done half a dozen things socially since we've known each other," says Johnson, who was a year behind Jones at Arkansas. And neither ever thought the other would wind up in football after college. Johnson, a psychology major, meant to take his people skills into business, as an industrial psychologist.

Johnson became a coach almost by accident. Coach Frank Broyles's Razorback staff often played host to groups of small college and high school coaches in miniclinics. Johnson so thoroughly comprehended the Hogs' defensive scheme—the whole thing, not just the linemen's assignments—that the Arkansas coaches would send him to the chalkboard to lecture. Louisiana Tech's staff was so impressed with him during one such visit that in 1965, when Tech's defensive coach had to sit out a season to recover from a heart attack, they talked Johnson, who graduated that year with a 3.2 average, into taking the post temporarily.

By the end of the 1965 season Johnson was hooked. But then he got knocked flat. In '66, Bill Peterson interviewed him for a job at Florida State, "but at the last minute," says Johnson, "he hired someone else." Jimmy jumped up, loaded Linda Kay and Brent and their belongings into a U-Haul, and went off to Picayune, Miss., to take a high school assistant's job. Because he didn't have teaching credentials, he had to monitor study hall. That's how badly he wanted to coach.

From there he plodded the assistant coach's trail from Wichita State to Iowa State to Oklahoma and back to Arkansas to work for Broyles, and there he got knocked down harder than he ever had. In 1976, Broyles decided to retire and "told the staff that he was going to make me head coach," says Johnson. But the last half of the season went badly, and Broyles, who was also the Razorbacks' athletic director, decided he needed a high-profile replacement. He hired Lou Holtz, who had been fired by the New York Jets with one game left in the '76 season.

Johnson was crushed. Jones, who was by then a prominent alumnus, could have lobbied Broyles on Johnson's behalf, but he didn't. Jones wasn't ready to invest in this promising property just yet. (Johnson now says that at age 33 he wasn't ready to be a head coach.) But Jones kept an eye on Johnson, who jumped up again and went to Pitt as Jackie Sherrill's assistant head coach.

Then, three years later, Jones made a personal investment in Johnson. An associate of Jones's in Oklahoma City, Kevin Leonard, was on the Oklahoma State selection committee that was looking for a new coach after the 1978 season. It was not a plum job, because the school was on NCAA probation and was facing additional sanctions pending the result of a new investigation. Moreover, the Oklahoma State coach had to recruit against titanic Oklahoma, then coached by Barry Switzer. The selection committee contacted Grant Teaff of Baylor, Hayden Fry of North Texas State and others, but Jones told Leonard, "The guy you ought to call is Jimmy Johnson."

Johnson took the Oklahoma State job mainly for the prestige that would come with proving himself in the Big Eight. Starting with about 50 scholarship players, as he recalls, because of probation limitations, he solicited walk-ons, patched together a team and won seven games in his first year. "It gave us some credibility," he says. But it wasn't that easy. His next three teams went 4–7, 7–5 and 4-5-2.

By 1983, after Oklahoma State had gone 8–4 and Johnson had signed blue-chip Texas high school running back Thurman Thomas, the program had turned a corner. Also in '83, Schnellenberger won the national championship at Miami and then left for the ill-fated USFL. The Hurricanes' athletic director, Sam Jankovich, went head-hunting at a coaches' convention and called Johnson aside for advice on some other coaches. Johnson said, "I wouldn't mind living on the beach, Sam."

It was more like hitting the beach. He walked into gale-force hostility from the media and the public, which resented Miami's hiring a country boy from a school that fell short of being a football power. And worse, he met resentment from Schnellenberger's old staff, which he was required to keep for one year. With the coaches divided, Miami went 8–5 in 1984 and lost its last three games notoriously: The Hurricanes led Maryland 31–0 at the half and fell 42–40 when the Terps staged what was then the biggest comeback in NCAA history; next they were beaten by Boston College 47–45 on Doug Flutie's famous Hail Mary pass; and finally they lost to UCLA 39–37 in the Fiesta Bowl.

After the season Johnson began to revamp his staff, hiring Wise and, later, Wannstedt, and Miami went 44–4 the next four years. Then the Cowboys came up for sale, and Jones finally played his hole card. "This was heart surgery for me," Jones says of buying the foundering pro team, "and I wanted to find the best heart surgeon." Friendship was a factor in hiring Johnson, but only in that Jones planned to be a hands-on owner. "I knew we could get back-to-back and work together," Jones says.

But mainly, Jones adds, "Jimmy was brought here because he'd been through adverse situations and jumped up and handled them. When we finished our first year together, I knew I'd made the right decision. I saw something during that 1–15 season that I couldn't have seen if we'd gone to the playoffs or walked into a honeymoon in Dallas."

SOLITARY MAN   Visitors to Johnson's big house in Valley Ranch have to stay on the balls of their feet, with their knees slightly bent, to keep up with him. His fist move is to check on his aquariums. "See that spotted brown one right there?" he says. "He eats a lot of fish. He's going to go hide now. He's shy. That's a marine beta. Here's another anemone, and there's a clown in there. Look at this damn thing hiding in there, 'cause these other tomato clowns will get after his ass." Johnson is partial to the tomato clowns, ferocious little defensive linemen. All-out rushers.

"And over here ... I put these pencil urchins in here to eat some of these algae. There's some tube worms in here, and he [an anemone] was heading over here, and I didn't want him to eat the tube worms, so I picked him up and put him back over there." Coaching. Always coaching.

"And over here ... " This looks like a designed route to the TV room, and if a visitor breaks in that direction right away, he might be able to cover. Don't buy the shoulder fake; Johnson's just picking up a speck off the spotless floor—"my raisin bran from last night"—because he's a neat freak of the first order. "Have you seen this movie?" asks Johnson. "*Terminator II*?" And there is Arnold Schwarzenegger's head, filling the big screen, and the floor and walls begin reverberating when *Bad to the Bone* pours through the sound system. Johnson is intense, waiting for Schwarzenegger to deliver the big hit. There it is: "Breakin' bones!" Johnson says with a gleeful giggle.

TV timeout! As Schwarzenegger kicks butt on the screen, Johnson settles down a bit. "This is kind of my world," he says. "My world is here, and over there." He gestures toward the Cowboys' complex. Both of his sons live in Dallas, and occasionally they come over. "Last Christmas we stopped by and watched football on TV and ate some ribs," says Chad, a stockbroker.

"Any special occasion we go get about a hundred dollars worth of Tony Roma's," says Brent, a lawyer turned short-story writer, "and everybody eats until they're sick."

Just some grown men kicking back together. "I think we're so much closer now than we had been," says Chad. "It's probably because I'm older now, and he can relate a little easier to me."

"I've had some of the best times with them in the last few years," says Jimmy. "We can do things and talk, and it doesn't have to be fatherly advice. It can be as a friend."

At the time Jimmy came to Dallas, Chad was just graduating from college. "The watershed time" in deciding to get a divorce, says Jimmy, "came when Brent and Chad were responsible for themselves. It was a combination of the boys' having grown, and my going into pro football, and my being to the point in my life that I ought to be able to do what the hell I want to do."

"Coming to Dallas, my mom and my dad were both kind of alone and left with each other, and they discovered that it wasn't what it once was," says Brent. The parting "wasn't traumatic, but it wasn't real easy for Mom. For 26 years she hadn't known anything else. I think she just didn't know what she was going to do. But once she figured it out, she was fine."

Last Memorial Day, on the porch of his cabin at Crystal Beach, Texas, Jimmy is looking out to sea, thinking of Linda Kay. He's drinking a beer, and he's gazing toward the southeast, past the offshore oil rigs on the Gulf of Mexico's horizon, in the direction of Venezuela. "It changed her life-style," he says of the parting. "Mine didn't change. I'm still coaching football. Still coming to the beach. Still drinking beer. Still laughing and cutting up with my family. And her whole life was centered around my job. And that's the thing I feel worst about."

Reached by phone in Caracas, Linda Kay says of her new life, "It's kind of wonderful." She teaches fourth grade at an American school for English-speaking children of well-to-do Venezuelans and foreign dignitaries. Now she travels wherever in the world she pleases. Of Jimmy's world, she says, "I don't miss it. When you're in football, you think everybody is interested. When you're out, you realize the circle is really small. You realize there's a group of people who are just as interested in ballet."

"To this day I care for her a lot," says Jimmy. "But I did what I had to do."

"It just happened," says Linda Kay. "I can't tell you why. Or when. I don't recall a discussion." Any resentment on her part? "Absolutely not," she says. "Never. Not from the beginning."

SWEET LI'L OL' BOY Johnson's hair is a mess, whipped every which way by the stiff winds blowing into Uncle Billy Sharp's yard at Crystal Beach. A family party—the Johnsons call get-togethers like this "cuttin' up"—is well into its third day, but there are still mounds of crayfish, pots of gumbo, pans of boudin and three brands of beer to be consumed. Jimmy is cuttin' up, telling loud stories, laughing louder, teasing his mama and daddy about how that li'l ol' dog of theirs will probably die any day now. C.W. and Allene don't drink, but otherwise they're right in the middle of the cuttin' up. Allene figures the ratio of dog-to-human years and says,

"Well, Jimmy, when you get to be 119, you'll probably teeter and totter a little bit, too."

"Mama, if I get to be 50, I'm going to be extremely happy,' says Jimmy. "And if I get to be 52 or 53, I'm going to be *ecstatic*!' He chuckles, but nobody else does. They know the strain of his work, know of his drive.

Uncle Billy brings the moment back from the brink of seriousness, "You can't kill these Johnsons," he says of his sister's family. "His bloodline'll take him to 90 at least. And when they get to be 110 you have to take a 20-pound hammer and beat their liver to death. Then you bury them, and you can still see the ground above them moving."

Jimmy so rarely comes home to the Gulf shore. Maybe once a year. He never remembers birthdays—"I'm not really sure when Mother and Daddy's birthdays are," he admits—and his Mother's Day, Father's Day and Christmas phone calls might come days after the holiday. He doesn't send Christmas presents.

Last year, a few days after his mother's birthday, she found a big box sitting on her porch. "I thought, Oh, Jimmy's remembered my birthday," she says. "I opened it, and there were power tools." Jimmy's TV show in Dallas was sponsored by a hardware chain, which had given him gift certificates. It was only a coincidence that he had sent the tools around the time of her birthday. "I called him and thanked him for my 'birthday present,' " says Allene. "Later, he did send me a present." She holds out her right hand to show a diamond cluster ring.

"I've been surprised out of the blue a lot of times," says Jimmy's girlfriend, Rhonda. "I appreciate that more."

"I want to do what I want to do, when I want to do it," says Jimmy. Then he takes a serious tone, and he tells the family, "I don't mean to be the way I am, but there's some things I got to do." The others go silent. "And there'll come a time," he says, as tears well in younger sister Lynda's eyes, "when I won't do 'em anymore." It's a promise to his family to come home for good.

"That'll be next year," says Uncle Billy, "when you get to the Super Bowl."

"I might go lie on the beach in five years," says Jimmy.

C.W. Johnson thinks back. "We went to a game in Dallas early in his first year," he says. "Of course, they lost. After the game, Jimmy said, 'Daddy, I don't want you to be hurt. But this year I'd rather you and Mother wouldn't come up here until we start winning. Let me suffer through this alone.'"

"Jimmy," says his mother, "is just a sweet li'l ol' boy." But she knows all about the bad raps. "The week he took the Cowboys' job, a lady from Dallas called our house. She said, 'You can just have him back down there in Port Arthur, because we don't want him in Dallas.' She said, 'They're saying this is going to put Port Arthur on the map. But I want you to know it's going to wipe Port Arthur clear off the map.'"

Port Arthur is still there. "You oughta see my bust in the library," says Jimmy. He sips on his beer and then holds his head up in a mock pose. "I got a bust, right there with Janis Joplin."

"They've got a display case," Rhonda cracks, "with Beat Weeds' panties in it."

"Beat Weeds' panties," Jimmy scoffs. "She never wore any panties." And to raised eyebrows all around, he adds, "From what I *understand*."

MILESTONES

◆ ◆ ◆

The Curtain Falls
on a Long Run

B Y   T E X   M A U L E

THE FOOTBALL WORLD WAS SHOCKED BY THE NEWS IN 1966
THAT JIM BROWN, THE DOMINANT PLAYER IN THE GAME, WAS
CALLING IT QUITS AT THE TENDER AGE OF 30 AND AFTER A
MERE NINE PROFESSIONAL SEASONS. TEX MAULE VISITED HIM
ON THE SET OF THE DIRTY DOZEN TO FIND OUT HIS REASONS.

The Cleveland Browns probably lost the championship of the
Eastern Conference of the National Football League on the
playing fields of Beechwood Park School for Boys near London
last week. That is where Jim Brown, the best running back in
the game for the past nine years, announced his retirement.

Brown was on location for his role as Robert Jefferson in the
movie *The Dirty Dozen*. Dressed in combat fatigues, Brown
called a hurried press conference, read a brief, rather formal
statement during the lunch break at the studio, then answered
questions for a few minutes before returning to the business of
making a movie.

The next day, working outdoors in a stockade, which is the
set for part of the motion picture, Brown was relaxed and
genial as he discussed his decision. He sat slouched in a can-
vas folding chair with his name on the arm and on the back,

while the movie crew worked on shots involving other actors.

"It was the right time to retire," he said thoughtfully. "You should get out at the top. And in the last three years, with Blanton Collier and Art Modell, I have been able to do all the things I wanted to do. Now I want to be able to devote my time to other things."

"Do you want to be an actor?" he was asked.

"I *am* an actor," Brown said irritably. "What does it take before you are an actor? One picture? Ten? Twenty? I have one picture under my belt, and I'm working on this one. I am being paid for it. I belong to the union. What the future holds for me as an actor depends on my producers.

"I've got a lot to learn," he continued, "but I'm working on it. I'm lucky. I've had two real good directors, and directors are everything to me. First Gordy Douglas and now Bob Aldrich. Gentlemen. They do things quiet and easy. And I'm fortunate to be working with what you might term the big boys, starting with Lee Marvin. But I've got a lot of the little things to learn on my own. When you're in a scene with another actor, it's competition, baby. You're competing with him. The oldtimers know all the tricks, and they'll do things to surprise you or take the attention away from you."

The scene was completed and a new one was begun. Brown turned the conversation back to football.

"I think the Browns will be all right," he said. "They may be even better without me because they will have a more diversified attack. Leroy Kelly will get a chance to play more now, and that's all he ever needed. And Ernie Green is a fine back. I'll be in touch all the time. Most of them are my boys, anyways, so I'll know what is going on. I may miss the action on Sunday afternoon, watching and thinking of the things I could be doing, but that's all. It would be different if I were out of touch, but they are my friends, and Mr. Modell and I are still friendly."

Robert Ryan, who plays a colonel in the movie, was on camera now. He is a heavy in this picture, and he delivered a short, ominous speech, which Brown listened to with admiration. "Now what I want to do," he said when it was over, "is spend time with my organization. That's the Negro Industrial and Economic Union. I'm chairman of the board, and John Wooten [an offensive guard for the Browns] is president.

"I got this idea about two years ago," he went on. "After the Pro Bowl Game in Los Angeles. There was a group of young, talented Negroes out there who had started a magazine called *Elegant*. It was a good magazine and a good idea, but they didn't have enough money. They were in debt to the printer, and they needed help. In my travels around the country with the Browns and when I worked for Pepsi-Cola, I ran into that situation a lot. I helped personally whenever I could, but it was too big a project for one man to handle. So I got the idea of forming an organization that would provide financing and technical help for Negroes. We formed our corporation about a year ago."

Brown was very earnest now, and for the first time he disregarded the movie activity going on around him.

"I worked it out with John Daniels, who was the editor of *Elegant*," he said. "Our attorney is Carl Stokes, who ran for mayor of Cleveland and only missed by a couple of thousand votes. But the officers and the executives are mostly athletes like me or Bill Russell or Mudcat Grant, and for a good reason."

A gentle rain began to fall, interrupting the shooting, and Brown got up to move his chair into a shed built as a prop in the stockade. He settled himself on the outskirts of a poker game going on among a group of extras.

"If everything opened up wide tomorrow, that is, if any position in the United States were available to a Negro, it still wouldn't be the end of the dream," he said. "You have to be qualified to fill the position, and that's what we want to do. We want to help the Negro from the beginning, open up schools and maybe even trade schools for the ones who do not want to go to college. The middle-class Negro does not need help, and the guy with a Ph.D. doesn't need it, either. We want to help the ghetto Negro, and we think maybe we can do it, because as athletes we can reach them.

"Look, to the Negro in Harlem the Urban League doesn't mean anything. To the Negro in the ghetto, Whitney Young is a name he hasn't heard. But he has heard of Bill Russell and Mudcat Grant and Jim Brown, and he feels like he knows us.

So he'll trust an organization we're in, and he'll come to us and maybe we can help him. We are sure going to try."

The rain has stopped and from outside an assistant director yelled, "You must all be bloody stone deaf! Will you be quiet? We're shooting!"

When the shooting ended, Brown resumed.

"We're getting cooperation from business men and professional men, and we'll get more," he said. "Arnold Pinkney is a big insurance man in Cleveland. He sold a million dollars worth of insurance himself last year. He's put on four or five guys to train in his business. We will have men who own garages and stores, attorneys, everything—so that when someone comes us to and wants training, we can send him somewhere. And we're working on building up capital so that we'll have money available for Negro businesses, too."

A man put his head in the shed and said, "Forty-five-minute break for lunch." Brown got up and moved slowly toward the dining tent.

Someone asked him about Main Bout, Inc., the closed-circuit television organization that handles Cassius Clay's fights.

"My role with Main Bout is a simple one," Brown said. "I am one of the officers. I own stock, and I am the individual who, more or less, put Main Bout together. Main Bout is not associated with the union, but it is an example of what Negroes should do and of what the union stresses. We have always been the gladiators in the ring, the men who were throwing the punches and getting a pretty good share of the money, but not the share of the money we would get with closed-circuit TV or network TV.

"We were able to get a company together that had both black and white, and it was the first time that black men were involved in that particular phase of the business. If you know anything about closed-circuit TV and that type of thing, you know that when you're talking about a big fight, you're talking three or four million dollars."

As for managing Clay when his contract runs out, Brown said, "That's very flattering, but it's the first I have heard about it. It's not in the plans as far as I know. I like the champ, and he stays with me in my apartment here sometimes, but I never heard anything about managing him. He is a gentleman. He thinks about people's feelings more than almost anyone I know."

Brown walked into the mess tent and sat down at a long table with several other actors. A waiter brought him a dish of turkey, with potatoes and cauliflower. He listened to an argument going on between some American and English actors on the difficulty of playing cricket and agreed he would play on an American side in the vague future. But his mind was still on the union as he left the mess tent.

"One thing you learn in football," he said, "one thing I learned: you must have respect. Liking does not matter, but you must have respect. Once you are on equal footing, then the rest can develop. Once you respect me and I respect you, then we can begin to regard each other as individuals. I don't look at you as white or black but as a man, and the individuality stands out. If liking comes after that, it is because of what you are as a person, and it all starts with respect. That is what we want to give the ghetto Negro—the opportunity to earn respect."

Bobby Phillips, who is one of the Dirty Dozen, walked beside Brown. Phillips was once a defensive back for the Chicago Bears and the Washington Redskins. He is now a good actor and has spent time coaching Brown.

"You looked good," he said to Brown. "Did you see the rushes?"

"No," Jim said. "I was worried about the first part. I didn't like the 'Who?' Made me sound like an owl."

They turned into the stockade, an enclosure about half the size of a football field, with a barbed wire fence surrounding it and three green, wooden structures inside, plus a welter of photographic equipment. Someone tossed Brown a football, and he caught it easily and threw it back.

"I used to get upset watching rushes," he said. "If I didn't like what I had done, I'd stay awake all night worrying about it. But you have to get over that. You have to be a little cocky to be an actor, same way you do to be a football player. When you get up before all these people and go through a scene, you have to feel sure that you are good, or you can't do it at all. And if you are doing a dramatic scene, you may have to do it over and over and bring it up from inside you each time.

Sometimes after I have been working all day on a scene like that, I'm more tired than I would have been if I had played 60 minutes of football."

The ball came back to him, and he threw a wobbly pass to Phillips, who caught it and faked by another actor.

"Come on," Bobby said. "We got a game, Jim. We're playing against John and Stuart."

Brown grinned and ambled across the lot to Phillips. They huddled briefly, then Phillips came out with the ball and snapped it back to Brown. John Cassavetes, another member of the Dozen, rushed the passer, and Stuart Cooper, a tall, thin red-bearded American actor who lives in London, covered Phillips, who slipped in his GI shoes when he tried to make his cut. Brown's pass sailed ingloriously over his head.

They tried again, with Phillips throwing and Brown receiving, and this time Jim ran a short hook and dropped the hard pass from Phillips to hoots from the other actors. The game went on for some 20 minutes before Brown caught a pass that gave his side at least a moral victory.

The cameras were set up again by now, and Brown, most of whose scenes had been shot earlier in the week, returned to his camp chair.

"I could have played longer," he said. "I wanted to play this year, but it was impossible. We're running behind schedule shooting here, for one thing. I want more mental stimulation than I would have playing football. I want to have a hand in the struggle that is taking place in our country, and I have the opportunity to do that now. I might not a year from now."

He sat quietly for a moment, his strong face intent. Earlier, another actor had said that Brown was a formidable competitor in a scene because of an intangible presence, due in part to his size but even more to the strength and dignity in his face. It was apparent now.

Phillips, who had gone off to appear in a brief scene, returned.

"You know a runner who reminded me of you?" he said to Brown. "He didn't look like you, and he wasn't as big, but somehow I thought of him watching you. Ray Nolting."

"Yeah?" said Jimmy, his face brightening. "I don't think I ever saw him, but he must have been close to the ground when he ran. I mean those babies," he said, looking down at his feet. "Most good runners run that way," he went on. "You have to keep your feet close to the ground so you can maneuver. If you lift your legs high and take a long stride, you get in this position and you can't move." He got out of his chair and demonstrated, taking an exaggeratedly long and high stride and keeping obviously off balance.

"Jim Taylor, Lenny Moore, runners like that, they stay close to the ground," he went on. "Lenny looked like he had high knee action, but that was just at the beginning, when he was looking for a hole. Later it was low. The thing you have to learn in the pros is to do what you want to do right now. Say you're running a sweep. Get on out there as fast as you can so you don't get caught by some big tackle busting through. Then when you get on the outside, you float a second to let the guard come out ahead of you. Then you make your move quick again. You do it *ahead* of the guard's block, not after."

He was demonstrating the moves, his powerful body graceful in the familiar patterns.

"You think you might change your mind and go back?" he was asked.

"No," he said, "I quit with regret but no sorrow."

It is possible, of course, that Brown *will* change his mind and that, when the Browns open their season on September 11 at Washington, No. 32, Jimmy Brown, will be in the starting lineup. In fact, some skeptics say it is probable, that Brown is simply getting valuable publicity for his movie. But watching him on location at the Beechwood Park School for Boys outside London, such a possibility seemed very remote.

Vintage Juice
1864 ... and 2003

B Y   R O N   F I M R I T E

IN 1973, O.J. SIMPSON HAD AS FINE A SEASON AS ANY RUNNING BACK IN FOOTBALL HISTORY, BECOMING THE FIRST BACK TO TOP THE 2,000-YARD MARK IN A SINGLE YEAR, AND THE ONLY MAN EVER TO DO SO IN THE OLD 14-GAME SEASON. RON FIMRITE WAS THERE TO RECORD THE MOMENT.

"Hey, man," a Shea Stadium functionary confided to a Buffalo Bill on the sidelines at last Sunday's Bills-Jets game, "the Juice still needs three yards."

"Four," said the Bill, brushing aside the impertinence.

On the next play, with four minutes and 26 seconds remaining in the first quarter, O.J. Simpson gratefully accepted blocks from the left side of his line and churned through the snow for six yards to break Jim Brown's 10-year-old National Football League single season rushing record of 1,863 yards. As befits an occasion of such historic moment, Referee Bob Frederic stopped the game and ceremoniously returned to Simpson the ball he had carried seconds before, whereupon the Juice toted it to the sidelines for safekeeping while most of the 47,740 fans rose to applaud.

Simpson's teammates seemed curiously unmoved, however.

They dutifully clapped him on the shoulder pads and noisily extolled him "Way to go, Juice"—but there was little pizzazz in the celebration. It was obvious then that they were looking beyond this achievement to others just ahead.

"More, Juice, more," they chanted as Simpson jogged back to the huddle in his lazy-dog style. "Let's get more."

There was much more. And when, with 5:56 remaining in the game, Simpson burst over left guard for seven yards to the New York 13-yard line, the Bills stormed onto the field and hoisted him to their shoulders in a scene reminiscent of an old Jack Oakie picture. For now the Juice had done it: he had surpassed a hitherto unthinkable distance— 2,000 yards—and he had triumphantly closed out a season unparalleled in the history of professional football. There was no need for more.

In this game alone, Simpson had exceeded the legendary Jim Brown's records not only for yardage gained, but for most carries in a season. He surpassed Brown's 305 carries on the same play he surpassed his 1,863 yards and he finished the season with 332 attempts, an average of nearly 24 a game. He had gained 200 yards for the second game in succession and for the third time in a season, both records, and he had enabled the once derided Bills to become the game's first 3,000-yard rushing team, replacing last year's Miami Dolphins as the NFL's alltime top rushers. Earlier in the year he had set two other records by running for 250 yards against New England and by carrying the ball 39 times against Kansas City. Preeminently, though, he became pro football's first 2,000-yard man, a 2,003-yard man, in fact, when statistics were revised after the game that, incidentally, the Bills won 34–14 to close out the season with a 9-5 record, their best in seven years.

What is perhaps most remarkable about Simpson's record spree is that it was made possible by two games played on fields of such Siberian frigidity they were fit only for eluding wolves. It snowed throughout the game the previous Sunday at Buffalo when Simpson gained 219 yards against New England and, if anything, it was snowing even more fiercely in New York City last Sunday when he gained 200 yards. While teammates and foes alike were battling futilely to gain

purchase on the frozen tundra, Simpson, a native San Francis-
can who played for USC in the tarnished sunlight of Los
Angeles, traversed the snowscape as swiftly and as surely as
an avenging Cossack.

The Juice is really more than a record-breaking record
breaker; he is a swashbuckling runner who calls to mind the
derring-do of Hugh McElhenny, Jon Arnett, Willie Galimore
and Gale Sayers. The 228-pound Brown, who retired in 1966
after nine seasons with the Cleveland Browns to pursue cinematic immortality, was a punishing runner with breakaway
speed. Simpson, while no wraith at 212, is the sort of escape
artist beloved by fans.

"O.J. senses tacklers," says Houston Oiler Linebacker Dick
Cunningham, a former teammate. "He makes cuts that are
uncanny. It's almost like the guy coming up behind him is
yelling, 'Here I come. You better go the other way.' "

Or perhaps he is, as Hall-of-Famer McElhenny once saw
himself, "like a little kid walking down the middle of the
street after a scary movie. He can't see anything in those
shadows, but he knows something's there that he'd better get
away from."

Simpson admits to such sensitivity. No matter how low
the temperatures—and they can be cruelly low in Buffalo—
he always wears short-sleeved jerseys, exposing bare arms.
"I can feel the tacklers better that way," he says. "I can feel
their touch, and in a football game I just don't want to be
touched. The more I feel that way the better the game I
play."

He is hardly an untouchable socially. In contrast to the frequently surly Brown, he is relentlessly congenial. And, if that
were not enough, he also seems genuinely humble.

The Jet publicity people, anticipating the record onslaught,
had set aside a special interview room for Simpson after Sunday's game, where he could preside with Kissingerian imperi-
ousness over the press corps. Simpson entered this chamber
with his entire offensive team in tow. "These," quoth he,
"are the cats who did the job all year long." And he introduced them all—Wide Receiver J.D. Hill; Flanker Bob Chan-
dler; Tight End Paul Seymour; Tackles Dave Foley and Don
Green; Guards Reggie McKenzie ("My main man") and Joe

DeLamielleure; Center Mike Montler; Quarterback Joe Ferguson and Fullback Jim Braxton.

"O.J. gives credit where credit is due," said Ferguson, a
rookie whose unfamiliarity with NFL defenses hampered the
Bills' passing game, permitting opponents to stack their
defenses, albeit unsuccessfully, against the Juice's flow. "He's
helped me on the field and off. Nobody here is jealous of
him. He hasn't got an enemy in the world. All of us wanted
to see him get the yardage."

"A record is a collective thing, anyway," says McKenzie,
echoing the sentiments of the runner he blocks for. "I'm just
thankful to be on the offensive line that broke Jim Brown's
record."

Simpson himself is not convinced the record is etched in
granite. When asked after the game if he thought 2,003 yards
would last, he commented quickly, "No, someone will come
along and break it, but I hope to stay in the league until
these guys [his offensive line] get so old no young back can
get behind them to break my record."

The pressure of record-breaking may have reached him this
past week. He refused to accept telephone calls at his New
York hotel and protested mildly when photographers hounded him during the game. "Look, man, I can't do that here.
C'mon now, no pictures now."

Throughout the season, O.J. had fought to banish the accu-
mulating figures from his mind, even to banish the thought
of Jim Brown. There is a peril, he discovered, in keeping
tabs on oneself.

"If you think about how much you're gaining," he said
recently, "you're not thinking about winning the game. Actually, people are always asking me what I'm thinking about
when I'm running. The answer is nothing. Or at least it used
to be. But when you get close to a record, you think to
yourself, 'If I'm this close, I might as well get it.'

"But I still try not to keep track. Once during a game I
heard the guy on the P.A. system announce that 'O.J. Simpson has such and such yards.' It scared me. I went down to
the end of the bench and just batted myself in the ears, trying to get it all out of my head. Football is a team game. You
can't be thinking about these other things."

It is unlikely,, however, that "these other things" escaped Simpson's attention last Sunday. They were definitely on the minds of his teammates, who continually exhorted each other in the bitter cold to "open it up, open it up for the Juice."

Simpson steadfastly avoided such chatter. Huddled in his parka, he sat mostly in solitude on the bench, occasionally exchanging views on blocking assignments with Braxton or Hill, avoiding always the obvious.

But even he gave way to the occasion when Ferguson leaped high after first examining the yard markers to make certain that his friend and teammate had exceeded 2,000 yards. Hoisted aloft by his pals, Simpson raised his left fist in triumph. It was over, and he was through for the day and for the season.

There were no characteristic Simpson long-gainers in this game, his lengthiest run being a 30-yarder on the second play from scrimmage. The nearest he came to bursting free was on a patented sweep of right end in the third quarter. He seemed to be on his way down the snow-packed sideline when he was finally hemmed in by the Jet secondary after a 25-yard gain. It was one of three runs he had during the day of more than 20 yards. Against New England the week before, he had broken loose on a magnificent, snow-churning 71-yard dash. This day he was more workmanlike, more Brownlike.

There are similarities between the game's two supreme rushers. Simpson wears Brown's number, 32, and, like the older man, aspires to a show-business career when his playing days are over.

"Actors have an air about them that athletes don't have," O.J. said the other day, looking decidedly untheatrical in his USC warmup jacket. "You know how people look at Jim. He's that tough guy beating up on everybody, throwing women out windows and shooting up all those people in the movies. Really, he's a good guy. But he has a very forceful way about him and people keep their distance. With me, well....

"But it's a real trip being somebody else. I've done a few things in the off-season and I have my broadcasting with ABC television. When I was at SC, I used to work in the studios and I'd watch some of those directors. I think I learned a lot, a lot of technique. I want to play at least two more seasons, until I'm 28. In two more years I'll be financially able to do what I want to do, even if it's nothing. Of course, if we're close to the Big One, I'll want to be there."

Brown, who performed in the pre-Super Bowl era, retired when he still had playing time left, but Simpson insists the actor has never influenced him in anything concerning his affairs. They are friends of a sort, near neighbors in Los Angeles and Simpson occasionally plays basketball at Brown's house. They will talk sports, "although never business," says O.J., "business being football."

Brown is under the impression he first met the man who broke his records when Simpson was an All-America and a Heisman Trophy winner at USC in the late '60s. But Simpson recalls an earlier meeting.

"I really first met him when I was just a kid in San Francisco. It was after a 49er game—I was a big fan of McElhenny and Joe Perry—and a bunch of us had gone across the street from Kezar Stadium to an ice cream parlor where we hung out after games. We were just messing around in there when who should walk in but Mr. Jim Brown himself.

"Well, you know how kids are. We started fooling around, mumbling things, and finally I just walked right up to him and said, 'Mr. Brown, someday I'm going to break all your records, wait and see.' I know it sounds unbelievable now, but I was just kidding around.

"Brown hardly looked at me. He just kind of walked away smiling. Now that we've gotten to know each other, I felt I could ask him if he remembered that time. Naturally, he didn't remember it at all. Why should he? Just some dumb kid."

Mr. Brown might have occasion to remember it now.

Up and Over, to the Record and Beyond

BY RICK TELANDER

WALTER PAYTON HAD BEEN CLOSING IN ON JIM BROWN'S ALL-TIME RUSHING RECORD FOR SEVERAL SEASONS. ALONG THE WAY HIS SKILLS AND THE CLASS WITH WHICH HE CARRIED HIMSELF HAD EARNED THE RESPECT OF FANS AND PEERS ALIKE. IN 1984 RICK TELANDER CHRONICLED HIS CROWNING ACHIEVEMENT.

With 14:11 to go in the third quarter of the Chicago Bears' game with the New Orleans Saints at Soldier Field Sunday, Walter Payton ran past Jim Brown and into a shimmering new realm. He gained six yards on a Toss-28-Weak—the 2-back, Payton, wide left through the 8-hole on the weak side—and thereby increased his career rushing total to 12,317 yards, five more than Brown gained in his nine seasons with the Cleveland Browns. At that instant Payton, in the sixth game of his 10th NFL season, officially became the top runner in the history of pro football.

The record fell on Payton's second carry of the second half, his 17th of the day. The ball was on the Bears' 21, second-and-nine. Chicago was leading 13–7—and would go on to win 20–7—and a gray sky was promising rain. There was nothing special about the call; the Bears have used the play dozens, perhaps hundreds, of times during Payton's career. Payton was the I-back in an I-Right formation, and flanker Dennis McKinnon went in motion from right to left, crossing in front of Payton and fullback Matt Suhey as quarterback Jim McMahon shouted the signals.

At the snap, left tackle Jim Covert and tight end Emery Moorehead blocked down. Left guard Mark Bortz pulled, and he, McKinnon and Suhey led into the hole. Payton skittered along in the backfield, holding the ball like a potato in his right hand, the way he likes to do it, surveying the scene before him. Then he tucked the ball away, squared his shoulders to the line and headed for history.

For weeks Payton had been trying to ignore the pressure building around him. Before the Dallas game the previous week, Payton had been so pumped up with anticipation he'd nearly passed out. "I've never felt like that before," he said. "It sort of scared me. I really couldn't see anybody unless they were two or three feet in front of me."

He'd needed 221 yards in that game to catch Brown, and in the Cowboys' 24-year history only one person had ever run more than 200 yards against them. That was Jim Brown. But there was no betting against Payton. He holds the NFL single-game rushing record of 275 yards, and when he takes off, as teammate Al Harris says, "he runs with a fever." He gained 130 yards on 20 carries in the first half against Dallas, but for some reason was called on to carry the ball only five times in the second half and finished with 155 yards, 67 short of what he needed to surpass Brown.

Gaining 67 yards "isn't like falling off a log," coach Mike Ditka pointed out to the swelling media contingent gathered at the Bears' training camp in Lake Forest on Thursday. "Multiply that times 16 games, and see what you get." What you get is 1,072 yards, a tidy sum. But not for Payton, who has gained more than that in all but two of his pro seasons—his rookie year and strike-shortened 1982.

"The pressure goes with the job," Payton said late in the week. "It's just when I'm driving home and there are two or three guys following me with cameras hanging out their windows, waiting to see if I'll signal when I make a right turn, that it gets tough."

One night during the week, Payton watched a TV highlight

film of the NFL's greatest running backs, and for the first time
in his life he studied the man he was about to pass. "Jim Brown
was big and strong and quick," Payton observed. "And he even
made a one-handed catch. Hey, that's what football's all about."
That and staying healthy, which was one of Brown's attributes
and certainly is one of Payton's. Sunday's game marked Payton's
126th consecutive start for the Bears.

When Payton's transcendent moment arrived, however,
Brown was nowhere in sight. In the last few months, he had
made so much fuss about the manner in which his record was
being approached—about the overall *worthiness* of Payton, Franco
Harris, Earl Campbell, Tony Dorsett, John Riggins—that the
Bears' management felt it would be best if he didn't attend the
game. "We want it to be Walter's day," said club president
Michael McCaskey.

And it was. Payton finished the game with 154 yards rushing
on 32 carries for a grand total of 12,400 yards. It was his fifth
consecutive 100-yard-plus game and the 59th of his career,
which broke another of Brown's records. Payton now holds 21
Bear records and four NFL records, and another five NFL
career marks are within his reach, including most rushing
attempts, most rushing touchdowns and most 1,000-yard rushing
seasons. Moreover, he leads the NFL in rushing this season with
775 yards and is off to the best start of his career, averaging just
over 129 yards per game. At his current pace he'll pass O.J.
Simpson's record of 2,003 yards for a season in the second half
of the Bears' last game, against the Detroit Lions.

"What he's going to do is put the career record so far out
there, that yours truly won't have a chance," says the Cowboys'
Dorsett, who's currently sixth on the alltime list with 8,769
yards and is the man generally considered to have the best
chance of passing Payton someday. And Dorsett is correct. Payton is running wild. He says he's headed for 15,000 yards, and
it's hard to believe he won't get there. "I had my 11,000-mile
tune-up in the off-season [arthroscopic surgery on each knee],
and I feel great," he says. "The way you think is the way you
are. And I think I'm 23."

"He's running as well as he ever has," says Bears veteran Brian
Baschnagel. "He ought to set his goal at 20,000 yards."

Typically, when Payton's moment of glory came, he wanted

the game to continue. He rose from the pile of New Orleans tacklers—linebacker Jim Kovach had hit him first—ready to run again. "We had momentum," Payton would explain later. In the pregame warmup, Payton had told his teammates to forget about his impending record and just win the game. And some of his teammates listened. "It was just a regular sweep," said right guard Kurt Becker. "We weren't thinking anything special."

"I don't even remember what I did on the play," said Covert. "I didn't know it was the record until I saw all the people on the field."

The people, mostly photographers with cameras firing madly, charged Payton in a reckless wave. Seeing the on-slaught, he dashed to the Saints' sideline, where he shook hands with coach Bum Phillips. "He's a perfect gentleman, and I respect him," Payton explained. Then Payton circled deftly away from the mob and cut to the Bears' sideline, where he handed the ball to offensive backfield coach Johnny Roland. Roland tucked it away and carried it to Pete Elliott, the executive director of the NFL Hall of Fame. The ball will go on display at the Hall in Canton, Ohio until the end of the season, at which time Payton will get it back in exchange, says Bears p.r. director Ken Valdiserri, "for Walter's uniform."

Up in a sky box, Payton's support people opened a bottle of champagne and toasted their man. Among them were Payton's wife, Connie, his mother, Alyne, former Bear teammates Roland Harper and Mike Adamle, his former high school coach Charles Boston and his agent Bud Holmes. They're the folks who keep Payton humble, who help him keep his achievements in perspective while so many others are losing theirs. "People say, 'You're married to *him*!' And all I can think to say is, it's no big deal," says Connie, a delightful woman of unfailing candor. "It's like my father said, 'He's lucky to be married to *you*.' "

Holmes, the Mississippi lawyer who helped negotiate the clause that specifies a $100,000 bonus for Payton from the Bears for breaking the rushing record—he'll get a $125,000 midnight-blue, 12-cylinder Lamborghini Countach-S from the Kangaroo Shoe Company, too—is equally low-key. "Hey," Holmes drawled after strolling into the Bears' locker room after the game and finding his client buried under microphones and notepads. "Whatcha been doing today?"

What Payton demonstrated most of all on Sunday is that he's an old-fashioned credit to the game, if that kind of morally atavistic notion still means anything. At a time when so many pro football players seem to be engaged in as many battles in court as they are on the field, here's a man whose chief vice is lighting firecrackers; whose favorite drug may be the cheeseburger; who says, when asked what political party he belongs to, "I'm an American"; who developed his awesome stiff-arm, he says, to keep kids from messing up his clothes while playing sandlot ball back in Columbia, Miss.

Against the Saints he bashed and crawled for every inch he could get, dealing some furious blows en route. On one seven-yard gain in the first quarter, he hit safety Frank Wattelet smack in the chest and knocked the poor man four yards downfield. Just before the half he launched himself into the air, tucked into a cannonball and landed hard in the end zone for the Bears' first touchdown. His style of running isn't glamorous, but it's so honest that even battered opponents come to appreciate it.

"So far, people have never tried to just hurt me, to put me out of the game," he says. "And I guess that's because of the way I play." Indeed, that explains why, when Payton broke the record, even the Saints applauded him.

Boston recalls that even back when he was coaching Payton in high school, Payton's attitude and skill could have a powerful effect on those around him. "When we first integrated around 1970 and combined the black and white school systems in Columbia, I remember we played Prentiss High and beat them 14–6," says Boston. "Walter had the two touchdown for us, one of 65 yards and the other, 95 yards. That did it for integration. Those people in the stands didn't see a black boy running with the ball. What they saw was a Columbia Wildcat."

"I really don't think people realize what a great person Walter is," says Suhey. "He's got a tremendous ego on the field, but he also has a great sense of humor, an ability to say something light at the right time. When I dropped a pass against the Colts, on the way back to the huddle he said to me, 'You can always get a paper route or join the Army.' And he's a good imitator. He does a great Ditka and a great Buckwheat."

After the game, when Payton was handed a telephone and told that President Reagan wanted to talk to him, he took the phone and, without batting an eyelash, said into the receiver, "The check's in the mail." And he was funny, and perhaps a bit truthful, at an earlier press conference when he said he didn't care who broke his record once he retired, "as long as it's my son."

In a way, of course, the humor is a mask. "It's a defense mechanism to relieve pressure on him and the whole team," says Baschnagel. In the past there has been a need for that. The Bears have fielded some pretty bad teams during Payton's career, and often the press has clamored for him to say something critical about his teammates. Sometimes he has, and has been hurt by it. But now the Bears are 4–2, and nothing can really detract from Payton's efforts.

"You cannot overemphasize what he's done," says Dorsett. "You can't make too big a flap about it."

The amazing thing is that athletes usually are in steep decline when they approach career records. That, of course, is the touching part of the chase: the getting used up. Just look at Pete Rose. But Payton is in his prime. Baschnagel even goes so far as to say, "He hasn't reached his peak."

In a way, Brown has clouded Payton's heroic effort somewhat. A remarkable runner, Brown nevertheless chose to stop playing football at a time when he could have continued on for years and possibly established a record so high that Payton would only be passing its midrange just now. Or Brown could have been injured and forced to retire. Who knows what might have happened? Yet somehow the myth has grown that Jim Brown was Superman, that every time he touched the ball he ran for 50 or more yards.

He didn't. In 1957 against Philadelphia he ran 19 times for 28 yards. In 1958 against Washington he ran 11 times for 12 yards. In 1960 against the Giants he carried the ball 11 times for 29 yards. In 1961 against Washington he ran 17 times for 24 yards. In 1962 against Baltimore he ran 14 times for 11 yards. And he had other bad days, too.

Jim Brown was fabulous, but human. He's a proud man, and he sometimes talks about making a comeback, even at age 48, to add to his rushing total. If he starts right now he'll only be 88 yards behind Walter Payton.

He Quit, for
Pete's Sake

B Y   P A U L   Z I M M E R M A N

AS IDENTIFIED WITH HIS SPORT AS ANY COMMISSIONER IN HIS-
TORY, PETE ROZELLE SHEPHERDED HIS GAME THROUGH
GROWTH AND TURMOIL, FINALLY SEEING IT BECOME THE
WILDLY SUCCESSFUL SPECTACLE IT IS TODAY. IN 1989, AFTER 29
YEARS AT THE HELM, HE DECIDED TO STEP DOWN.

With 2¾ years to run on his sentence, Pete Rozelle opted for
parole. For more than 29 years he had been commissioner of
the NFL, the best commissioner in the history of sport, many
people felt. Franchises were selling for $1 million or so when
he took over in 1960. The last one to change hands, the Dallas Cowboys, went for a reported $140 million-plus last
month. Rozelle brought pro football into the living room and
into prime time. He negotiated TV contracts that now guarantee each team close to $17 million a year. He successfully
lobbied Congress for the revenue-sharing plan that made the
owners rich. He gave reporters an endless supply of copy,
always handling his press conferences with style, class and
humor.

Then came the lawsuits, the endless rounds of depositions
and court dates, the lawyers who would get a little publicity

for themselves by attacking the NFL and its commissioner, owners who sued one another and the league (or threatened to), a Management Council that couldn't or wouldn't, make a collective-bargaining agreement with the players. Rozelle's term as commissioner had become a prison sentence. So on a brilliantly sunny day last week in Palm Desert, Calif., he told the world what he had told his wife, Carrie, five months earlier. After 29 years, he had had it. *No más.*

As a 22-year-old student-publicist at the University of San Francisco, he would walk into a newspaper office with an armful of releases and try to hustle up space, any kind of space, for his Dons. Rozelle remained a fan, and he loved nothing better than sitting around swapping stories about Gino Marchetti or Ollie Matson. Then the job wasn't fun anymore. Where's the fun in a lawyer's office or a courtroom?

"I didn't want to die in office like Bert Bell did before me," he said on March 23, the day after he announced his retirement at the NFL spring meetings in Palm Desert. "I'm 63. I can't remember the last time Carrie and I had a real vacation. I've got to get out while I can enjoy some years without stress."

But why the urgency? Why not finish the term that would have ended after the 1991 season? "Because now, in my 60's, I realize that I'm not going to get everything cleared up," he said. "I look back on the 1960s and 1970s as, well, the Eisenhower years compared with the '80s. Sure, we had problems, but nothing compared with what followed. All those days dealing with lawyers—you're playing defense all the time rather than working on anything constructive. My eyes were bloodshot. I wasn't getting enough rest. I looked bad, felt bad. I was smoking two packs of cigarettes a day. I asked myself, Is that all there is to life—work, die and never experience retirement? I wanted at least a few years of leisure without stress."

After enduring three court cases in six years—two involving the Raiders' move to Los Angeles in 1981–82, and then the USFL trial in '86—he looked terrible. The old image of the suave, nicely tanned young man was gone. "Hell, I haven't had enough sun to get a tan since the 1970s," he says. He always looked tired. Sometimes he slurred his words. An

NFL assistant would have to prompt him. How many years could he go on like that?

"What you saw," says Carrie, "was the combination of fatigue plus cigarettes. He says he smoked two packs a day, but during that period it was probably three, maybe even more. He'd devote a whole day to depositions, to attorneys who didn't understand sports or couldn't care less about football. He'd come home at night and go to bed at around 11:30—he always wanted to watch the 11 o'clock news—and two hours later he'd be up, roaming around, smoking one cigarette after another, working things out on a legal pad."

The start of a new season was generally an upper for Rozelle. But when the '88 season began, he faced a daunting stack of problems—the unresolved collective-bargaining agreement, the drug controversies, the growing specter of steroids and even a threat to his authority. Tampa Bay Bucs owner Hugh Culverhouse had gained enormous influence during his 13 years in the league, and he had become the dominant force in the six-member Executive Committee of owners, which oversees the Management Council's dealings with the Players Association. An insurgent group led by Cleveland Browns owner Art Modell was preparing to mount a challenge to Culverhouse's power in an attempt to resolve the impasse with the players. The owners were a house divided.

"It really got to Pete last fall," says Carrie. "It finally reached the point where he was sick and tired of going to the office every day and dealing with problems that couldn't be resolved and trying to keep these people from killing each other off."

So one day in October he decided to quit. He asked Carrie to sit on his decision for five months, until he could tell the owners as a group at their annual meetings. He said he owed it to the people who employed him to tell them before he told anyone else outside the family.

He told his daughter, Anne, and his stepchildren in December. A week before the spring meetings were to begin, on March 14, Rozelle called his longtime friend Wellington Mara, the owner of the Giants, and set up a meeting for the next day in the Manhattan office of Jet owner Leon Hess.

"Leon negotiated my last contract," says Rozelle. "I wanted to work out a consultant's contract this time, should the league want me to stay on in that capacity."

"The meeting was for 10 a.m.," says Mara, "but I got there early. My first thought was that it was something involving the two New York teams. Pete said he wanted to talk to us face-to-face, not over the phone. Then he told us that after 29 years he was leaving. My first reaction was shock, the kind of feeling we've come to expect lately—how many more things can go wrong now? Pete broke down once or twice, but the real sadness of it didn't fully hit me until he told the entire owners' body a week later. That's when I got misty-eyed, along with everyone else."

Rozelle told his staff shortly after noon on March 22, just before the owners went into an executive session. His announcement to the owners took barely more than a minute. He had tears in his eyes when he left the room. Raider owner Al Davis, Rozelle's bitterest foe, shook his hand on the way out and then embraced him. Rozelle went directly to a press conference, which lasted 10 minutes, until someone asked him, "Was it very emotional when you told the owners?" Rozelle broke down.

There was a rush to the pay phones. "No, we don't have enough tape," said a TV man. "How the hell did I know this was coming?"

Mara then spoke to the reporters, saying, as his voice broke, "I believe Pete Rozelle forevermore will be the standard by which all sports commissioners will be judged."

A six-man search committee was formed to pick a successor. Mara, the NFC president, and Kansas City owner Lamar Hunt, his AFC counterpart, are heading it. The rest of the group consists of Modell, Buffalo owner Ralph Wilson, Pittsburgh president Dan Rooney and outgoing Green Bay president Robert Parins. The idea is to find a commissioner by the start of the 1989 season. Rozelle will remain in office until the new man takes over and will serve as a consultant "for as long as he feels I'm needed."

"I'm going to propose something I've thought about for some time," says Modell. "Divide the areas. First, get rid of the Management Council, which has been totally ineffective, and appoint a league man to deal with labor-management concerns. He'll be the owners' representative. Hire someone else to deal with the game itself, the integrity of the game, drugs, steroids, whatever. A Whizzer White type. It's too much to ask of one person to do everything. We shouldn't have asked that of Pete."

"You need a litigation specialist to take that kind of pressure off the office of commissioner," says Bob Wallace, counsel to the Cardinals. "Then I think you need two league presidents who are really presidents, as they are in baseball, not just club owners who happen to have the title, as in the NFL."

"It should be like a president and his cabinet," says San Francisco general manager and former coach Bill Walsh, "with the areas divided, but one chief executive who's clearly in charge."

Dividing the commissioner's duties among two or more executives makes sense. The NFL is a far different league from the one the 33-year-old Rozelle captivated in 1960. One man shouldn't have to deal with the conduct of the game itself and its finances and its litigation, which will start again when the Players Association's antitrust suit goes to trial in November.

Walsh was one of the people mentioned early as a possible commissioner, however the job is defined. "That's clearly speculative," he said. "There will be hundreds of names brought up, every day a different one."

The name mentioned longest and loudest last week was that of former AFL quarterback Jack Kemp, who is now secretary of Housing and Urban Development. He quickly stated that he was "happy in his job." A year ago he had said he would welcome being commissioner.

Only one current NFL executive has ever been a league commissioner. Davis briefly headed the AFL before the 1966 merger with the NFL. He is well versed in all football matters, including litigation. He successfully sued the NFL and was a witness for the USFL in its suit against the league. Some team executives said privately that he would make a terrific commissioner, but it is hard to imagine the owners going for someone who played a leading role in causing Rozelle's resignation.

What will be Rozelle's legacy? Solvency, certainly. And parity. He envisioned a league in which the rich would never gobble up the poor, in which football would be decided on the field instead of in the bank. And public awareness. No one ever promoted a sport more effectively.

But decency was always there, too. Rozelle loved the game, and he shepherded it through the 29 most dramatic years of its history. He chose to leave it before it destroyed him.

THEY ALSO SERVE

◆ ◆ ◆

The Scout Is a
Lonely Hunter

BY   GEORGE   PLIMPTON

FAR FROM THE GLARE OF THE SPOTLIGHT, AN UNSUNG CREW
OF WEARY WANDERERS LABORS TO FIND THE PLAYERS THAT
POPULATE THE PROFESSIONAL GAME. IN 1976 GEORGE PLIMPTON
DID SOME BIRD-DOGGING OF HIS OWN AND RETURNED WITH
THIS MEMORABLE PIECE ON THE LIFE OF A SCOUT.

The scout had good reason to be tired. He had been on the
road for almost four months. He had called on almost 50 colleges. He had "visited"—which is the best way to describe it—
with a couple of hundred coaches, and he had seen, by his
own reckoning, about 35 miles of football film, some of it of
such murky quality that the action seemed to be going on in
the depths of a fishpond. He stretched his legs out in front of
him. What was going to be the best thing, he said, was getting
into a different set of clothes, and especially putting the attaché
case with all its scouting paraphernalia in the back of the closet
where perhaps he could forget about it.

He began talking about the trademarks of his profession—the
cowboy boots, which were sensible because they could be
buffed up a bit and worn in a motel breakfast room and yet
were fine for standing along the sidelines of a practice field in

bad weather. Most of them came from Tony Lama's in El Paso, the scout said, because the proprietor takes as much as 60% off the price of boots if a scout visits with him and talks football. Leather, that was the other sartorial telltale—soft buckskin jackets, and suede, and often stiff new leather pants that creaked when the scout walked through the motel parking lot to his car. At the practice field he often wore a stopwatch hanging on a lanyard around his neck. That marked him, unless he was a track coach dawdling on his way to practice. A scout, that magic word; the players on the field would catch sight of him on the sidelines, the helmets turning just briefly. "They really begin to perform," the scout said. "I'm surprised that coaches don't use *dummy* scouts—just stick some cowboy boots, a buckskin jacket and a stopwatch on a janitor and set him out there on the sidelines and point at him. 'Look, everybody, look there, the guy from the Rams!' You'd have yourself some mighty fine practices. Of course, a kid will never let on that he knows a scout's there. But he'll miss a pass in practice, and you can tell by the way he stomps around and looks shocked that he is trying to tell you that it was only an act of God that he missed it. But he knows *we* know."

The scout was asked about the tools of his trade. "Well, in that attaché case you'll find a stopwatch. It's for timing pro prospects in the 40-yard sprints when the colleges have what's called Pro Day in the spring. Scouts put such stock in a guy's speed over the 40 that they'd time a prospect down an airplane aisle just to get a figure written on the performance sheet. And we use the stopwatch for checking the hang-time of punts, how fast a quarterback drops back and how quickly a center can get the ball to his punter." The scout laughed. "We've got to keep our stopwatch fingers in shape," he said. "Not too many beers, because you've got to time that center's snap to an accuracy of a tenth of a second. He's doing O.K. if he gets it back to the kicker in seven-tenths of a second, but he's on the border if it's nine-tenths.

"Now let's see. There's always a tape measure. We are always measuring people. Very important. I carry an architect's plastic drafting angle to use against the wall and get the kid's height exactly right when he's standing up there, because a lot of them will strain to get an extra millimeter or so, tilting their noses back, thinking that's going to heft them up a bit. In fact, it does just the opposite. You have to watch their feet, making sure they don't curl their toes under to push themselves up. Harley Sewell, the old Detroit Lion offensive guard who scouts for the Rams, told me that he always calls out, 'O.K., let's curl those toes up, son.' That stops 'em. But most kids these days are so damn big that you need to climb a ladder to measure them.

"Let's see. Some of us carry the Otis Self-Administering Test, which is a 20-minute exam that you can give a player. It will tell you for sure if you suspect he is an exceedingly slow learner, so that you can prepare for that when he turns up at your training camp and does the 40 in 4.9 and can truly run with the football but can't figure out what he's being told in the huddle.

"Now what else?" The scout pinched the bridge of his nose. "Usually, a scout has a pair of binoculars in his kit, seven power and never the opera type—not correct for scouting along the sidelines. Doesn't look right wearing all that suede and buckskin to be holding a li'l bitty opera glass and looking at some guy who weighs 270 pounds. A tape recorder. Legal pads. Pencils. Sometimes a pocket splicer for patching films. Eye drops. A roll of Scotch tape. That's for splicing broken film if you don't have a splicer—a junior-high splice, some scouts call it, and others, for reasons no one knows, call it an Al Davis splice, after the general manager of the Oakland Raiders. Whichever, the next scout who borrows that film from the athletic department will hear the splice rattle and chatter briefly in the machine before the film breaks, and the guy, with a good bit of cussing, reaches for *his* roll of tape.

"Then, of course, you carry a projector, a 16mm. motion-picture projector with the football club's decal on the carrying case so that when you walk through a motel lobby people will know that you're in football, not the blue-movie business. The projector is probably the most important device the scout has. With it, often in the coaches' conference rooms, but sometimes at the motel, the scout'll look at game films, reels that each college takes from up on the rim of the stadium of every game it plays. Each scout is supposed to see four game films on each prospect, which means that he'll see a player in action well over 100 times, and that's not counting the times that you flip the switch and rerun a play maybe a dozen times to check something out about the kid. And then you see him down on the practice field, maybe in a scrimmage, which is best. You might talk with him, just a few words, or, if he is a senior, you might *visit* with him, which is more of a commitment. You'll be trying to figure his attitude. And then you visit with his coaches. You have to be careful. Most coaches oversell their players. Obviously, they have a natural affection for them and will recommend someone totally unsuitable for the pros because of a great play the kid made in his junior year that may have saved the coach his job."

The scout grinned. "Sometimes the coach's reputation can get you into trouble. I've always been awed by Bear Bryant of Alabama. If he said, just in passing, that so-and-so could play football, well, I'd be inclined to rate the kid high even if what I was looking at weighed 92 pounds, was five feet tall and kept walking into things.

"So you have to make your own determination. Most scouts look for different things. Roosevelt Brown, who scouts for the Giants, looks for what he calls 'constant competitiveness,' never a guy who plays a quarter and loafs a quarter, but athletes like those Selmon brothers at Oklahoma who stay keyed-up high for an entire game. Attitude is a big thing for some scouts. I can remember Will Walls—one of the great oldtime scouts, the Red Grange of scouts some people call him—telling me about Duane Thomas. He saw him for the first time in a spring alumni game at West Texas State. Thomas carried the ball eight times, four for touchdowns, for a total of 210 yards. And yet his attitude was pitiful, wasn't it? Walls could never figure what had happened—maybe somebody promised Thomas something and had not given it to him.

"I myself put a tremendous premium on toughness," the scout said. "Perhaps more than I should, because an emphasis like that might penalize players who could go on to great things. Jimmy Orr, for example. He may have been different in college, but when I saw him he certainly wasn't anyone you would ascribe toughness to—a pussycat—and yet he was one of the best pass-catchers the Colts ever had."

The scout got up and mixed himself a drink. "Toughness isn't that easy to judge. We have these prospects we call 'Tarzan-Janes'—players who look terrific, built like Tarzans, but then after a while it turns out they play like Janes." He grinned. "There's a lot of terms like that ... a whole lingo that's evolved with scouting.

"Let's see. To begin with, everyone's called coach. 'Hey, Coach!' You look around and there's another scout. You shake hands and admire his leather jacket, and when you start talking football, about prospects, you begin talking in this special jargon. You use a lot of initials. 'J.O.P.' That means Jump on the Pile. Very disparaging term. It describes a guy who's never quite in the play and arrives late. 'Aw hell, that guy's just a J.O.P.' Or sometimes he's called a 'Flop-on.' Another one is 'C.O.D.' It stands for Change of Direction. 'The kid's got great C.O.D.' A word you hear a lot is 'quab.' It comes from quickness, agility and balance, which are categories on the Individual Player Form. You come up to a scout and you ask, 'Hey, Harley, how's this kid's quab?'

"The word 'numbers' refers to a guy's height, weight and speed, and you'll hear a scout say, 'I'm going to Boise, Idaho. The boss tells me a guy out there had interesting numbers.'

"Two classes of players that a club wouldn't want to draft are 'tweeners' and 'hammers.' A tweener is a player whose physical characteristics are just off for every position—too small for tackle but too slow for linebacker. And a hammer is a big, strong, ferocious guy who's too slow. If he gets there he really beats up people, but he can't get there.

"If you want to know how competitive a player is, you ask for a 'gut check.' 'Give me a gut check on this guy.' The answer will be that the kid is or is not a *competitor*. That's the biggest word, competitor. The scout will say, 'This kid is looking for something to hit; if it moves, he hits it. My God, I'm telling you this kid is a *competitor*.'

"The other big word is football. It's never 'This kid can run,' or 'This kid can throw.' It's always 'This kid can run with the football,' or 'This kid can throw the football'—just in case [the scout shook his head in wonderment] there was something *else* he might have his hands on. So you always have to specify that he's playing with a football. You get a couple of scouts on the sidelines, and one of them asks, 'Who are you looking at? Are you looking at someone who can play football?'

" 'Number 32.'

" 'Number 32 can't play football. There ain't but two players here who can play football. One of the kids who can play football is Number 8. He can *kick* the football.'

"We talk a lot about a guy's physical characteristics," the scout said. " 'Can he break down?' It means, 'Can a player attain a good hitting position?' If a couple of scouts are standing on the sidelines looking out, one of them will say, 'Big ol' legs. Nice arms, too. What a specimen.' You hear that a great deal, a specimen. 'That specimen's got a good pop—he's as strong as train smoke.'

"There's a lot about feet. There are three categories: good, adequate and no. A scout will look out and say, 'He ain't got no feet at all.'

"There's talk about hands. He's got 'soft hands,' hands like 'boards,' or hands that ought to be 'on a clock.' If a player's hands are good they're referred to as 'claws.' The fact is scouts look so much at a prospect's physique and what he can do with it, that at times we feel like inspectors from the U.S. Department of Agriculture, getting ready to hit a guy with a rubber stamp."

The scout went on to say that the sort of information that emerges from this jargon is carefully filled in on the Individual Player Form, or the Senior Ability Form (the names vary depending on the organization the scout works for), which the scouts mail to the home office. The forms are complex, designed to make available either by analysis or computer evaluation a near-palpable specimen for the home office to consider.

The average scout traveling in his own car will journey more than 12,000 miles during a season. "We check out quite a variety of places," the scout said. "The facilities differ considerably. You might drive up to a place like the University of Tennessee, pass playing fields with yards and yards of artificial turf laid down to practice on and park in the lot behind a gym the size of an ocean liner, with wide corridors hung with near-lifesize photos of its top athletes. There's a statuary of its 1956 SEC champion team, each player carefully sculpted, and the trophy cases, and you can hear the typewriters going like 60 in the athletic department, and the game films are filed, and the scouts can sit in a conference room in comfort and watch their prospects. Or you may arrive at a little college where you park out along a muddy lane and there's nothing much there ... you have to *look* to find the college.

"About the two worst athletic facilities in the East are Harvard University's—that's right—and Maryland-Eastern Shore's, which is a small, mostly black college in Somerset County where the saltwater bays come in from the sea. At Harvard the scouts look at films against a wall at the end of a corridor; there's a window right there without a shade, so that films show up ghostly and pale, as if the players were going at it in a snowstorm. The students, carrying their books, walk through the beam of light from the projector, saying 'Excuse me.' It's best for a scout to go to Harvard when the day is very murky so that the film will show up better on the wall. But the coaches are good to visit. They sit with you and lean forward and point out the work of Dan Jiggetts, who is one of the best linemen in the East. Another who should rate high is Don Macek, the fine center at Boston College.

"At Maryland-Eastern Shore this year there wasn't enough money in the athletic budget to allow the taking of game films. But that doesn't keep the scouts from going out across the wooden bridges that rattle under car tires. There's a strong smell of marsh grass—hell, there are places where the scout can expect to be poled across a tidal basin in a flat-bottomed ferryboat. A guy can hardly get there from *nowhere*. When he does, he stands on the edge of a practice field where the grass isn't cut and it comes up over the players' shoe tops. But the scouts all go because the school traditionally turns out fine football players: Roger Brown, the 300-pounder who played for Detroit, Johnny Sample, Charlie Stukes, Emerson Boozer. This year the school had a bad season, but it had another fine player in Carl Hairston, a big, fast defensive end. The scouts stood in the tall grass and looked at him. A lot of them went down to the Central Florida Classic on Nov. 29 in Orlando to watch him when Maryland-Eastern Shore played Bethune-Cookman. Bethune-Cookman won 67–0. But Hairston was all over the place that game, knocking down the Bethune people despite that terrible score, and that got him good marks in the gut-check department."

The scout reckoned that during the season more than 150 scouts were on the road checking out the colleges. The vast organization committed to scouting is a relatively new process. The scout said that scouting in the modern sense began with the Rams out on the Coast. Until then the coaching staffs did most of the scouting themselves. They went to college games on Friday nights and Saturday afternoons; they relied on what they could gather from talking to college coaches, what they read in the papers and sporting journals, and even on their mail from college alumni. "Because it was such a very low-pressure operation," the scout said, "the clubs made some whopping mistakes when it came time to draft. In the mid-'50s the Cleveland Browns picked a quarterback in the first round, and when he got to training camp the Browns found that he stuttered. That's right. He'd stand in the huddle and the players'd look at him and he'd say, 'Fl ... fl ... fl ... ' trying to say flank right something, and then finally the coaches' whistles began to shrill and they discovered what the problem was, which of course any scouting system would have turned up at the start.

"Until things like that happened, no one thought scouting was necessary. One of the main reasons was that there wasn't much need for players. The team limit for a while in the mid-'30s was only 24.

"But then Eddie Kotal, who had been an assistant coach in the Green Bay organization, was asked to scout full time for the Rams. In a couple of years the Rams had such a powerhouse that they had leftover guys like Andy Robustelli who later became All-Pros. So the other teams began to do it. Bucko Kilroy began scouting full time for the Eagles in 1955, and by 1960 they had a championship team."

The scouting process quickly became refined, and at present all the teams in the NFL with the exception of Oakland and Cincinnati not only have their own scouting systems but belong to scouting organizations whose function is to pool information for the use of the member clubs. There are four such systems: Galaxy, CEPO, QUADRA and Blesto.

Each has nearly a dozen scouts. Their services cost a member club about $100,000 a year. The operations are similar, though CEPO is the only one of the combines that pools scouting reports from all its members (the Packers, Giants, Cardinals, Patriots, Browns, Redskins and Falcons) in a procedure called "full disclosure." Each team is privy to information gathered by the others. The advantage of this system is that a great deal of manpower is supplied. Every team scout is morally obligated to tell CEPO at its meetings everything he knows about his prospects. "The CEPO people feel that they'd rather get a tremendous file on each player," the scout said. "Then it's up to the individual club to decide whether he can play Packer football, or fit into the Atlanta organization, or whatever."

The other combines do not function on a system of full disclosure. The member clubs like to think that their own scouts can find them a sleeper, a gargantuan tackle out in the sandlots somewhere, whose abilities they would want to keep very much to themselves until the draft.

Blesto (which serves the Bears, Lions, Eagles, Steelers, Vikings, Colts, Dolphins, Bills and Chiefs) is the combine especially known for its work with a computer; an optimum football specimen is programmed into the machine against which a prospect can be compared and graded. The scout matches the physical characteristics of his prospect on a chart (the computer offers six types of legs, five variations of the upper torso; for defensive tackles, say, it can bracket a height range of 5' 10" to 7 feet) and when the scout has finished feeding this sort of information into the machine, it offers up a final grade on a scale of 0 to 3.1. "We call the machine Big Dummy," the scout said. "Like something that stands in the corner and needs to be fed. I've seen it work. There's an operator who pushes buttons on a control panel. A lot of other things are being figured by Big Dummy at the same time. The day I saw it operating, the computer was also figuring what was called Mini-max Strategy for National Guard War Games. The stuff comes out of the machine as printouts. It keeps coming out and folding on itself in a metal basket, yards and yards of information and evaluation. The top mark in the Blesto system is 0, which is perfect. No one would ever get that. Superman himself would lose out; he'd get marked down for wearing a disguise and surely for undressing in phone booths. He'd probably end up with a mark quite a bit above O.J. Simpson, who was an 0.4 and doesn't, so far as we know, have curious habits like that."

The scout motioned with his glass. "But you still need the man who says, 'I don't give a damn what Big Dummy says; this kid can play football.' He'll probably be right.

"The computer misses them. Every free agent who makes a team—and 32 did last year, kids like Johnnie Gray, the rookie who made it as a safety with the Packers—shows the system isn't perfect. There's so much a machine can't define properly.

A kid can be a great football player without looking anything like the optimum programmed into the computer. There's no way a computer can field the data fed into it on a player like Don Nottingham, the 'Human Bowling Ball' who plays in the Miami backfield, and not shudder and come up the same recommendation it did in 1971—that he should be picked just where he was in that draft, number 441, the next to the last guy chosen. Would you draft a Lee Roy Jordan or a Nick Buoniconti? A machine wouldn't. I would. I played against them. The main trouble with Big Dummy is that it can't tell you anything about a guy's heart. So many good-looking football players turn out to have hearts the size of marbles. If a scout could only tell, if there was some way that heart could be measured—a white spot in the middle of a player's forehead that gave some indication." He shrugged. "Of course, that would finish off the need for scouts."

Cincinnati and Oakland feel that they can better prepare for the draft by concentrating on their specific needs rather than by digesting computer reports. Much of what a scouting combine provides can be of no use to a team—for example, all that energy to supply information about the nation's quarterbacks when the Cincinnati Bengals have two fine ones of their own (Ken Anderson and John Reaves). So the Bengals and the Raiders fend for themselves. The Cincinnati organization has eight weekend scouts, most of them originally Ohio-based and personal friends of Paul Brown, the recently retired head coach. The operation is marked by a strong family bond. Among them are a tennis-club manager from Nashville, Tenn., a dynamite salesman from Cleveland, an Arkansas cattle rancher and a humanities professor from the Colorado School of Mines who is called "Professor" by his fellow scouts and twitted for the patches he wears on the elbows of his tweed jacket. During the season each scout calls in to Cincinnati on Monday and reports his availability for the next weekend. He will be paid an average of $50 for each college game he scouts. One weekend last fall the dynamite salesman was stuck in Alaska, but he called on the University of Alaska where he had his photograph taken outside the athletic department building. He wanted the home office to know that he was on the job (even though football is not played at the university) and that if there were rumors of an Eskimo placekicker out on the tundra he was in a position to check it out.

The most vociferous disparager of the combine system that the Bengals and Raiders avoid is the legendary Fido Murphy, a Runyonesque figure who scouted on his own for the Bears with considerable success for many years, though he is perhaps best known in football circles for his ceaseless self-promotion. He claims that he invented scouting back in 1933. In fact, he claims responsibility for the combine system itself (he calls the organizations "combos"), which he says he originated in 1965 when Buddy Parker, the Steelers' head coach, suggested that he scout for Pittsburgh as well as Chicago. "That was the start of Blesto," Murphy says. (Actually, the Cowboys, Rams and 49ers had formed a scouting partnership three years earlier.)

Fido also claims the invention of the T formation (he says George Halas brought in Clark Shaughnessy to run it), the blitzing maneuver known as red-dogging, and even to have been the first to establish the 40-yard-sprint distance that scouts use to time prospects. He says, "In 1938 I timed Bill Osmanski at Holy Cross in shorts at 40 yards and in the fall of that year in full football gear. Forty yards seemed right for Osmanski and everybody else."

Fido Murphy's monologues, punctuated with an occasional "Got it?" have a certain Stengelese quality: "The combos are worthless. Their scouts rely too much on the computer. They don't know what you're talking about if you say that the trouble with the guard is that he leaves his foot in the trap. Imagine that! The college coaches know they're no good. They say to me, 'Hey, Fido, nine Blesto scouts were here yesterday and they all want to know who Fido likes.' 'Fido's been around? Oh God, who's he like? Please tell me who he likes?' Got it? I know where there are two defensive linemen like elephants. The Bears won't draft them. They rely too much on Blesto. The computers are beating the Bears. I tell them to stay out of the combos. I know where there's a football player better than Archie Griffin, who's an easy first-round draft pick, but the combos won't have the guts to rate the kid high. Of course, I'm not going to tell you his name, but I'll tell you he's like Mike Thomas, the little running back for the Washington Redskins. Got it? I know where there are two centers better than

Rik Bonness, that kid at Nebraska. The best field-goal kicker
I've seen is a mule called Gus who kicks a field goal in the last
minute of a Walt Disney film starring my wife. She's made 188
films. Gus plays for a team called the Atoms and he wears a red
blanket. The combos'll never pick him up. They rely too much
on stopwatches and computers. You have to have the personal
touch, to find out if the kid's got heart and character. I rejected
Joe Namath when he was at Alabama. I didn't like the way he
took his eye off me when a coed went by. I knew O.J. Simpson was going to be great when he ordered a grilled-cheese
sandwich in the dining room of the St. Francis Hotel in San
Francisco. No pretensions about the guy. Character. Got it? I
sent that grilled-cheese sandwich back to the kitchen and
ordered him a New York cut steak. I called up John McKay
and told him there was this kid at City College of San Francisco, and that's how O.J. went to USC."

The scout laughed. "So you talked to Fido Murphy," he
said. "Everyone who is a scout knows Fido. Great character.
My theory has always been that Art Rooney of the Steelers
and George Halas of the Bears set him up to needle people
in the business." The scout grinned and stretched. "You meet
all sorts in the scouting business. I like it. Of course, some
scouts leave it. I remember Carl Brettschneider, the linebacker who later scouted for the Lions, telling me that one
time he took a look at all these scouts—a lot of them ex-head
coaches who'd had their day in the sun. They had gathered
around a huge tureen of shrimp at the Senior Bowl in
Mobile, a rain drifting against the window outside. It always
seems to rain when that game is played. And he suddenly
knew what these big men with shrimp clutched in one hand
and booze in little paper cups in the other were talking
about—quabs and Tarzan-Janes and C.O.D.s and whether this
guy could hit, and then after a while they would begin talking about why they weren't head coaches anymore and how
their careers had been soured by the press and the fans and
their players. Losers, that's what these men were, and
Brettschneider got so upset thinking about it that he quit
scouting and went into the jewelry business.

"Aw, it must have been the rain in Mobile that did it," the
scout went on. "It's a good fraternity of people. There's a

glamour in it. You can stand around at a cocktail party with a lot of automotive VIPs and if it gets around that you're a football scout, you've got instant-celebrity status. The pay's good—$18,000 and up. But you've got to love football. If you are around scouts, what else is there to talk about except football? Sometimes you pick an all-star team of the worst players in the NFL and you kid a guy if he touted any of them. They're good people—great ex-head coaches like Jim Lee Howell of the Giants and Red Hickey of the 49ers, great players like Harley Sewell, Rosie Brown, guys who got into it from high school and college coaching and built their reputations as scouts by having great eyes for talent, and then there are the people just starting off, like Donny Anderson and Bill Curry from the Packers.

"You meet them on the road and you sit and visit. It makes the travel easier. That's the worst thing about scouting, the travel. Motels. Not a surprise in any of them. No 30-year-old 19-year-old blondes in the lobbies. No surprises in the hotel rooms either. The purple bedspreads. The paper band across the toilet. Those huge brown lamps. I finally reckoned, after years of staring at those lamps, why they're so big—it's to keep scouts from taking them apart, packing them up and bringing them home. They're mammoth. An average Ramada Inn lamp would rate an easy 0.9 in the Individual Player Form in several categories: stamina, toughness, balance—they are nailed down half the time—durability, poise...."

The scout began to talk about the more agreeable aspects. It was awkward for him. The best moments were when someone he had seen on a practice field, or among the welter of shapes moving against the screen, or the pinned-up sheet in the motel room, made him lean forward, the words already forming in his mind how he would describe this phenomenon to the home office, play after play verifying what he had in mind. And then having his opinion realized and perhaps hearing the name of the player coming over the car radio a year or so later perhaps the star player now and being interviewed before a Sunday afternoon game, and the scout would say aloud to himself as he drove (there was never anyone else in the car, so he could not be embarrassed), "I'm telling you that kid would hit anything that moved, always did, and I said from the very first time I ever saw him on that crazy little practice field that he was a *competitor.*"

Gimme an 'S',
Gimme an 'E',
Gimme...

BY   BRUCE   NEWMAN

THE GAME OF PROFESSIONAL FOOTBALL SEEMED TO HAVE
EVERYTHING—GRACE, VIOLENCE, DRAMATIC FINISHES. BUT
ISN'T THERE SOME OTHER AMERICAN PASSION NOT REPRESENT-
ED HERE? AH, YES: SEX. IN 1978 BRUCE NEWMAN REPORTED ON
THE GROWTH OF CHEERLEADING IN THE NFL.

One day, long after the National Football League has finally
abandoned football altogether and turned into a coast-to-
coast string of peep shows, someone will make one of those
37-part made-for-TV movies about the Great Cheerleading
War of 1978. They can call it *Boots*, the story of sexy, yet
wholesome, young Linda Sue Ann Cheri Jo, who travels to
her ancestral homeland in Dallas where she finds the secret
to her past by unearthing the fossilized brassiere of her great-
great unbelievably-great-grandmommy, Dana Debbie Sue
Tammy Lynn.

It's something the NFL ought to be thinking about as it
boogies on down the road to perdition and Super Bowl
XXX. Goodness knows, the only thing anybody talks about
anymore is S-E-X and the Dallas Cowboy cheerleaders. Just
last week, Ann Landers had to contend with an enraged

reader complaining about the trend toward "older, sexier, and more naked cheerleaders" in the NFL. "Talented baton twirlers and really good dancing ... don't mean a thing," the infuriated correspondent said, asking Ann how she felt about such an "appalling commentary on American taste." How Ann felt was that such preferences were the "last gasps of a dying civilization."

Right. Certainly, whatever the Dallas cheerleaders started six years ago, with their plunging necklines and winking belly buttons, has spread through the rest of the NFL like a social disease. Which, of course, is exactly what a lot of people think it is. But as Vince Lombardi almost said, "Sinning isn't everything, it's the only thing."

The truth of the matter is it's hard to believe you could shake a "two bits, four bits" out of the dozen or so so-called cheerleading squads that have reared their lovely heads in the NFL in the last year or so. But never mind. They've got their vinyl boots and their pompons and Niagaras of blow-dried hair cascading down their backs, and you could just go to pep rallies and commit the cheers for Sunday's game to memory. Life is a series of small concessions, and this is one you can enjoy.

Recently Los Angeles Ram owner Carroll Rosenbloom proclaimed, "Cheerleaders are now an intrinsic part of the NFL." He said this about the same time Bill Allen, director of Miami's Dolphin Dolls, vouchsafed that "Cheerleading is becoming nothing more than a battle of belly buttons, busts and backsides," or words to that effect. If it follows that Allen's three B's are now at the heart of NFL efforts, then pro football must be just the thing for people who like a little sex with their violence.

Something is afoot. Last April 24, CBS's *National Collegiate Cheerleading Championships* went head-to-head with ABC's *Monday Night Baseball*, and won. The cheerleading show drew 37% of the viewing audience, baseball only 22%. And this is the National Pastime we're discussing here, not a couple of refugee jai alai guys on cable TV.

Moreover, last month in Chicago, 1,500 young women applied for 28 spots on the Chicago Honey Bears. Los Angeles recently selected 24 Ram Sundancers from a field of more than 800 candidates. In Baltimore the Colts have signed 45 girls to wear uniforms almost identical to those worn by the Dallas Cowboy cheerleaders.

"Everyone is trying to out-Dallas Dallas," says Atlanta Falcon Assistant GM Curt Mosher. Indeed, the Cowboys are usually a year or so ahead of the rest of the league in everything, and cheerleading is no exception. It was back in 1972 that Dallas General Manager Tex Schramm professionalized his squad by hiring eight girls from the dance studio of choreographer Texie Waterman. Suzanne Mitchell, who came to the Cowboys in 1975 as Schramm's secretary and has since become the cheerleaders' full-time manager, agent and martinet, is now, more or less by default, the arbiter of taste and decorum for the whole league. "Obviously we don't put the girls in those uniforms to hide anything," says Mitchell. "Sports has always had a very clean, almost Puritanical aspect about it, but by the same token, sex is a very important part of our lives. What we've done is combine the two."

This state of affairs may be to some degree a result of the influence of television on sports. TV did not create the Dallas Cowboy cheerleaders, but its unblinking eye drove the number of applicants for the 37 spots up from 250 in 1976 to 1,053 this year, and it is responsible for the recent demise of the Dolphin Dolls, a precision dance team of conservatively dressed teen-age girls. The Dolls had been with the Miami franchise since its inception in 1966, but choreographer Allen claims he was told twice by network cameramen that the Dolls wouldn't be shown on camera until they wore skimpier costumes. Now the Dolphins are going to older, sexier girls, who will be choreographed by the legendary June Taylor. The plan is to put them in bathing suits and have them cavort in an end zone around a pool containing the legendary Flipper.

With few exceptions, cheerleading for a pro football team is hard, demanding, underpaid work. Dallas cheerleaders get only $15 per game ($14.12 after taxes), must clean their own uniforms, attend innumerable practices (miss two and you're out), and be at the stadium two hours before each home game. Other teams pay even less and perks are minimal. Dallas may hold the record for penury by bringing their girls to New Orleans a few hours before the Super Bowl and sending them right home afterward on the pretext that there had been no hotel rooms available.

When not being penurious, the Cowboys try very hard to put their girls over as not only beautiful but also bright. Mitchell is forever trotting out Connie Dolan, a nuclear-medicine technologist, and Shannon Baker, a 4.0 student at SMU who just happens to have danced a solo turn with the Bolshoi Ballet.

The tryouts that have been taking place in NFL cities all over the country this spring are an indication of what lies ahead, and of how the professional cheerleading war is hotting up. The Atlanta Falcons auditioned more than 150 girls for 18 to 20 cheerleading spots. Three of them somehow managed to wiggle out of their tops, and only one bothered to stop dancing and regroup. One entry arrived with her record broken, but disported herself with such charm that the platter problem was overlooked. In Baltimore they're "definitely showing more skin this year," according to the Colts' front office, and in Cincinnati even conservative old Paul Brown has given the O.K. to a plan to dress the Ben-Gals in sarongs decorated with hand-painted tigers.

Still, a girl can't make it on the three B's alone. Last week at the final tryouts in Dallas, the contestants were interviewed, took a written exam on football and the Dallas Cowboy organization, and then pranced in groups of four onto a makeshift dance floor. There, in a swirl of disco music, they proceeded to dance their brains out, which in some instances did not take very long. Two networks and a film crew from UCLA were on hand, and Fleet Street was represented by a man from the London *Daily Express*.

These tryouts are a one-day, now-or-never proposition, with no consideration for the fact that even cowgirls get the flu. "Most of these girls would be here even if they were having an appendicitis attack," said Suzanne Mitchell.

This year's candidates began converging on Texas Stadium at 8 a.m. last Saturday, 78 of the fairest and finest tributes to the American cosmetics industry the world has seen. High cheekbones, higher cheekbones, cheekbones as high as an elephant's eye, all of them seeming to shimmer like sunlit promontories under the high-intensity movie lights.

Many of the girls had been unable to sleep the night before, but there was so much adrenaline flowing in the try-out room you had to be careful not to step in some, slip and break your concentration.

Contestant No. 3, Suzette Scholtz, was smiling so hard she nearly drove her eyeballs into her forehead. Eva Stancil had come all the way from her home in Alabama, ready to move to Dallas—as the rules required—if she was selected. She wasn't. Nineteen-year-old Robin Sindorf, a striking brunette, had tried out because cheerleading for the Cowboys would be "something to do," and because her heart belongs to daddy. When her name was announced as one of the chosen 37, she kept repeating, "This is going to make my father so happy. He's a big Cowboy fan."

It's hard to say where all this will lead. As Shannon Baker has noted, "Even Charlie's Angels could only stay on top for so long." But Oakland Raider Coach John Madden, holding forth on the subject of cheerleaders the other day, had what sounded like a good guess.

"I can see what this game is coming to," said Madden. "Choreographers instead of coaches. It will be a contest to judge which set of girls gets more TV time. After the gun sounds, the losing choreographer will tell the press, 'We lost our momentum. We couldn't maintain intensity. That's the name of the game—intensity. We'll have to regroup, go back to fundamentals. Put it in the paper, we'll be back.' The losing side will complain about the judges' decisions and the case will go to the commissioner, who will appoint a seventh judge. And after the girls have competed, the football players will come out at halftime for their exhibition, but the press won't notice because they'll be too busy watching replays of the cheerleaders."

Busman's Holiday

BY PETER KING

IN 1990 PETER KING HAD THE PLEASURE OF VISITING WITH JOHN MADDEN, AMERICA'S FAVORITE FOOTBALL ANALYST AND COAST-TO-COAST COMMUTER. ADDING TO KING'S ENJOYMENT WAS THE FACT THAT HIS VISIT TOOK PLACE ON THE ROLLING TOUR BUS CUM LIVING QUARTERS KNOWN AS THE MADDEN CRUISER.

When I was very young and the urge to be someplace else was on me, I was assured by mature people that maturity would cure this itch. When years described me as mature, the remedy prescribed was middle age. In middle age I was assured that greater age would calm my fever and now that I am fifty-eight perhaps senility will do the job. Nothing has worked.... I fear the disease is incurable.

—John Steinbeck
Travels with Charley

John Madden, 54, has a job most of us would love to have. He sleeps as late as he wants and wears whatever clothes he wants almost every day of his life. He eats what he wants, when he wants. He *has* to be somewhere, with a tie on, for only three hours a week. He makes much more than a million dollars a year. To do this job, he crisscrosses the U.S. six months a year in the greatest bus you've ever seen. It is a hotel suite on wheels.

Madden, the CBS-TV color analyst who along with Pat Summerall forms the preeminent NFL broadcast team, is a big, friendly, surprisingly tranquil lug of a guy who sees his country as few other Americans do—from the ground floor. "People used to say to me, 'It must be great coaching and traveling and seeing all the things you do,' says Madden, who piloted the Oakland Raiders for 10 years (1969 to '78) and to a Super Bowl championship. "Well, I'd get on the airplane, and then I'd get off the airplane, get on a bus and go to the hotel. Then the stadium, then the airplane again. I thought I'd traveled all over, but I hadn't seen anything. You've got to be on the ground to see things."

Madden is not talking about sightseeing. He's talking about being a witness to America—the land, the people, the life-styles, the thoughts and the emotions that make up a society. He loved stopping at the Tastee-Freez in Sidney, Neb. (pop. 5,834), a few years ago to watch *Monday Night Football* on a small black-and-white TV, with a group of townspeople that included the coach and players of the local high school basketball team. He discovered great Mexican food in Van Horn, Texas (pop. 2,772), at a restaurant called Chuy's (pronounced CHEW-ees).

One fall he was walking through a Green Bay neighborhood and stopped to watch someone rake leaves; being a California guy, he had never raked leaves. While spending four days in Longboat Key, Fla. (pop. 8,000), between assignments last season, he was drawn every day to the Gulf Coast shoreline, where he watched the fishermen. You have to move around, overland, to see these things.

There have been circumstances in all of our lives that have placed us where we are today. There are reasons that Madden tours America on a bus. Twenty-eight years ago, as a myopic head coach at Allan Hancock College in Santa Maria, Calif., he read *Travels with Charley*, Steinbeck's rediscovery of America, and vowed one day to see the country. Madden tired of coaching after the '78 season and took a flier on a TV analyst gig with CBS in '79. Three attacks of claustrophobia while traveling to assignments forced Madden off airplanes and onto trains.

However, the Amtrak schedules weren't always convenient. The TV gig turned into a second career, one that has increased his wealth and fame more than he ever expected, and in '87 Greyhound offered to customize a bus for Madden and supply him with drivers for three years in return for promotional and speaking appearances. After three years, the bus would be his. It's now known as the Walker Advantage Muffler Madden Cruiser (a new sponsor, to cover expenses, you know), and Madden is one happy claustrophobic.

Sometime after dawn of every morning spent on the bus, while Madden sleeps soundly on a queen-sized, ultrafirm bed in the rear third of the vehicle, the driver stops to pick up a *USA Today* and whatever local paper is available. When Madden awakens, he picks up the intercom phone, calls one of his two drivers and asks, "Where are we?" And Dave Hahn or Willie Yarbrough might say, "In the middle of the Sierras, just past Reno," or, "Below Cleveland, almost into Pennsylvania."

Madden moves forward to the codriver's seat, puts his feet—in untied shoes, with no socks—on the railing near the windshield and digests the sports sections of the papers. During the day he eats, reads, talks and, for at least three or four hours, while sucking on an unlit Macanudo cigar, just peers through the front windshield and the huge side picture windows as America rolls past. He spends some time going over press releases and newspaper clippings about the teams playing in the game he'll be working that Sunday. Often he'll pick up the cellular phone and call his agent, Sandy Montag, in New York, or his wife, Virginia, in Blackhawk, Calif., or the coach of one of the teams in Sunday's game. At night he stops for dinner somewhere; rarely is it planned. Back on the bus he switches on one of his two 20-inch color TVs and pops a game tape into the VCR. He might watch two. Because it's his life, and he can do what he wants.

What follows is an account of his most recent coast-to-coast trip, from his house outside Oakland to his apartment on the Upper West Side of Manhattan. The Madden Cruiser left the East Bay area at noon on Wednesday, Sept. 26. It pulled in front of Madden's New York City apartment building at 10 p.m. on Friday, Sept. 28. I was on the bus with Hahn and Yarbrough, who split the nearly nonstop run into shifts;

Madden's 25-year-old son, Joe, who is traveling with his dad this fall; and Madden's California neighbor, David Liskin, who was taking the long way to see family in Englewood Cliffs, N.J. The trip took 55 hours and covered 3,016 miles, but who's counting? Not Madden.

DAY 1: BLACKHAWK, CALIF., TO THE NEVADA-UTAH BORDER
We know so little of our own geography. Why, Maine extends northward almost to the mouth of the St. Lawrence, and its upper border is perhaps a hundred miles north of Quebec. And another thing I had conveniently forgotten was how incredibly huge America is.
—Travels with Charley

On the bus's digital temperature gauge, the outdoor reading is 79° and the indoor reading is 59°. No wonder Madden used to stalk the sidelines in shirtsleeves in December. The rules of the bus are made clear: "Don't wait for anyone, finish any bottle of water you start, drink right out of the bottle, and never take I-80 in or out of New York—there's always construction." Madden doesn't like the clutter of plastic bottles. One problem: The bottles each hold 50 ounces of water.

Soon the Madden Cruiser headed into the web of California freeways, turning onto I-580 and then onto I-205 in the San Joaquin Valley, where endless fields of vegetables were being irrigated. South of Stockton the bus picked up I-5, the freeway to Sacramento, which would connect with I-80, the highway Hahn and Yarbrough would drive for 53 hours. "Now, you don't think," Madden said, an hour from his front door. "You've got to turn off your brain for 50 hours."

On the right side, about mid-bus, is a table with two bench seats, and Madden, five deep slugs into his first bottle of water, sat on the bench facing the front. To his right were miles of fields. Straight ahead was road. He was the tour guide, and he relished the role. A passenger found out soon enough that one of Madden's favorite topics is America. He talked about its wide-open spaces with the same fervor he uses for a chalkboard description of a Lawrence Taylor sack. He is loquacious and engaging, but he doesn't burst through walls—as he was portrayed in the famous Lite beer commercials—and he doesn't wave his arms. That is Madden shtick. Madison Avenue Madden. This is the real Madden. On the whole trip, I counted only two booms, no whaps and no significant rise in his voice, You know, as in, "SeeTaylor-comingpastLacheyandBOOM!HelevelsBynerandWHAP!Rypien's down!"

"If anything will impress you as you go across the country, it's how much space there is," he said. "This country, you'd think it was crowded, but you cross it, go for hours, and not see anything. You realize the only places that are truly congested are the big cities. Between congestions are just wide-open spaces. There's a hell of a lot more wide-open spaces than congested cities.

"That's why I've always said that before someone can be a congressman or a senator or president or vice-president, the person should ride across this country. Not drive, because you can't see when you drive. You have to ride, either like this or on a train. If you fly into Washington from New York, or from San Francisco or L.A. or Chicago, how the hell do you know? If a person can't see the country, how the hell can he represent it?"

He sounded like a father taking his seven-year-old son to see the Chicago Cubs play at Wrigley Field for the first time. "Wait until you see it at all," he said.

Ninety miles outside of Reno, I asked the tour guide, "How did you get so interested in seeing the country?"

"*Travels with Charley* influenced me a lot," Madden said. "I always wanted to travel, because I'd never seen anything. He was a great storyteller, John Steinbeck. I read everything of his. What happened was, my wife was taking this class for her master's or something. It was a literature course, and she had to study an author. She picked Steinbeck. One of things she had to do was go up to Monterey, where Cannery Row was, and I did the stuff with her. She'd read the books, and they were just lying around, so I'd read them. The Monterey Peninsula, Cannery Row, is still my favorite place in the whole world.

"If the claustrophobia thing didn't happen, I wouldn't know what this country is, or what these people are like. I would have been like everybody else: run, run, run. Airport,

airport, airport. Hotel, hotel, hotel. City, city, city. I wouldn't have found time to see things like I see them now."

The bus was climbing into the Sierras, and the temperature outside had dropped to 66°. "John Robinson and I were coaching together [with the Raiders in 1975] before he went to USC, and we used to ride to work together," said Madden. "He once said to me, 'You've changed. It's like you live in a tunnel. You don't have any idea what's going on in the world.' It was true. He thought I'd lost my sense of humor, my inquisitiveness. It got so I knew nothing other than football and the Raiders. I'm not criticizing that in myself; it's part of the job. You focus in so much, and you miss life."

In Nevada the bus sliced through mountains that were a mile and a half high. Yucca plants and paintbrush shrubs were the only things growing here, and Madden saw a solitary ranch about 500 yards off to the right. It consisted of a small house, two trailers, some farm machinery and about 600 head of cattle.

"What do they do at night?" he said, nodding toward the ranch. "No malls. No movies. No TV, it looks like. No neighbors. Where do they get groceries? If there's anything I'd really like to do, I'd like to pull into a place like that, knock on the door and say to the guy, 'What do you do? How do you live? God, I go to movies, restaurants, ball games, plays, the gas station, the market. You don't do any of those things. What do you do?'"

At about 5:30 p.m., he adjourned to his bedroom for a nap. When he returned an hour later, the sun was setting and the bus was passing through low clouds on a mountain pass. A voice on the CB piped up. "Breaker, breaker one-nine," a trucker said. "Is that the John Madden bus?"

"Affirmative," said Hahn.

"What game's he doing this weekend?"

"Giants-Cowboys in New York."

"Holy cow! That's a long way! Well, I enjoy listening to him."

We stopped for dinner in Elko, Nev., at a Red Lion Inn with a mini casino and sports book in the lobby. Madden walked through the casino, stopping at the sports book. The guy behind the counter was thrilled to see him. He started grilling Madden about who was going to win Sunday's games, and Madden, who doesn't gamble, kept telling the guy that he didn't know, that whatever he said would be only a guess—and he meant it.

"How can people bet on this stuff?" Madden would say later. "Nobody knows how these games are going to go."

Elko County is wider than Connecticut, and the town of Elko is the only place for 100 miles in either direction that has anything resembling shopping or something to do. It was 9:30 p.m., and Madden wanted to walk before eating. A shopping center was nearby, but most of the stores had already closed. The doughnut shop was still abuzz, and in the beauty shop a woman in a white uniform painted one last set of nails. Madden laughed. "God, are these things popular or what?" he said. "Every town in America has a nail shop, and somebody is always in 'em."

After Madden made a run through the Red Lion salad bar, the bus headed off into the night, and he broke out the tape of the Dallas-Washington game from the previous week. At 2 a.m., somewhere in the Great Salt Lake Desert, he turned off the TV and went to bed.

DAY 2: GREAT SALT LAKE DESERT TO OMAHA

I discovered that I did not know my own country…. I knew the changes only from books and newspapers.

—Travels with Charley

At 6 a.m., Madden was still sleeping, but the sun was coming up over southern Wyoming. We had slept through Utah. Now the eastern horizon was slightly pink with wispy clouds. It was as if the horizon were a stage and the curtain was opening an inch a minute, revealing a work of art. "We see those things," Hahn said from the driver's seat, "but unless you mention them to me and Willie, they kind of go right by us. Now that you mention it, it's incredible, isn't it?"

We were near Rawlins, Wyo., more than a mile high, traversing the Rocky Mountains. But aside from a truck stop every 40 miles or so, nothing was out here except hills and rocks and mountains, which is why the surroundings are so pretty and so desolate at the same time. Through Bitter Creek, Table Rock, Wamsutter. So wide open. We had just left Sweetwater County. Delaware and Rhode Island together could fit in Sweetwater County. Delaware and Rhode Island have a combined population of 1.7 million. Sweetwater County has 42,347.

In the morning light Hahn pointed to antelope, 50 yards from the road, eating brush. Soon we saw deer and jackrabbits. Yarbrough woke up—drivers and guests slept on fold-out beds and shelves with mattresses—and went to the front of the bus in time to see a pack of wild horses grazing half a mile off the side of the road. "I remember John bringing a producer from New York on the trip once," Yarbrough said. "He'd lived in New York all his life. He gets out in this part of the country, and he says, 'Man, there's sky all over the place.' We got a good laugh out of that."

After a 9:15 a.m. stop in Laramie, Wyo., so Madden could use a pay phone to do his daily five-minute spot for KSFO radio in San Francisco, he took his seat on the padded bench as the bus passed through the southeastern edge of Wyoming and headed for Nebraska. "Have you ever heard of whiteout?" Madden said. "Whiteout happens around here in winter. It snows, and it blows so hard you can't see. Everything is white. If it's too bad, you can't drive." The Madden Cruiser was caught in a whiteout once. Hahn drove two miles an hour until he got through it.

We passed some tepees on a hill by the side of the road. "We're coming up to Pine Bluffs, Wyoming, now," Madden said. "That's where the missile silos are. Once we were coming through and stopped at a 7-Eleven or something, and we see all these things—not cars, I don't know what you'd call 'em."

"Armored personnel carriers?" someone said.

"Yeah, yeah. Well, [the troops] didn't come out of doors. They came out of holes in the roof of the carriers, and they climbed down on the side. And they go into the 7-Eleven for coffee. I was worried. I thought some gray-haired guy should be sitting at the controls, but these were just kids eating nachos in the morning in Pine Bluffs, Wyoming." Off to the right were the silos, built into the ground, with a lot of fence around them.

After another hour or so, we hit the cornfields of Nebraska.

"We had to stop in Beaver Crossing, Nebraska [pop. 480] once, to use the phone for the radio show," Madden said. "It's near Lincoln. Some guy comes across the street from a gas station and introduces himself. Roger Hannon. He was the mayor, and it was his gas station. The next thing I know, we're in front of city hall, and the people start coming out, and they want to see the bus. One woman brought me a rhubarb pie. I didn't even know what rhubarb pie was, but it was great. The whole town came out. There were only about 10 of them, but they were the whole town. I remember asking them, 'What do houses sell for here?' They said the last house that sold was right down on the corner—three bedrooms, three baths, a picket fence, for $8,000."

Two days after Madden's visit to Beaver Crossing, the *Omaha World-Herald* ran a story on page 3 with the headline: MADDEN STOPS TO USE THE PHONE.

"Sometimes I just like to break up the trip, and Omaha's kind of halfway [across the country]," Madden said. "So I stayed in Omaha one night, and we went to see the minor league baseball team play. Anyway, they have a raffle for a case of pork and beans. It's the seventh inning, and everybody's excited. They pick the winner, and the guy's sitting right behind home plate. His name is Elmer something, and he's jumping up and down. To him it was like a trip to Hawaii or a new car or something. It was just a case of pork and beans. That was great."

He read all the press clips and news releases sent to him by the Cowboys, and then he looked out the window some more. When we saw some red wildflowers by the side of the road, Joe fetched a coffee-table book, *Wildflowers Across America*, to identify them. The book had been a gift from Joe to his father. How many former NFL coaches would be caught with a copy of *Wildflowers Across America* in the drawer next to the Giants media guide? Joe found the wildflower in the book: spotted knapweed.

In Brady, Neb., we saw the strangest sight of the trip. We pulled off the highway, emptied out of the bus and looked with the same fascination we would have if we had seen a UFO. It was an animal farm, with a long ranch-style house and a grazing pen that was home to one gray burro, two dozen deer, five dwarf ponies, five llamas, one crossbred deer-llama and several crossbred animals that resembled llamas with very thick necks.

"He looks like he's on steroids," Madden said of one thick-necked llama-lookalike. There were no signs, no explanation of what this farm was for. A man staring at us from the picture window of the house wouldn't come out to answer our questions.

Madden still hadn't gotten over the weird animals when we stopped for dinner at Grandpa's Steakhouse in Kearney, Neb. He asked a woman who had come to our table for his autograph if she knew why the animal farm was there. "I just think he has them for personal pleasure." she said.

While we were eating, the Kerry Kimple clan of Kearney collected near the bus, waiting for Madden. "Nebraska loves John Madden," said Kerry, whose son, Travis, 10, got Madden's autograph. "He's a common-sense, say-what-he-thinks guy."

Back on the bus, Madden watched the Giants-Dolphins game tape. Around midnight, somewhere just over the line into Iowa, he said, "We really saw a lot of stuff today, didn't we? Think of all the things we saw that we wouldn't see on a plane."

DAY 3: COUNCIL BLUFFS, IOWA, TO NEW YORK CITY
There are customs, attitudes, myths and directions and changes that seem to be part of the structure of America.
                                        —*Travels with Charley*

From some point just east of Des Moines to a rest stop south of Cleveland—a stretch of 640 miles traveled in 12 hours—Madden slept. He missed the early rush hour in the suburbs south of Chicago. He missed South Bend, Ind., waking the echoes on a brand-new day. He missed the heart of the Rust Belt. He missed most of Ohio, including 19 consecutive American cars passing the bus in the westbound lane in Maumee, a Toledo suburb. He missed the colorful foliage of Sandusky County, Ohio. He missed Liskin, his amiable neighbor, talking about what a great time he had had seeing America.

"I don't want it to end," Liskin said. "I want it to keep

going. I just called my brother in New York. He's an investment banker. His voice was so tense. He told me that with the Iraq situation, the world's going crazy. I told him, 'Not where I am. Everything seems fine here.' He told me, 'Ahhh, you don't understand reality.' I feel great now, like I just came back from Hawaii."

At 10 minutes past noon, with the bus pulling into the rest stop near Cleveland, Madden stirred. "Sleep," Madden said a few miles into Pennsylvania, "is the key to the whole thing. If you finish a trip and drag in like a washrag, it's not going to work. I sleep better on the bus than I do at home, I think. I've been on it so much, it truly is home."

We stooped for lunch in Clarion, Pa. (pop. 6,664), and Madden strolled the sidewalks. Two men were sitting on a bench in the center of town when Madden passed. "That's the Ace Hardware guy," one said.

"No, he's the football announcer," the other replied.

Madden loved the sights, but he likes being invisible, so he doesn't walk the streets in small towns as much as he once did. When we were a few hours outside New York City, he was asked about the states he slept through. "It seems that Iowa should be the capital of small-town America," said Madden. "Every town is so nice. Illinois is Chicago to me, Michigan Avenue—one of my favorite cities. Indiana is Notre Dame. Ohio is Youngstown. [San Francisco 49er owner] Eddie DeBartolo's from there, and he's always telling me, 'Stop by, come and eat, I'll cook for you.' Pennsylvania, trees. Look at this foliage. I mean, people pay money to take tour buses to see scenes like this."

We were in a long, deep canyon of red, green, yellow and brown, driving on a ridge just below the Moshannon State Forest in north central Pennsylvania. The trees looked like pom-poms.

Against his better judgment, Madden agreed to break one of his cardinal rules. He told Hahn and Yarbrough they could take I-80 all the way into New York City. Naturally, the highway was under construction in northeastern Pennsylvania, and the bus crawled for two hours. "No more of this — — road, ever, into New York," said Madden before retiring for a quick nap.

When we reached the congestion of eastern New Jersey, it reminded Madden that he was closing in on his home away from home. He reflected on the trip and the country he had crossed. "I think we're in pretty good shape," he said. "The thing that's always amazed me is how it works. People who live on farms don't want to live in big cities. People who live in big cities don't want to be farmers. If everyone wanted the same thing, or wanted to live in the same place, the thing would never work. There are people who are as happy as hell living in Kearney, Nebraska, and eating at Grandpa's. There are people who are as happy as hell living in the middle of nowhere.

"Probably above that, what I've learned traveling around is this: People are nice. You go to a big city, and you hear the world is going to hell, but it's not true. Small parts of it are; the whole isn't. Hey, all we have to do is spread out a little bit, because we have a lot of space. You get out there, and it makes you feel better about America. The thing works."

From start to finish, I found no strangers.... These are my people and this is my country.

—Travels with Charley

One to Remember

BY RICK REILLY

WITH THE CREATION OF THE WORLD LEAGUE OF AMERICAN FOOTBALL, THE PRO GAME FINALLY WENT GLOBAL. BUT WHAT RICK REILLY DISCOVERED WHEN HE COVERED THE FIRST TITLE GAME IN 1991 WAS THAT CALLING SOMETHING THE WORLD BOWL DOESN'T NECESSARILY MAKE IT SUPER.

What? Do I remember the first World Bowl? Like it was last week, kid. Those were great days back in 1991. Those were young days 20 years ago. The fans and the game and the players all had a freshness to them, as though nobody had told them the game didn't matter. Not like now, not like the monster hype vehicle you see today. You know how many American sportswriters flew to London to cover the first World Bowl? One. Me.

You laugh, but I'm serious. This was before the shoecam and the pigskincam and even the pom-pomcam. The World League of American Football was zilch back then. I'll never forget the week before the World Bowl. At a charity dinner, the WLAF president, Mike Lynn, bumped into Prince Charles, whose charitable trust benefited from the game. Lynn says to the prince, "So, you coming to the game?" And the prince goes, "What game?"

Those were the days when nobody was sure whether the World League was football or something held over from the Wilson Administration. The WLAF was sort of like Jerry Lewis—very big in France but couldn't get arrested in the States. That made media access to the players ridiculously easy. I rode on the London Monarch team bus back to the hotel one day. Can you imagine that now, with the, what, 3,000 reporters around? The Moscow coach would have you hung in Red Square if he caught you on his bus.

There was even a question of whether the first World Bowl would be a sellout. The WLAF tried just about everything to get one. "We're ready for the New England Patriots," said Monarch general manager Billy Hicks in the week leading up to the game. "We could hold our own."

Of course, they almost did sell all 63,500 seats. Wembley Stadium was rockin' that day, with 61,108 banner-waving, mostly pre-40, American-pop-freak fans ready to make history. Here's how new everything was: The MVP of the game, London cornerback Dan Crossman, didn't even know that he got a $16,000 van for winning the award. "Guys kept coming up to me during the game, telling me I was going to win the car," Crossman would say later. "But I thought they were kidding. I mean, I'm thinking, This isn't the Super Bowl."

He was right. This was more fun than the Super Bowl. When London won—21–0 in a blowout over the Barcelona Broncos, er, Dragons—the Monarchs did something I'd never seen in pro football. They went into the stands to get their trophy from Lynn. They they romped around Wembley carrying it over their heads, dancing to excruciatingly loud music, waving the Union Jack around as if it were their very own (all but four players were American) and generally carrying on as if they cared, which—and this is the funny thing—they really did. The fans cared too. Twenty-five minutes after the final gun, maybe 1,000 people had left.

In those days, the World League broke all the rules. The Monarch players spent the season living in some 100-year-old, vacant university dorms, which were a £30 ($50) cab ride from town. It was quite lovely. The dorms had shower heads at navel level, no telephones in the rooms, one television in each lounge, next to no heat, even less hot water and, as the sole source of amusement, a bedraggled dart board. It inspired various tournaments of backward darts, blindfolded darts, steeplechase darts (competitors had to come running into the room at full speed, leap over a couch and fire) and, of course, lucky darts, in which outside linebacker Danny Lockett, who also happened to be the league's defensive co-MVP that first season, would suddenly decide to bury the darts as hard as he could into a wall and everybody in the room would duck to avoid being punctured.

The other coaches in the league, whose players lived in hotels and apartments, said the Monarchs had an advantage in enduring this hell, because they "lived together, like a family." Right. "We were lucky to keep them off each other's throats," said the Monarch coach, London Larry Kennan. Actually, they weren't that lucky. The Monarchs had half a dozen shouting matches on the sideline during the year, plus one in the *huddle* during a game. Didn't bother Kennan much. He once had been an assistant coach with the L.A. Raiders.

Back in 1991 the World Bowl was practically run out of the back of a VW. The stadium crew at Wembley couldn't even begin painting the WLAF logo and the team names on the field that year until a schoolboy soccer match ended at five o'clock the night before the game.

And even once the historic event began, you weren't sure what in the world was going on. For instance, after London fumbled away the opening kickoff, Barcelona lost 12 yards on three plays and screwed up a field goal try. The holder dropped the snap, and kicker Massimo Manca tried to kick the ball while it was squirting on the ground, figuring the big guys chasing it would leave him alone. London recovered, went nowhere and punted, and then Barcelona was intercepted. Anyway, after almost 15 minutes, the score was 0–0, so, naturally, the soccer fans at Wembley felt right at home.

But on the last play of the first quarter, a pass from the London 41-yard line, Monarch wide receiver Jon Horton—yes, *the* Jon Horton; believe it or not, at that point in Horton's career, the NFL didn't think he was any good—totally embarrassed Barcelona cornerback Charles Fryar (Irving's cousin), letting Fryar think he had an interception, then stealing the ball out of his hands at the Barcelona 19. Fryar fell down, and the safety sideswiped Horton and missed. Horton could've scored the first World Bowl touchdown in a Beefeater's uniform: London 7–0.

Every fifth catch Horton made that year was a touchdown. Not bad for a guy who couldn't make it through one season in the Canadian Football League and had to make a living playing pro basketball in Mexico, eh?

Barcelona quarterback Scott Erney threw his next two passes to Crossman, the second of which was returned for a score. Crossman just sneaked inside a down-and-out, "squeezed the ball like a baby," he said, and floated in for a 20-yard TD. Crossman would get a third interception later in the second quarter. Up in the royal box, actor John Cleese and the Moody Blues (who did *not* lip-sync *God Save the Queen*) were having a bloody good time. London was up 14–0.

Then, with 52 seconds left in the half, Monarch quarterback Stan Gelbaugh threw a rope to halfback Judd Garrett—they hooked up 12 times that day—for a 14-yard touchdown. Bring on the marching band from Central State University, in Wilberforce, Ohio, which the Wembley crowd greeted like a Beatles reunion. London 21–0, and you know the rest.

Back in the States, you probably could've heard the Nielsen ratings dropping through the floor, but in London, what one veteran Fleet Street writer called as "fine a celebration as ever seen at Wembley" was building. When the game ended, the idea was for Gelbaugh to go into the stands and accept the trophy, a 40-pound glass globe (it lit up, too) from Lynn and his pals Pete Rozelle, Tex Schramm and Tom Landry. However, Gelbaugh's shoulder was hurting, so he asked Crossman to accompany him into the stands and help him lift the globe. Next thing you know, all 41 players and the coaches were stomping up to the royal box to get their big paws on the globe. Then came the Stanley Cup lap.

"The NFL should do that," I remember Lynn saying afterward. "The NFL just goes in the locker room, and nobody gets to see the celebration."

That's the way that first World Bowl went down, kid— almost 25 years to the day after the NFL and the AFL agreed to merge—in front of a crowd that was 838 short of the attendance at the first Super Bowl, in Los Angeles, in 1967.

There was something wonderfully honest, low-rent and delicious about World Bowl I. Afterward, the Monarchs, who finished 11–1, dressed in a "locker room" that was nothing but some partitions put up in the middle of a giant exhibition hall, with portable showers trucked in for the World Bowl. The game was dreadful and terrific at the same time: You didn't know whether it was the beginning or, who knew, the end of something.

"If that wasn't big-time football out there," said London Larry, "I don't know what is." Across the way, Monarch head trainer Mayfield Armstrong was showing off his new and very permanent tattoo, a Monarch logo on his butt.

And to think England's favorite sport used to be soccer.